# PRAISE FOR SPITTING IMAGE

"Levi paints a picture honoring strong, beautiful, courageous women. A baby once abandoned finds his deep roots and an understanding of unfathomable bravery. This book is a dive into a complex and rich history, one of courage, sadness, joy, understanding, and redemption. Take the time to read these words and journey into the past, the present, and the influence of determined and strong women, mothers that shape the future through their love for their children even in the most devastating of circumstances."

**—HEATHER BURNER, National Safe Haven Alliance**

The journey of this foundling serves as a light post to anyone "in search of". For Ron, it was birth parents. Be it lost family, lost loves, or lost innocence, by taking us along his personal journey, Ron gives hope and inspiration to anyone who has missing puzzle pieces or unexplored questions about their past. His experience proves that voids can be filled, wounds can be healed, and God is real.

**—AÏDA OWENS**

# SPITTING
# IMAGE

*A Foundling's Memoir of*
*Faith and Gratitude*

**RONALD G. LEVI JR.**

All Bible scriptures are taken from THE KING JAMES VERSION (KJV), Public Domain.

This is a work of creative nonfiction. Some parts have been fictionalized in varying degrees, for various purposes. The events and conversations in this book have been set down to the best of the author's ability, although some names and details have been changed to protect the privacy of individuals.

First hardcover edition November 2020

*Contributing researcher Frances Lillian Stephens*
*Edited by Critique Editing Services, Herndon, VA*
*Cover design by 5Mediadesigns*

Hardcover ISBN:  978-1-7358805-2-5 (Jacket)
Hardcover ISBN: 978-1-7358805-5-6 (Case Lam.)
Trade Paperback ISBN:  978-1-7358805-0-1
eBook ISBN:  978-1-7358805-1-8
Audiobook ISBN:  978-1-7358805-4-9

Published by Alba-Lu Press, San Antonio, TX

# DEDICATION

In *Catch the Fire*, Poet Sonia Sanchez implores us to find our fire and pass it on. She names it the fire of living, of loving, of Blackness – the "beautiful fire" that gives light to the world. This story is my fire, kindled to warm you and to illuminate your path. I dedicate this fire to motherhood - to the mothers who prayed me into existence, who have sustained me and continue to lend me their hope and courage, and to those future mothers who will be my legacy.

# Preface

*And there went a man of the house of Levi, and took to wife a daughter of Levi. And the woman conceived and bare a son: and when she saw him that he was a goodly child, she hid him three months. And when she could no longer hide him, she took for him an arc of bulrushes, and daubed it with slime and with pitch, and put the child therein; and she laid it in the flags by the river's brink.*

*And the daughter of Pharaoh came down to wash herself at the river; and her maidens walked along by the river's side; and when she saw the ark among the flags, she sent her maid to fetch it. And when she had opened it, she saw the child: and, behold, the babe wept. And she had compassion on him."*

Exodus 2:1-3, 5-6

# PROLOGUE

⁊ᕤ⁊ᕤ

Reading the accounts of adoptees who searched for and found their biological relatives, I was struck by the number of disappointments and tragedies recounted. So many begin their search with wide-eyed optimism, nurturing the fantasy of a hero's welcome or at least a congenial acknowledgement. Even those with modest expectations tell of the devastating impact of being rejected twice: at birth and again when finally finding a long-hidden truth. I never expected to find a perfect beginning. I am a romantic who loves happily-ever-afters, but I always assumed that the circumstances that lead parents to abandon or give up their children for adoption are complicated to say the least and almost universally born of adversity. My analytical self determined that adversity and deprivation must exist for us to recognize and appreciate peace and prosperity. Darkness gives meaning and context to light. As much as the tribulations of my existence continually tempt me to seek respite, I have come to accept if not welcome them as harbingers of inevitable growth. In 50 years of seeking myself in every foreign and familiar face, of searching for a piece of myself that had been missing since birth, I discovered that the courage to embrace my truth requires a willingness to see it naked without flinching. What is the worth of effort and expense if upon discovery, I shrink from or ignore the bald truth? I steeled myself for every outcome my long-suffering imagination could muster. Hoping for the best and preparing for the worst, there were so many unknowns, so many questions. I knew that the answers I sought could as easily be horrific as they could be heartening. What I could not imagine, however, was the journey through centuries and cultures I was about to embark upon. When I logged in to view the results of my DNA test I had no idea that a teaspoon of spittle could transform my views of race, relationships, and gender so quickly after having arrived at them glacially.

According to the Adoption History Project by the University of Oregon:

> *We know one thing with certainty on the basis of historical statistics. Adoptions were rare, even at the height of their popularity, around 1970. What is paradoxical is that adoptions have become rarer during the past several decades, just as they have become more visible. A total of approximately 125,000 children have been adopted annually in the United States in recent years, a sharp drop since the century-long high point of 175,000 adoptions in 1970. Growing numbers of recent adoptions have been transracial and international— producing families in which parents and children look nothing alike—and the attention attracted by these adoptive families has led many Americans to believe that adoption was increasing. The adoption rate has actually been declining since 1970, along with the total number of adoptions.*
>
> *Estimates suggest that adoptive families are atypical as well as few in number. Approximately 5 million Americans alive today are adoptees, 2-4 percent of all*

*families have adopted, and 2.5 percent of all children under 18 are adopted. Adoptive families are more racially diverse, better educated, and more affluent than families in general. We know this because Census 2000 included "adopted son/daughter" as a kinship category for the first time in U.S. history. It is possible that the demographic profile of adoptions arranged many decades ago was just as distinctive. We simply do not know.[1]*

My story is one of adoption into a loving, if imperfect family. It is one of abandonment and reconciliation, and it is complicated greatly by America's longstanding obsession with the social construct of race. Until I began searching, I could not have fathomed the diversity of experiences related to adoption. In my self-centeredness, I never pondered the difficulties faced by families who adopt transracially—or any family that adopts a child who looks conspicuously different from parents and siblings. *Matching* was a purposeful act in my process. My parents brought pictures of themselves and their families to the adoption agency, which sought to find them a child that *fit in* well. As much as racism has devastated the descendants of slaves in particular and our nation in general, colorism ironically helped me enjoy the most "normal" and healthy adoptive experience any child could have. Most outside observers would agree that I look somewhat like many people in my adoptive family—even if they "can't quite place" the resemblance. *Racism,* as I use the term, refers to beliefs and behaviors that contribute to and support the persistence of institutionalized policies and practices that limit and harm people of African descent. *Colorism,* as I use it, is the largely self-inflicted discrimination of people of African descent against one another

---

[1] https://pages.uoregon.edu/adoption/topics/adoptionstatistics.htm

based on the visible concentration of melanin in their skin—usually favoring lighter brown or nearly white complexions. Without these distinctions, the reader may misunderstand the intent of passages related to these terms, so they are worthy of mention at the outset.

Contrary to the early misgivings and protective psychology I created for myself, my story is also one of tremendous hope and miraculous Grace. It is the evidence of things not seen. It is a story of providence and the hand of God at work in my life and in my heart. I hope that my story will encourage someone who is struggling with issues of identity, race, faith, or love. The child within the adult adoptee or foundling naturally longs for closure. It is easy to lose hope and often seems that the road to truth is paved with one insurmountable obstacle after another. To that child I say, "Don't give up." To that child, I say "Stand fast. God is working on your behalf, arranging the pieces so that they are available to you when you are ready, and He is closing doors which do not benefit you. Remain open to the possibility that if you are meant to know, there will be learning and growth involved. If you are not meant to know, you have already received a far greater blessing."

# PART I

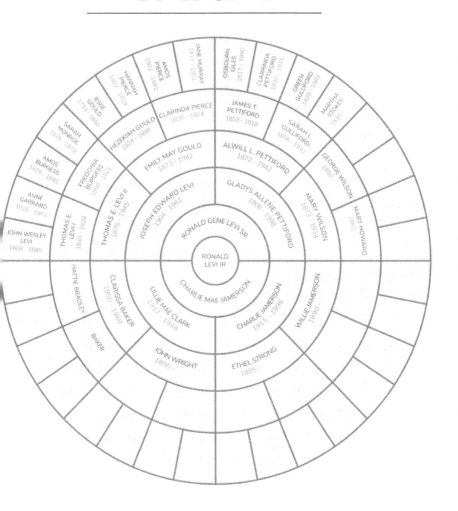

*Figure 1 Adoptive Family (1808- Present)*

# CHAPTER ONE

---∂૭∂૮---

# THE ANNOUNCEMENT

M y worldview was not particularly complicated or unusual for someone of my background. Growing up in an African-American working-class family of the sixties and seventies, I breathed the smoke of the Detroit rebellion, drank from the clear fountain of civil rights activism, and ate the sweet fruit of equal opportunism. My views were shaped by injustices I witnessed personally and those that were recounted by my mother and others. All white people were privileged, and few could understand or empathize with the indignity experienced by black people in the North let alone those still living in the South. The bus I rode to a private suburban school for so-called *gifted* children meandered through our post-rebellion enclave, abandoned by most of its white prior inhabitants, up Livernois Avenue to the solidly middle-class and still largely white university neighborhoods before making a right turn onto 7 Mile

Road and then into the decidedly wealthy, professional oases of Palmer Woods and Sherwood Forest.

When I boarded, there were a few other brown-skinned kids scattered about. Steve and Jeanine sat in the first row. Greg and Georgia sat in the back. I usually plopped down somewhere near the middle row. In Palmer Woods we took on a few more white kids than black, but by the time we crossed 8 Mile Road and headed into Birmingham and Bloomfield Hills there were no more black kids getting on the bus. It was all white from there on out. North was up, white and good. South was down, black and bad. So, in spite of or because of my interactions with white and black people in Detroit, I concluded that there were indeed two separate societies and that all white people had an easier row to hoe. It was my early understanding that there were good and bad people of all pigmentations and persuasions. I was fortunate to have friends and enemies on both sides of that narrow divide, but I also noticed that the white people I knew clearly had advantages and privileges that black people—even professional ones—did not. It wasn't fair, but that's the way it was and it was up to each of us to figure out how to cope with that reality and make something useful of it for ourselves, our family, and our community.

I didn't experience overt bigotry or bullying daily or I failed to recognize it as such; however, the practical experience of living in this racially semi-segregated reality had an effect. I find myself able to unpack the effects only decades later, after experiencing so much of life, raising a family of my own, and discovering the truth of my genetic identity. I never suspected that the image reflecting from the bottom of a tiny tube of spittle would be so different from the one I always had of myself, of my family, of our nation and our world.

What would my biological parents say if they could see what I've become? I like to think they'd be filled with pride, and that they'd be amazed by stories I'd tell them of the places I've been and the things I've seen. What would they tell me of their own lives and what would they withhold out of shame or vanity? How did they meet? Was their union a passionate moment of indiscretion, a forbidden love that could never endure, or a violent confluence of tragic misfortunes? If God really exists and has a plan for us all, how and why do I find myself precisely here and preci145sely now? Where am I headed? By the time I began searching in earnest, I had lost interest in the hows and felt that I would be fully satisfied with finding two names—those of my biological parents. I dared not hope to learn much beyond their ethnic origins, but their names and ancestral lineage would be worth the time and effort of seeking them. Pictures or anything more would be a happy bonus, I decided.

All stories begin in, end in, or otherwise involve cars when you're from the Motor City. If you weren't conceived or born in a car, you certainly lived, learned, loved, or lost something in one. Whether it is innocence, a sense of invulnerability, connections to the past, or dependence on others, with most losses we also gain something. Losing a sense of invulnerability often engenders greater responsibility and respect for ourselves or others. Sacrificing some connections to the past opens doors to broader opportunities in the future. In post-war Detroit, the ubiquitous automobile inevitably had a peripheral if not central role in these events. Our lives were intertwined by the capillaries and interstate arteries like the Lodge, Fisher, Ford, Jeffries, and later the Reuther freeways. While most freeways have numbers, ours have also had proper names as long ago as I can remember. I didn't learn the numbered names US-10, M-12, I-96, and others until after I learned to drive. It's no surprise then that our cars had not only brand and model names like the freeways which they plied, they were often bestowed proper personal names not unlike members of our families. Old Sylvie was our padded vinyl-top, silver Buick Electra 225 in 1974. She was a shiny land-yacht with fender skirts which had to be removed before a flat tire could be changed. Mom bought the car second-hand from a physician who was trading up. It was a grand floating parlor with air conditioning and power windows—features that were new experiences for our family. The icing on the cake for me, however, was those red tufted velour power bench seats. Soft, comfortable in every temperature, they wrapped me in warmth in the Michigan winters and were soft and cool in the middle of July once the A/C levelled out. Mom and I went everywhere in that boat of a car. School, work, grocery shopping, visiting family members, you name it. Her job, my school, our home and Grandmother's house were 15-30 miles apart from one another, so we spent almost as much time going to and from as we spent in our own home during the week. On the weekends, we did our grocery shopping and other errands that often took several hours. Comparison shopping and bargain hunting in the days before cell phones and global positioning systems was an auto-equestrian sport for my mom, and the deuce and a quarter was her trusty steed. Most of our conversations took place in the car, so it's no surprise that the announcement was made there. I don't remember where we were going or from where we had come, but it was a sunny day and I was nestled in those velour tufts with the plastic directional A/C vents pointing slightly to either side of my head. I was staring out the passenger window fooling with the power rearview mirror when I heard the words.

> *"You know that I have always loved you and I always will. I am your mother and you'll always be my son ... Maybe you already guessed it, but it's right for me to tell you that you were adopted. That doesn't matter, though, because you belong to us—to our family—and we love you as much or more than any parent can love any child. If you ever have any questions, you know you can always ask me anything, right? I love you."*

In retrospect, I imagine any reactions other than those I actually felt might have been more natural. One might expect that such a revelation would elicit shock, anxiety, anger, sadness or fear. None of those describes how I felt, however. It was more of an exhalation for me. Not a relief, just an exhalation. It was as if I had been unintentionally holding my breath and become suddenly conscious of the fact. I don't know if there's an ideal age to find out that one is adopted, but it probably depends on the child's and parents' level of maturity and personal sense of security perhaps giving greater weight to the former.

The news explained a few things at least temporarily in as much detail as my 11-year-old mind needed. I never doubted my mother's love for me, but I had begun to notice differences among family members. My parents were asked to bring pictures of their family members to the adoption agency, where they were used to match children—not very unlike paint samples at Lowes or Sherwin Williams. Unlike some transracial adoptions of African or Asian children by white families, my adoption was a conscious attempt by all parties to fit me into a "similarly appearing" family.

Although my skin was nearly the same tone as that of my grandparents and many other members of my extended family, I strained to find any greater resemblance. While some adoptees grapple with constant questions about obvious ethnic differences from their parents, my questions developed gradually and much more introspectively. It wasn't forced upon me, but I somehow sensed it without yet having a name for it. My hair was a pile of big, shiny brown curls that I would later brush and train into gentler waves despite their obstinacy. I resembled many in my adoptive family closely enough that I don't recall ever being asked by anyone if I was adopted, and I never felt out of place or unusual. But I did wonder.

From the day I learned I was adopted, things made a little more sense. I felt a little more "true." As an only child, the first thing I

5

wondered was if I had any siblings. Was there another boy or girl somewhere in my city or the world beyond who looked more like me than the cousins I'd always known and loved? Was there an uncle whose ears were a little more like mine, a grandmother with my nose or an aunt with my hair? Maybe I even had an identical twin! That would be *so* cool! Whenever we went shopping, I studied faces for any resemblance. People must have thought my staring impolite, but I was quite oblivious to any non-verbal cues my behavior elicited.

My childhood was, I assumed, about the same as most kids I knew. The first schools I attended where quite diverse, but white flight to the suburbs was set in motion by the *riots* of '67. One of my earliest memories is of watching the National Guard trucks roll down streets like Linwood and Dexter while Mom was taking me to or from school or Grandmother's house. Mom worked as a surgical technician at Martin Place Hospital. She prepared operating rooms with the instruments and supplies for surgeries and passed them to the surgeons as they were needed. She started working at the hospital in the cafeteria soon after graduating from high school in 1955 and worked her way up within a few years to helping in the operating room.

I was very proud of what she did, although she worked long hours and often took "call" which means she made herself available to be called in after normal work hours to assist on emergency surgeries. Sometimes she'd get called in and drive all the way to the hospital to find that the surgery had been cancelled. It broke up her day, but she didn't complain because she was paid to be available. That's why she took *call* so much—she had to be available to get to work at a moment's notice, but she was paid for those hours whether she was called in or not. While working those long hours and taking call, Mom also found a way to attend school and earn a professional certification, "Certified Operating Room Technician," which later became "Certified Surgical

Technologist." All the while, she never lost sight of me. In fact, I often went into work with her. I studied, watched television or slept in the nurses' lounge while she worked. I don't know how she was able to keep it all together, but she did and I never felt short-changed—at least not by her.

We were never wealthy, but we always had a roof over our heads and a meal to satisfy if not fill our bellies. I was thankful for leftovers when we had them, and I don't recall ever going to bed on an empty stomach. Because mom worked so much during the week, she'd often make big pots of stew, spaghetti, soup or other things to last us through the week. It's amazing all that she accomplished and how hard she worked, but when you're born a preacher's daughter in Jim Crow Mississippi around 1934, you get busy doing what you need to do. She didn't dwell on the past and there was little time to research it or wear it on her sleeve because she was so consumed with making the best of each day as it came.

She kept my routine as normal as possible. Normal for me was waking before sunrise, eating breakfast and getting dropped off at Grandmother's house about an hour before anyone else was awake. Kiss goodbye from Mom, trudging up the walkway and steps of the two-family-flat often through snow, I was met by my cousin Jenny—a few years older than I—who dutifully and reliably unlocked the door and let me in before sleep-walking back to her bedroom. Back then TV was live, and I remember arriving before the stations began broadcasting. I turned on the TV to see a black and white Indian head test pattern. At 6:00 am, the morning programming began with the playing of the national anthem and the shades of gray image of a billowing flag.

In 1975, lingering questions about my genetic origin were not easily answered. Although Mom invited me to ask, I learned as the years passed that the subject was something she preferred not to discuss. She did so reluctantly and always with the punctuation, "I am your mother," as if it were something that could be forgotten

7

like last week's headline or a fleeting fad. Sometimes she said it with such careful deliberation I wondered if she doubted my mental acuity to grasp and retain such a simple fact.

I knew early on that although she didn't say so directly, Mom was deeply concerned that she would be replaced. Even though I knew that could never happen, no matter how I would assure her, she bristled at any talk about learning the identities of my birth parents. By the time I was in high school I had given up asking her, but unanswered questions like missing puzzle pieces have always irked me. I can push them aside for a while, but they are as insistent and persistent as those unruly curls atop my head.

My granddad Rev. Dr. Charlie Jamerson was born in 1915 in Winona, Montgomery County, Mississippi. Little is known about his parents, but his buckskin complexion and features made him somewhat racially ambiguous. When he was young, his fine, black hair was easily parted with a comb leaving restless undulations in its wake. Granddad never passed for white and as far as I can say, he never gave such a thing a thought. Perhaps his pedigree was well known in the rural confines of Winona never allowing him the option, but even after moving North, he never pretended to be anything other than what he was. After the War like many others, Granddad struck out for better conditions for himself and his daughter up North. His wife died in her prime and my mother was a young child whose earliest years were spent with her maternal grandmother while her father was making a place for them in Detroit.

While my grandfather attended barber college and seminary in Detroit, my mother lived with her grandmother in little Itta Bena, Mississippi. I called it "Itty Bitty." My mother went to school in a one-room schoolhouse; she did not have shoes until she moved North to join Granddad. Her grandmother's home was one room with a potbelly stove in the center for heating and cooking, a bed for her grandmother and one for my mother and a cousin. There

8

was no indoor plumbing. There was an outhouse behind the home and a pen that housed several hogs.

Mom's memories of these times were those of a child who had no point of reference for comparison. She didn't think of shoes as a necessity or luxury. She had no concept of indoor plumbing or heating other than from a wood-burning fire. Her childhood memories were absent of self-pity, shame, or deprivation. She spoke with pride about the way her grandmother could make something to eat out of "a little of nothing." Anyone who knew her casually as a young adult would never have guessed the scarcity from which she emerged.

While my grandfather lived nearly 50 years after leaving the deep South, he never abandoned his thick southern affect. He became a very diligent student and earned a Doctorate of Divinity after becoming an ordained minister. His vocabulary had become immense and his oration was always inspiring and profound, yet the Mississippi accent, which lent him great warmth and sincerity, persisted until the day of his great reward. His daughter, on the other hand, lost that accent like a pound on a treadmill. Every once in a while, an old phrase or word would turn up in her speech, but you can be sure that it was spoken with a well-practiced Yankee dialect.

She recalled one such incident when she walked into a store in Detroit not long after arriving from *Itty Bitty*. She asked the shopkeeper if he had any nigger toes. She did not ask it ashamedly, she did not whisper, and she gave it no other thought until she caught the glare of the man to whom she spoke. He told her kindly, but there was no mistaking the gravity of his entreaty, "Miss, that's not what we call them here. They are called Brazil nuts. Please don't ever use that term again." Perhaps it was the look on his copper face or the tone of his voice. It was not to frighten or shame her, and she never forgot the lesson.

9

Although she spoke fondly of her childhood, especially the friends and family who lived there, she spoke of the times themselves and the surroundings very matter-of-factly if not nostalgically. It's easy to picture her walking the dirt roads to school in a plain home-made dress sewn from sackcloth by her grandmother, shoeless, skipping and leaving a cloud of dust behind her with every care-free hop. She didn't even blink as she told me about the Nigger Tree when I asked what she remembered about segregation in those days. There was a tree where they hung black folks for any real or perceived transgression. This was not 1800 or 1870. This was in the 1940's. I asked if she had ever seen anyone lynched or hanging from that tree, and she said that she had not, but the idea that a child could remember such a frightful appellation with clarity and without wincing speaks to the enduring horror of Reconstruction and the Jim Crow era. She didn't even blink. "That's what it was called." She shrugged.

# CHAPTER TWO

## THE QUEEN'S BUSH

Ronald Sr's family came circuitously to America by way of Ontario, Canada at one of the most precipitously perilous times for Blacks of the 19th century preceding the Civil War. Intolerance and persecution of free black people was at a fevered pitch. On January 21st of 1831 the Courier, a newspaper in Portsmouth, Ohio, published an article notifying all that the "Black Laws" enacted in 1804 would now be stringently enforced. These laws forbade any black or mulatto to live or even work in the state without written proof of their freedom from the county clerk. Over 80 African Americans, "all the colored people of Portsmouth," were forcibly expelled from the state. Exactly 10 months later on August 21st, 70 enslaved men rose up against their tormentors in Virginia, methodically proceeding from one plantation to the next murdering over 75 men, women and children. The Nat Turner rebellion ended with the hanging of him and 17 of his followers, and the lynching of 40-100 enslaved

Ronald G. Levi Jr.

people who had nothing to do with the uprising. According to a 1930 article written by John W. Cromwell in the Journal of Negro History,

> *Turner was skinned to supply such souvenirs as purses, his flesh was made into grease, and his bones divided as trophies to be handed down as heirlooms.*

These were the times in which my second great grandfather John Wesley Levi came of age. Either, both, or countless other similar events conspired to push him from the land of his birth to Ontario, Canada. Born in Maryland in 1809, if he had been a slave he was free and literate by the time he crossed the border. He was among a hardy band of runaways and free people who were compelled to hew their future out of the untamed wilderness rather than face the continued persecution of their birthright.

Upon arriving in Canada, John and his compatriots remained vigilant to preserve their freedom. They took whatever work they could find and educated one another on the news of the day. There were stories of slave catchers prowling the border towns looking for runaways they could return to bondage. The band of men and women knew they must save enough money to buy tools and provisions to set out as far as possible from town where they would not be seen or found. They needed a place of refuge where white southerners dared not follow and one from which they could defend themselves from marauders.

Being free in Canada did not mean free of discrimination. They were not welcomed in many places and they endured insults often, yet they were able to bond with one another and they understood that they were much stronger united than divided. John assumed a position of trust and leadership in this group. He sufficiently impressed and married Ann Garrad on October 1, 1835. Ann was born in and had recently arrived from England. When provisions and tools were secured, the group set out for the wilderness of Canada West. Before Ontario existed, there was the

12

Queen's Bush—a no-man's-land of timber and wildlife. Into this shroud the band forged, hiding themselves from the outside world and setting themselves to the task of building new lives. In the eyes of the government, they were squatters, but every risk the true pioneers took was freely chosen and gladly so.

John and Ann were my third great grandparents who by 1845 were raising one daughter and four sons in the home they were making for themselves. The settlement had grown to nearly 500 souls, and the men realized the risk they faced by continuing to improve lands without permission of the Crown. To mitigate this risk and preserve their investment and livelihood, over 160 heads of households signed the Petition of Wellesley and Peel, requesting permission to buy the land which had been offered for sale. To His Excellency, Sir Charles Theophilus Metcalf, Governor General of British North America, they requested an extension of the period in which to make payment:

> *"We your petitioners, inhabitants of the Township of Wellesley and Peel in the Wellington District being a few days since apprised of the fact that the land in the aforesaid Township is advertised for sale on the 15th [inst] and the conditions of sale being such as to render it impossible for us in so short a time to meet its demands, therefore we humbly petition Your Excellency to grant us a longer time to pay for the land. Your Excellency may not have known the difficulties we have had to surmount in settling these Townships. A majority of your petitioners fled to this country from American oppression and consequently had no funds to commence with. As we came into this wilderness, we were obliged to cut our roads and for the first year were under the necessity of going to the neighboring settlement the distance of 14 miles and bringing in our provisions on our backs. While our food lasted, we labored with persevering industry to*

*clear the land and then went again for a fresh supply. In this way we have been able to clear a few acres so as to begin to raise our own provisions. We have averted ourselves to the utmost to obtain stock and farming utensils as mills are a great distance and consequently much time is consumed in getting our wheat made into flour. Our families have hardly been comfortably provided for.*

*Having these difficulties to surmount your petitioners have been unable as yet to acquire money to pay for the land. Your Excellency is aware that if two hundred families are left at this season of the year without any home, our sufferings will be extreme. A single glance at our prospects urges us to lay our situation before Your Excellency, hoping that you will listen to our petition. And for which your petitioners will ever pray.*

The petition was granted and many of the settlers were able to raise the money to purchase their land. Those who did remained there for many years. John and Ann's family held their land for over a century. A portion was sold in 1949 to Charles Price as witnessed by John Evans, but the descendants of John's son, Wesley, still live on the land, which has become the town of Dresden, and is home to the Uncle Tom's Cabin National Historic Site. Josiah Henson's autobiography was the inspiration for Harriet Beecher Stow's title character and he was the father-in-law of John's granddaughter Estella Levi.

John and Ann added 5 more sons to their family in the years from 1848 to 1855. Like many of the early refugees, John and Ann set aside as much as they could to donate to a formidable new cause led by a woman in nearby St. Catherine's known as Harriet Tubman. Knowing the difficulty of his own journey to freedom from Maryland 15 years earlier, John felt deep admiration for Harriet who returned to their shared place of birth to free others. It was no small accomplishment to carve a community out of a wilderness in the midst of persecution, but to willingly return time and again to the most frightful, loathsome, and lethal locations to free others was a heroism John could barely comprehend. Young Harriett was his idol and the photo of her published in the Dresden paper was preserved in a glass frame for many years.

As the children came of age, so did industry and the wilderness their parents penetrated became cities of some substance. The French who founded Détroit chose the name for its location on the river which connects Lakes St. Clair and Erie. The "straight" as it is translated became known as the Detroit River, and upon it the late 19th century commerce bustled by steam. Paddlewheel boats, barges and ferries of all kinds moved passengers and freight north and south between the two border countries decades before there were bridges and tunnels connecting them. Detroit is the only city in the United States that is north of Canada (Windsor Ontario).

My second great grandfather Thomas Sr was the first of the Levis to repatriate. Following the Civil War, Thomas married Fredonia Burgess and moved from Ontario to Detroit where they began their family in 1872. Detroit was becoming a magnet of industry by the 1880's and there was no shortage of jobs for those able and willing. Opportunities were limited by race as well as education, but Thomas's family set about making a way and transforming themselves from farmers to wage-earners eagerly. Thomas Jr. worked as a cook on one of the steamships that filled the Great Lakes channel. The work was hard and the hours long, but Thomas was thankful to have an occupation that paid enough to support his new wife Emily Gould. My grandfather, their first son Joseph, was born in 1904. Thomas's 8 siblings traveled between Ontario and Michigan commonly. While Thomas worked on the steamships, Emily and Joseph ferried back and forth from uncles and cousins to his parents. These were hopeful times for the mobile family, but none of them foresaw the event that would change Thomas's fortune and re-establish the family as U.S. citizens for decades to come.

The luxury steamer of the Great Lakes in late 19th century did double duty as a passenger and freight carrier. Steamboat lines were established by railroads to join railheads in the 1850s. The service transported passengers and materials from the east to adjoining spurs headed West. Thomas gained employment with the Detroit and Cleveland Navigation Company (D&C), aboard one of the largest and most luxuriously appointed steamers at precisely the time leisure cruising crested in popularity for travel to summer resorts away from the congested industrial hubs. Many of the excursions were overnight sailings arriving the morning after departure. Thomas's ship was described in company brochures:

> "...[It] is without doubt the most palatial steamer on the lakes. It is representative of the company's ideal to serve the public well. The City of Detroit III is a splendid example of marine architecture, beauty and science combined. Power and grace are written into her sweeping lines. The waters of all the world boast no sidewheel steams as large. From stem to stern over all she measures 500 feet, or the length of two city blocks. In beam she is 100 feet wide or the width of a generous city street. At the stem she has a depth of 29 feet 3 inches and at the stern 25 feet 3 inches."

What the kitchens lacked in luxury, they recompensed in functionality. There was no shortage of appliance, ingredient or tool, and Thomas learned his trade from the best chefs and cooks in the region as the City of Detroit III ferried some of the most powerful and influential personalities of the era. D & C policy forbade the mingling of kitchen staff with passengers, so it was with great concern that Thomas answered a summons by one of them. He was not part of the wait staff and not adorned to be present in the dining salon, so the patron was seated in the office of the kitchen smiling with a ship's officer. Before they noticed his approach through the office windows, Thomas recognized the man immediately as none other than Henry Ford. "Lord, save me," he thought. "Please don't let me have offended this man with my cooking or in any other way." The officer opened the door and the eccentric titan stood and smiled warmly. The exact words Henry Ford uttered were shared with family but faded in the cacophony of so many others which followed because Thomas would spend the rest of his career in the employ of the Fords at their new estate, Fair Lane Manor in Dearborn as their personal chef.

Ronald G. Levi Jr.

# CHAPTER THREE

꩜

## GOULDTOWN

Thomas's wife, my great grandmother Emily was a descendant of a unique tradition in New Jersey which was first formally documented in the book *Gouldtown, a Very Remarkable Settlement of Ancient Date* by William Steward and Theophilus Gould Steward published in 1913. The Goulds and Pierces were descendants of Elizabeth Fenwick Adams of England and Abijah Gould, a free black man. John Fenwick and his family arrived in West New Jersey aboard the Griffin in 1675. In his will he bequeathed his holdings to them with a notable exception for his granddaughter:

> *"I do except against Elizabeth Adams of having any ye least part of my estate, unless the Lord open her eyes to see her abominable transgression against him, me and her good father, by giving her true repentance, and forsaking the Black that hast been ye ruin of her, and*

18

*becoming penitent for her sins; upon the condition only I
do will and require my executors to settle five hundred
acres of land upon her."[2]*

Upon learning of her grandfather's exception in 1683, Elizabeth arranged a marriage of convenience to Anthony Windsor on August 23rd only 16 days after the will was signed. After the will was proved Elizabeth Fenwick Adams and Abijah Gould ("the Black") produced a son, Benjamin Gould who inherited the lands secured by his mother. Benjamin married Ann of Finland and their seven children were the foundation of curious racial balancing over many generations. Brothers Richard and Anthony Pierce of Barbados arrived in New Jersey with wives Hannah and Marie Van Aca of the Netherlands. The children of the Pierces who were double cousins (each set of parents were siblings of the other) married the children of the Goulds. The small interracial community was large enough to maintain genetic diversity and consciously selected mates to preserve their light skin and distinctive features. While some found white husbands and wives and moved away to blend in with the majority populace, a few also married darker-skinned black mates. This Colorism was a source of contention in the community for decades. They did not want to be *all white*, they did not want to be *all black,* and they used social and peer pressure to propagate this to the shame and pain of many descendants.

Ronald's grandmother, Emily Gould Levi was born in Michigan after her parents and siblings Eva and John migrated from Gouldtown to Sanilac County. Her father found work in the Clough & Warren Organ Company where he met Eva's future husband, Joseph Hunter Dickinson. Joseph was born in Canada and through hard work and talent became an accomplished inventor owning many patents including an improvement to the player piano which controlled the loudness or softness of the key

---

[2] Gouldtown, a Very Remarkable Settlement of Ancient Date, William Steward, 1913, p. 48

strikes and which could play the sheet music from any point in the song. After marrying Eva, Joseph partnered with her father in the Dickinson & Gould Organ Company. The team exhibited one of its organs at the Word's Fair in New Orleans in 1884. Emily married Thomas Edward Levi Jr. and their sons were Joseph (my grandfather) and Lawrence. Like their parents, these young men were very fair-skinned. Photographs of Lawrence are most always mistaken as those of a white man. Aunt Eva and Uncle Joseph had their fill of racial persecution and returned to New Jersey to live as a white family with their children. They were successful at this and even had German housekeepers, but when their nephews came to visit, Eva hurried them into the garage and closed the doors lest any neighbor recognize them as Negroes. This cruel irony was never forgiven by her sister. "How could she, having understood and fled the oppression of racism, inflict it in any measure on her own nephews?" Emily reasoned. Great Grandmother never forgave her sister for this transgression and my grandfather never visited his aunt in New Jersey again.

It is this context of American racial identity and conflict that Ronald's personality was forged. One side of his family the descendants of persecuted pioneers who left America only to return years later at the feet and in the service of industrial power and the other a tradition of unusual racial homogeny and self-inflicted discrimination. The rarely-spoken and little-understood ramifications of these circumstances are as deep and wide as the oceans, rivers and mountains that connected them. Some found strength and raison d'etre in this history: over time the memory of these names and events faded but the impact to generations echoes on.

# CHAPTER FOUR

───── ঌ ૭ ૯ ─────

# PARADISE LOST

M y paternal grandmother was an articulate, musically talented woman with a warm chuckle that drew a smile from anyone who heard it. To all who knew her, friends and family, she was always known by her middle initial, *A*. The vocal tone of Gladys Allene Pettiford was slightly nasal with a timber as warm and comforting as a cottage fire. As she aged, her voice soothed like a hot toddy and emitted a barely perceptible vibrato that gave the impression she might lapse into Shakespearean grandiloquence at any moment. Her voice and speech were a uniquely Canadian-American amalgam of Downton Abbey's Maggie Smith and songstress Eartha Kitt. She never spoke of it in my presence, but one of the most iconic images of Jim Crow evil scorched in American memory is a stark reminder of the conditions that prompted her father Alwill Pettiford to move to Canada in the early 1900s.

Ronald G. Levi Jr.

The evening of August 6, 1930 in Marion, Indiana, 3 black men were arrested and charged with robbing and murdering a white factory worker and for raping his girlfriend. A photo taken by Lawrence Beitler the next evening reveals a huge crowd of white faces with one man wearing a snot-brake mustache pointing at two of those men bloodied and hanging by ropes from a tree. Beitler sold thousands of copies of the spectacle lynching that inspired the poem "Bitter Fruit" written by Albert Meeropol and popularized by Billie Holiday as "Strange Fruit." One of the men lynched was J. Thomas Shipp. The other was Abraham (Abram) S. Smith, son of Luzenia Pettiford, great grandson of Edmund Pettiford, my fourth great grandfather and second great grandfather of Grandmother A. If her father Alwill Pettiford had not fled reconstruction era persecution of Indiana to Canada at the turn of the century 31 years before this infamous photo was made, perhaps he would have eventually met a similar fate as his second cousin Abram.

Grandmother was not one to gossip, and she was regarded as quite proper and reserved. She didn't go in for the whooping and hollering or the cavorting of the younger generation. She fed her eight children the same foods, bought their clothes from the same stores or made them from the same cloth when they were young. They attended the same elementary schools, and participated in most of the same activities. She kept a tidy home when her four boys and four girls allowed dust to settle beneath them, which was increasingly rare as they came of age. It amazed and at times frightened her how different they all became from one another in spite of the homogeneity of their formative experience.

Emmeline and Lawrence (Buddy) were the eldest and set a high standard for their younger siblings to follow. Uncle Buddy was the first baby to cross the Ambassador Bridge when it opened 12 days after his birth on November 15, 1929. The first underwater tunnel connecting two countries was opened the following year.

giving my grandparents and their children a third conveyance to visit family back in Ontario. Great grandparents Thomas and Emily, along with their siblings and cousins made the journey by ferry at the turn of the century, but the dawn of the Great Depression arrived on wheels in the Motor City. Whether crossing above the water or beneath it, there was no need to stop or transfer on the other side for anything more than a customs check. As the economy recovered from its collapse, commerce and private travel via the bridge and tunnel quickly eclipsed the steamship era.

The boys were too young to enlist when War came. Ronald was the youngest boy of the eight children, but he was old enough to understand the frustration and anxiety his father and uncle faced. Neighborhoods were entirely segregated then. As men left to fight overseas, the vacuum of the war machine sucked in over 400,000 Americans of both races emigrating from the rural south to fuel the Arsenal of Democracy, Detroit's assembly lines. Housing shortages and competition for space and jobs escalated rapidly. The oldest and cheapest housing in the city was originally named by the French for its fertile topsoil, *Black Bottom*. The region north of the River was a cultural cradle of Blues, Jazz and Swing music in those days and became widely known as Paradise Valley. To alleviate congestion and ease tension among the disparate ethnic groups, a federal housing project named Sojourners Truth was created for black families. City and state police guarded moving vans that transported furnishings and belongings to the new homes, but white protestors rioted against the infiltration and had to be forcibly dispersed by police. This was the first salvo in the war within the War. Fifteen months later the allies would be bombing Italy, Detroit would be the fourth largest city in the nation, and Michigan Governor Harry Kelly would be calling in the National Guard.

Grandpa Joe took Ronald to Belle Isle Park for fishing after church, and if he was good, Ronald knew he would get an ice cream bar on the way home. Grandpa, like all Negroes—as they were called in 1943—was wary of interactions with whites in general and with the police in particular. The Ku Klux Klan had a significant presence in Detroit at this time, and Grandpa's experience with his mother Emily and Aunt Eva was a constant reminder that no matter how light his complexion, he was still a colored man and subject to indignity and cruelty at any time. He never took this hypersensitivity for granted, which is why he was keenly aware of a gathering of boys several years older than his own sons, about 30 to 40 yards to his east. When Grandpa and Ronald arrived and dropped their fishing lines into the water, there were a few dozen teenagers sharing tables under a park picnic shelter. School was out for the summer and Grandpa noticed that the kids were grilling hotdogs. He could not hear their conversation or see any disturbance from this distance, but he could see that they were mostly colored boys and girls and there looked to be three or four white boys in the group.

The fish were biting, the June weather was perfect and Ronald was on his best behavior. He shrieked at the sight of the red and white cork float bobbing in the green water offshore, "A bite! A bite!" Grandpa raised an index finger and Ronald knew to be quiet and to watch. He kept one eye on the bobber as it zigged and zagged, and one eye on Grandpa as he grasped the bamboo pole and gently began to pull. Grandpa kept one eye on his son and one on the boys as a larger group of white students arrived and engaged the squatters.

Grandpa didn't need to hear the conversation to understand that an eviction was imminent. He helped Ronald pull in his catch—a respectable yellow perch—and deposited it in the cooler with the bluegills and walleyes they'd already caught. He briskly packed up their folding chairs, poles and cooler and hurried Ronald onto the

Detroit Street Railway bus. He was horrified to see punches being thrown as the bus began distancing them from the spectacle. He pounded his knee in anger. If he had been alone or with other men, he might have tried to intervene to diffuse the antagonism, to help the colored kids find another spot, maybe. That's what he would have wanted someone to do if his sons were being attacked. But he would not take such a chance on his own with his small son and a crowd of agitated young people. Ronald never saw the melee behind them as he was fixated on the glassy-eyed stare of his victim peering through the shaved ice. He was proud, victorious and looking forward to that ice cream bar, "This is the best day ever!" He smiled at his perspiring father.

The ride between Belle Isle and their home required one bus, two street cars and a five-minute walk. To get there, it took them about 40 minutes that summer afternoon. Grandpa's throat parched as the bus slowed to a stop and he saw mounted police and Ford panel vans with their bulbous fenders gleaming and lone red lights flashing urgently atop the roofs racing to the scene they left minutes earlier. National Guard tanks were swerving from Jefferson Avenue onto the bridge. Traffic leaving the island was bumper-to-bumper. Grandpa considered getting off the bus and walking, but they were probably safer minding their own business on the back of that bus than exposed to the hostilities outside. Bicycles and motorcycles were leaving the island in droves, squeezing between and weaving through the belching cars and buses.

As the bus turned onto the bridge to leave the island, Grandpa could finally see the pandemonium in the vicinity of the picnic shelter. There were far more than a few dozen kids brawling now. There were at least one hundred men and boys throwing fists, garbage cans, rocks, tree branches and more. There were not enough police officers on the island to quell the violence by the time the bus exited the bridge. Grandpa opened the window a little more and told Ronald to stop sticking his finger in the bluegill's mouth, "Leave it be now. That's our dinner. Mama will fry it up good. I can smell it already, can't you?" he forced a smile. His face did not reveal the dread that had begun to set in.

Grandpa Joseph's father Thomas warned him how he had been harassed and abused for simply driving in Dearborn to his employer's home on several occasions. Were it not for a personal call from Henry Ford to the chief of police informing them of his personal chef's legitimacy, Thomas said, "They would surely have strung me up sooner or later." Grandpa was angry that his family had to endure this treatment after having voluntarily repatriated and having worked so diligently to better themselves and their community. The persecution had not ended with his father, and it would not end with him or his sons, he lamented. The white community, as diverse as it may have been ethnically, seemed unanimous in its regard for Negroes. The monolith made no distinction between northern blacks born natively or emigrated from Canada and those exiting reconstruction and the Jim Crow South.

As they transferred from the bus to the street car on Gratiot Ave, Ronald saw crowds gathering and the men looked angry. They were shouting things, but there was so much noise, Ronald couldn't quite make it out. The street cars were open to the elements and normally Ronald enjoyed the wind, sights and delicious smells from restaurants and street vendors, but something wasn't right. He felt uneasy and tugged Grandpa's elbow. "What's happening?" he asked. "Some boys started fighting on the island, and it looks like the word is spreading. You stay close to me and do everything I say immediately; do you understand?" "I'm scared." "It'll be ok. You carry the fish and I'll carry the chairs and poles. We don't have too much longer." Ronald had forgotten about the ice cream bar by now. The *best day ever* was vanishing as miraculously as it had dawned.  They transferred to the final leg of their journey home almost 2 hours after packing up their gear.

The streetcar stopped at an intersection and Ronald looked ahead in amazement as another coach crossing their path was consumed by a hoard of grotesquely distorted white faces. Ronald grabbed his father's hand, but he could not look away as he saw a colored man pulled through the open side of the car as easily as that yellowfin had been plucked from the green water of the great river. Ronald winced as he witnessed white men pummeling and kicking the fellow. His face and shirt collar were covered in blood and Ronald strained to see if there was some cut or why there was so much bleeding.

Just as he noticed the man's nose was terribly shifted to one side of this face, Ronald was airborne. He was dangling by one arm floating above the ground. He slammed into someone's body, was pulled over another's head and jostled against a few more before his feet finally felt something solid beneath them. "I told you to keep your eyes on me," Grandpa said sternly and kneeled to eye-level with his son. "We're not far from home, but it's too dangerous to stay on the street car. We'll stay off the main roads and cut through the alleys. Can you do that with me?" Ronald felt the wetness of his face and realized tears had been flowing—he had been crying without realizing it. He wiped his face with his hands and arm, sniffed and nodded.

Neighborhood streets were separated by narrow alleys where garbage was collected in galvanized steel cans. The homes were built back-to-back and the yards typically abutted an alley where garbage trucks drove to empty the cans. This novel design maintained curb appeal and kept refuse, rodents and scavengers out of sight. For this reason, they were rarely traveled by pedestrians and could not easily be seen from the main streets. As chaos erupted around them, Grandpa and Ronald walked quickly and single-mindedly for the safety of home. As they

27

crossed the last street before reaching their home, they saw smoke billowing from the five and dime—the "dollar store" of the 1940s. Ronald saw men jumping through a broken glass window of the grocery where Grandma sent him and Buddy for Pall Mall unfiltered cigarettes all the time, and he heard the deafening sound of shots being fired—bang! bang! bang! He saw Gerald from across the street fall and he heard the thud and crack of his skull as it met the cement curb. The "army man" killed Gerald, the paper boy. He shared penny candy with Ronald every week when he delivered the Sunday edition of the Detroit News. He had the best knock-knock jokes of anyone Ronald knew. Gerald's blood emptied into the gutter. The riot lasted for 3 days, became fodder for Japanese and German war propaganda to sow dissent among American troops, and was the utter end of innocence for one little boy. He learned many lessons in his formative years, but the first race riots of Detroit set a few tenets in motion. He would never be abused, he would always have the upper hand. Violence and pain are potent motivators, and if it ever happened again, he would be ready for it.

# CHAPTER FIVE

## CHARLIE MAE

When the sun was shining and Mom was happy, I never gave my biological origins a thought. I don't think my adolescent angst and sophomoric woes were any more severe than other children of my age and socio-economic circumstance, and for the most part I felt fortunate. One might think loneliness would be common among only children, but I don't think it was any more pronounced in me than in others with siblings. Once in a while I wondered if there were another child out there that looked like me—if I had a sibling somewhere in the world—but I didn't dwell on it and the thoughts were not caused by loneliness or boredom. I spent so much time travelling to and from grandmother's house and school that I was always with someone: Mom and her carpool, Grandmother, cousins, aunts and uncles... there was always someone around. The neighborhoods had plenty of kids and we all knew one another and played together often, especially when the weather warmed up. If I got bored, all I had to do was walk two houses in one direction or three in the other and there'd be someone to race, ride bikes, or play kickball and two-square. As long as we were on the porch of our homes by the time the street lights came on at dusk, we were allowed a lot of independence.

One summer weekend Mom and I were on our regular shopping errands and we stopped at her favorite second-hand store that sold everything from appliances to clothes, and of course, toys. I never minded going in there with Mom because the toy room was always full of things I could try out while she was looking for bargains on other things. She'd pick out a shirt or pair of pants for herself or for me, I'd try them on and then head back to the toy room to continue my adventures. By the time I was entering Jr. High School, it occurred to me that many kids never bought anything second-hand. I didn't see much difference between the used things I had and the new things other people had—for the most part, I couldn't tell the difference. As a matter of fact I found it amusing that kids would get new things and come up with creative ways to "age" them.

Whether blue jeans or a baseball glove, I figured it was a lot easier to have fun with something that was already broken in. So, having things that were not brand new was never a source of shame or longing for me. Once in a while, however, there was something that captured my attention completely and the 5-speed bike with the gear shift on the cross bar, the padded banana seat and the tall sissy pole on the back was it! There were always bikes in the toy room. The store was good about cleaning them up, but they were usually nothing special. Pedal brakes, baskets or bells on the handlebars, that was all kid stuff to me. But this red boy's bike with the hi-rise chopper handlebars had to be mine. Instead of shifting gears on the handles, this one had a lever on the cross bar that looked like it belonged on a car. Instead of P, N, D, R, it had 1, 2, 3, 4, and 5 and you better believe my mom haggled over the price to get it for me. Never mind that the bike was used and already marked down to $10 or $15. Mom never missed a chance to save a little more. I don't know what the final price was, but I know it wasn't what was marked and I wouldn't be surprised if she convinced them to throw it in with the rest of her purchases for free. That was how my mom rolled.

I loved that bike and I rode it every single day. I rode with friends and rode all by myself. I rode it from one end of the block to the other and everywhere in between. I wasn't allowed to leave our block, so it was a little like being a hamster on a treadmill, but I had the coolest bike anywhere and if they took away all the streets in the entire city of Detroit I would have been content just sitting on that bike and going nowhere at all. I rode to the Standard gas station on the corner of Linwood Avenue where the attendant Mr. Williams sold me penny candy. The chewy Mary Janes and Squirrel Nut Zippers were my favorites, but he wouldn't acknowledge my presence (or anyone's) unless we first extended a proper greeting, "Hello, Mr. Williams. May I have...." was the only way to be noticed. Any other words or behavior apparently rendered us completely invisible.

I must have been invisible one afternoon when I rode to the station and popped the kickstand to go hunting for crayfish in the ditch by the railroad tracks. There was an oil refinery behind our neighborhood and a railroad track separated it from our alley and the backs of our homes. You could dip a jar in the muddy water two or three times and almost always come away with one or two little crawdaddies—not to eat but to look at and throw back. It sounds quite strange now, but it passed for great fun back then.

As I walked back to my bike from the ditch, I noticed a big burly kid crossing Linwood heading straight toward me. An awful dread overcame me and I was frozen with fear. I don't know where Mr. Williams was or if the gas station was closed, but I felt completely alone and was unable to look in any direction other than the face of this huge, dark menace. The skin around his eyes looked purple almost as if eye shadow had been applied. I remember his exact words as he grabbed the handle of my bike in the fat meat of his palm, "I'll count to 3 for you to get off this bike. 1...2..." and I gave it up. I watched his hippo hind parts rise and fall with each turn of the pedals and my bicycle disappeared with him.

When they were out of sight, the flood gates opened. I turned and ran home—less than 20 yards—in complete hysterics. "He took my bike!" I cried to my mother. After calming me and coaxing the entire story out of me as well as a description of the thief, my mother went to the home of every child on our block—not to accuse them but to enlist them. She offered a reward to anyone who would tell her where the bike was. She asked them to go out and look everywhere they could, and the first one to give her the correct information would get the reward. She didn't go to the police—she went to the kids and parents—our neighbors.

We found the bike. One of our neighbor kids reported that he saw the thief riding it only a few blocks away, and at that very moment the bike was parked in the detached garage of his home. My mother thanked the boy, gathered me and her purse and promptly drove us right over to the scene. She knocked on the door and a woman answered—the thief's mother. She rejected the accusation, "My son? Oh no, you must be mistaken. He would never do anything like that." The hippo became a sheep before my very eyes. Guilt was written all over his face whether his oblivious mother could see it or not. "Oh, he did it alright!" my mother insisted, "and the bike is in your garage right now!" I don't know if his mother's surprise was feigned or real, but when the garage door opened and we put the bike in the trunk of our car, I never looked back.

I was so proud of my mom and thankful for her. She said we were going to get that bike back only a few days earlier, and she meant every word of it. Maybe that's why I never doubted her. If Mom said she was going to do something, I knew it was as certain as the sun and moon. If she said I was going to get a spanking, there was no chance she was going to forget about it. If she couldn't do it immediately, it would find me later. *Yes* was always *yes* with her and *no* was always *no*. It stayed that way well into my high school years before I ever had reason to question her resolve.

# CHAPTER SIX

———————— ༺༛༺ ————————

## TOYLAND

The Detroit of my youth may be romanticized, but everything I confide to you here is verifiably true. Detroit was invigorating, exciting, beautiful and frightening long before it was defiant, frightening, resilient, and resurgent. The Detroit of my youth was after-church meals with Granddad at the Flaming Embers restaurant on Grand Circus Park, weekend shopping for furniture at the J.L. Hudson's warehouse on Woodward Avenue with Mom, winter ice skating at Palmer Park and Belle Isle with cousins, and ripping and running in the streets and alleys with friends and neighbors whenever allowed. In those days, ladies and gentlemen dressed in their finest clothes when shopping at department stores like Hudson's or on the *Avenue of Fashion* named Livernois Road. Women wore white gloves, gentlemen wore ties and hats, and children were equally accessorized.

Mom took me to Hudson's where we rode the attended elevators to the children's shoe floor. A uniformed attendant closed the doors to the compartment, rotated a lever, the lights on the ornate brass panel alternated 1, 2, 3, 4 as the cabin rose and she politely announced, "Children's Shoes." She opened the inner accordion gates, then the outer door, and we stepped into the majesty of the modern American department store as only Detroit and J.L. Hudson's could conjure. There was a floor for everything at Hudson's, and children's shoes was complete with a bridge and mirrors that allowed parents (mothers) to study the gait of their toddlers walking. The bridge was a novelty that distracted the objects of study (us children) from the act of being studied. The result was a flood of mothers who appreciated the recognition of their passions and who rewarded it financially.

My Stride Rites were thick-soled, stiff, bulky white leather ankle-high boots. Cute is a matter of perspective, but what isn't cute on a toddler with the newfound ability to stand upright? When your child was important, and you had the means, you got thick-soled, ankle-high, polished white leather Stride Rite shoes for their proper physiological development. That's what they were selling, that's what my mom bought, and I can't argue the fact because I've never had a problem with my feet, arches, gait, stride, or spine. In my long-earned wisdom, I recognize that perhaps my podiatric good-fortune had more to do with genetics than with the good people at J.L. Hudson's or Stride Rite, but most of all it had to do with Mom's prioritization of her life. She sacrificed a lot for me and of all the doubts I have ever had, one has never been her ability to prioritize her life. I was always at the top. There's never been a close second, and there's never been a question of that matter. She did her very best to give me the best of everything the world had to offer. She'd work extra hours, take extra call, postpone buying something she needed or wanted, in order for me to have not just any pair of shoes, not just any education... but the best pair of shoes any toddler could have, the best education any elementary school student could have.

J.L. Hudson's was also the perennial home base of Santa Claus and the Thanksgiving Day parade in Detroit since 1924. This was not a fake Santa Claus, a stand-in or a look alike. The real, actual Santa Claus left the North Pole and traveled all the way to Detroit to live for a whole month. All of the other children in the entire world had to settle for a stand-in while Detroit hosted the real Santa from Thanksgiving until Christmas. Today the start of the Christmas season is dictated by the retailer who announces the biggest discounts first. It seems to begin earlier each year and Christmas carols can be heard on the radio before Halloween candy is fully digested by most trick-or-treaters. In the '70s, Christmas didn't start in Detroit until Santa stepped off his sleigh on Woodward and into the open window of Hudson's after accepting the key to the city and "the hearts of good children everywhere." The parade on Thanksgiving Day marked the beginning of Christmas and the Mayor welcomed Santa to town and parents and children to *Toyland*.

Toyland at Hudson's flagship store was the most wonderful, magical place on earth! Sparkling garland, twinkling lights, fluffy never-melting permanent snow overflowing everywhere, proudly prancing reindeer perched strategically, peppermint and evergreen swirls of color, oversized ornaments of silver and gold, and meticulously costumed elves and matching retail helpers transported boys and girls who waited in line for seemingly hours to the transplanted North Pole at J.L. Hudson's Department Store. Toyland *was* Santa's workshop and if you didn't believe it, all you had to do was wait in line for an hour or so and you'd see him face to face—you'd sit on his lap, tell him what you wanted, and then slip down a slide into your parents' waiting arms ready and assured that this would be the best Christmas ever.

On one of our weekly shopping excursions downtown, which included the Eastern Market, E.J. Korvette, Cunningham Drugs, and a quick stop at S.S. Kresge, we found ourselves at my favorite, Hudson's. As Mom was trying on leather gloves at the ladies accessories counter, I found myself transfixed by the escalator carrying shoppers from the main floor to upper echelons. I was old enough to read, but apparently not old enough to reason well. There are two moving rails on either side of the metal escalator stairs. In the lower right corner of the right rail, near the floor there was a square sign marked Do Not Push. I don't recall if there were any other words written on that sign, but I do remember the words were written in red on a white background, and I was captivated by a curiosity for an explanation. "Do Not Push," Why? What will happen? If we shouldn't push it, why is it there? It can't be too bad, or it would be hidden from view.

I wish I could say that I hesitated or considered the possibilities more thoroughly, but I was drawn to the button as to a black and white hypnotic spiral spinning that drew me inescapably nearer. I squatted down and pressed the square button, and suddenly the moving stairs stopped. Dozens... maybe hundreds of white faces turned and looked down... all the way down the long moving stairway at the little barely brown face with big shiny curls, wide-eyed and mouth agape. Some of those eyes pierced me hatefully, some of the gasps singed me, some looks were a tangle of bemusement and frustration, but none were happy, joyful or thankful. I quickly and easily disappeared into the crowd behind me, navigated the knees and hips in the undulating mass returning to the glass counter where my mother was completing her purchase. I never told her of my curiosity or the lesson I had learned.

# CHAPTER SEVEN

—⌒⟁⌒—

## RONALD GENE

Ronald Gene was the youngest boy and 7th of 8 children born to Gladys and Joseph Levi. His brother Buddy noted that Ronald always had a contrary streak in him. If he couldn't get others to see or do things his way, he'd go without them. *Meatball* was what his father called him, but after Grandfather Joe died in 1961 the nickname was retired permanently. Ronald was his own man and no one else's. He made his own rules and as far as I can recall, he never apologized to anyone for it. After graduating Northern High School in Detroit, he wanted a car of this own. His parents refused and his defiant response was to enlist in the Air Force. He served four years as a military policeman without any particular mishap or distinction and was discharged honorably. That's about the last time he ever served anyone other than himself.

He was a self-professed hustler and inordinately proud of that fact. When he returned from service he took jobs delivering ice and fish to homes, and he saved and borrowed enough money to buy a tidy two-story on Doris Street near Oakman Boulevard. Mr. and Mrs. Painter, an elderly white couple lived next door and welcomed him and his new wife to the neighborhood warmly. Ronald wasn't much for making friends with neighbors, however. He was all about the *hustle*. While Mom worked her way out of the kitchen and into the operating room at the hospital, he started his own security business out of his new home. He bought badges and starter pistols and hired himself out to local businesses—groceries, dry cleaners, and gas stations. The badges and pistols were used to project an image of authority and power where little if any truly existed. That was the hustle, but he worked it to great effect.

He quickly set about hiring men to watch businesses while he transitioned to an executive role in the company he named Inner City Security. In the days before electronic surveillance, video cameras and recorders, security monitoring was performed contemporaneously by human eyes and ears. In larger properties, keys were permanently attached at strategic points throughout the building or campus. Guards made rounds with a mechanical watchman's clock to record their movements. The key inserted into the clock made an imprint on a paper disc recording the time of the event. In this way, the boss knew if his guards were making rounds as scheduled or if they were falling asleep on the job. Ronald's business grew as he executed contracts with insurance, retail and manufacturing facilities throughout the city of Detroit.

The first extended interaction I had with white people was with our neighbors, the Painters. Mrs. Painter often invited me over to bake cookies (or eat cookies which she baked). In their basement, Mr. Painter had an electric train with its own little city of buildings, trees and lights. I can still remember the smell of the "smoke" expelled from the engine as it came through the mountain tunnel with its little HO gauge headlight blazing the way. The excitement of running the train never faded for me, and eating cookies after a hard day at the train yard was just about Heaven. When I was very small and Mom was called into work, Mrs. Painter would babysit me. Other than the freak death of my pet Beagle who was shot in the eye on a New Year's Eve by a stray bullet, mine was in every way an idyllic toddler-hood. That was before the Rebellion.

If Inner City Security did well before the riots of '67, also known as the Rebellion, it really took off afterward. As businesses and residents fled the city in droves for the suburbs, they left their assets behind. For those who decided to hold on to their investment, securing their interest became of paramount concern. For those who wanted nothing more to do with the city, the glut of property and plummeting demand ushered prices right down the drain. Ronald was able to buy a 4-bedroom mansion with servants' quarters for a paltry $12,000 cash in 1972. As we drove south on Linwood Ave., made a left on LaSalle Gardens and a right on LaSalle Blvd, the size and beauty of the homes made no impression on me. It was my mother's optimism and ebullience that outshone every other hint of opulence and grandeur. Whatever this new home was, the move was making Mom happy, and her happiness was my happiness.

As I grew up in that home, I learned much more about the history of Detroit and the significance of the neighborhood. It was several years before I noticed the large caliber divots in the facia and masonry of a home on the opposite, north corner. Surrounded by a towering black wrought iron fence, it was a beautiful property, but the holes which had escaped my attention when we first moved in were permanent reminders of the violence that precipitated our good fortune. I never learned the details of the siege. Rumors were that the home had been used as a base of operations for those resisting the oppression of a corrupt legal and enforcement bureaucracy or that it was a depot for weapons and drugs. Whatever the case, it was clearly a corner whose current beauty and tranquility belied a dark and extremely loud past. None of the other homes on that block or the adjacent ones sustained similar scars. Including the shell-pocked southwest corner of Lamothe and Lasalle Blvd.; the neighborhood remained an oasis for many years before it would face the despair of the1980's.

The neighborhood was the geographic epicenter of social and racial change in Detroit. Our Mediterranean white stucco masterpiece with black trim was within short walking distance of the corner of 12th Street and Grand Boulevard where the Rebellion was sparked, Hitsville USA (the first home of Motown and Tamla records), and Olympia Stadium, the home of the Detroit Red Wings. Next door to the home of Rev. C. L. Franklin and the childhood home of his daughter Aretha, our expansive back yard nurtured mature maple and elm trees, a two-story carriage house and several iron horse rings anchored in concrete blocks from the era before automobiles ruled the roads. Before we finished moving in, an in-ground pool ten feet deep had been installed and a 12-foot chain-link fence had been erected around the perimeter of the yard. Anyone who offered counsel as to the error and offense of such a change to the very traditional and historic neighborhood risked no end to the peace of mind and obscenities they would receive from Ronald. His disinterest in neighborly pursuits was interpreted disdainfully by some who welcomed his changes by throwing bags of garbage over the fence into the yard on several occasions. This was answered by an additional 12 inches of height and barbed wire which seemed to do the trick for a while.

Still a hustler at heart, Ronald had become a bona fide entrepreneur, employing scores of men and women. Whether the

Ronald G. Levi Jr.

IRS was on his heels, or dissatisfied customers & employees sought legal remedies, Ronald would simply change the name of his company first to Nu Way and then to Prudential. He opened a bar with his brother on the eastside. They bought Duke, a Doberman Pinscher, to "guard" the property. Within a couple of years, the dog had been poisoned and the bar burned to the ground. I was never privy to the machinations of his businesses; however, I knew that he worked long hours, often slept at the office and drank a lot.

I quickly learned to distinguish sober frustration and anger from drunken rage. When he was sober and angry, he was quiet and unapproachable. When he was drunk he was confrontational, paranoid, exceedingly bitter—and unapproachable. His drunken rage was terrifying when I was young, but it became exhausting as I matured. The best memory I have of him is a late summer evening when the lights of the pool he built danced in the canopy of trees above. Mom had forgotten how to swim many years prior. She said that she once knew how, but a boisterous dunking scared the ability from her forever. Ronald was a strong swimmer and watched as I paddled back and forth wearing floaties on my skinny arms and waist.

He shouted encouragement from his chaise lounge and that was about the closest I ever felt to him. He acknowledged me and that was far more than I usually received from him, so it was memorable. As I dried myself from my self-inflicted swimming lesson, we noticed a bird dive-bombing the water. It was fast and it skimmed the shimmering surface but the flight pattern was erratic. Ronald recognized it not as a bird but as a bat. The poor creature oblivious to its own fate, ironically in search of life-giving water and insects met its end when Ronald caught it with the extendable leaf-skimming net. Mom and I shrieked as the doomed creature circled and dove one, twice, three times, skimming the water for a drink. Thwaccckk! Knocked from the sky, its sonar useless and its blindness exploited, its freedom was snuffed from the sky—suffocated in shimmering aquamarine.

Fascinated, I knew Mom had access to formaldehyde at work and asked her to bring some home so that I could have more time to study the little brown bat. Was there anything in the world my wonderful mama would not do for me? If so, this was not one of them. I had that bat in a jar the next day and watched him for weeks...turning and twisting that jar to view every angle. I marveled at the leathery web of its wings and was amazed by the use of its claws for climbing, crawling and hanging. I wondered the purpose of its eyes since it was nocturnal and blind and was duly impressed by ears that were independently capable of locating and processing sounds in ways I could only imagine. I knew it depended on echo location and I wondered how it could recognize its own family or if that need were even present in the species. The closest I ever felt to Ronald was the night I swam in floaties and he killed a living creature right in front of my eyes.

# Chapter Eight

───────── ༁ ༁ ───────── 

## Unbearable Lightness

The preschool, kindergarten and elementary schools I attended in the early '70s were, I thought, racially diverse. To understand the obvious as well as more nuanced differences between diversity and integration, is to fully appreciate Detroit's hard-won infamy as the most segregated city in the North. Until 3rd grade, the schools I attended were all within the formal boundaries of the city of Detroit. None were suburban, all were private, and I always thought they had a nearly equal representation of black and white students. I pulled up a class picture from 1969 and to my surprise the only white face was that of our teacher, Mrs. Wells. Pictured are 26 students, 2 teachers, and 2 administrators—only one of them was white. Somehow in the intervening 45 years, I have unintentionally lightened the complexions of 13 people! In a city of 1.5 million, 839,000 were white. Detroit was extremely diverse, but the ethnic groups were largely stratified, each with its own cultural enclave.

Springwells, which was originally an independent German-speaking community of Lutheran protestants, was annexed by Detroit in 1849. The Great Irish Potato Famine of the 1840s became the great immigration of County Cork to West Detroit where half of the population of the 8th ward comprised Corktown. From 1904 – 1925, Detroit's Polish population grew from 13,000 to 115,000 and the Dodge Brother's Hamtramck plant became the cradle of Poletown. Before the German immigrants pushed out to Springwells, they inhabited much of the fertile area between Lafayette and Jefferson avenue. As they shifted southwest in the 1840s, newly arrived Greek immigrants filled in behind them and the area remains known as Greektown. The most recent immigrants to add their culture and color to the saga of Detroit have snuggled right up to the aging and evacuating Springwells, and have carved out of it Mexicantown.

Germantown, Corktown, Poletown, Greektown, and Mexicantown are all within the city limits. It can reasonably be argued that Detroit was one of the most cosmopolitan cities in America in every manner—especially in the arts. culinary, music, visual and performing arts—we've always had an embarrassment of riches from which to choose. A different kind of embarrassing is the manner in which redlining contributed to the marginalization and near complete destruction of one of the oldest and most tenacious of all ethnic groups to set foot on her soil, the African-Americans.

In the early 1800s Poland was not yet an independent country. Slovakia and other Eastern European countries were part of the Austro-Hungarian Empire. Many who arrived from those regions in the mid-1800s were listed as German or Hungarian, but their ethnicity—their culture and language—tells a different story for those caring to listen. For them the transition, if not assimilation, to American life was as complicated as walking through a well-lit open door. Many Poles, Slovaks and Hungarians spoke German. Transacting business between those communities was natural or easier for them than for the Greeks, who had to be more self-reliant. The Irish came in such numbers and had the benefit of a nearly common language—English. To be sure, there were misgivings or animosity between some of these factions, but none more easily identifiable for the purpose of discriminating than those whose skin was darker.

This is the context of a young boy who sees the differences in skin color and features of black and white people, but who has not yet attached any significance to them. I recognized the differences early, but did not draw correlations until my subconscious adaptations failed one sunny summer day in my 3rd grade year.

It wasn't until 3rd grade that I felt the pain of exclusion and otherness. Before moving to the Mediterranean on LaSalle, little Doris Street with Mr. Williams at the corner gas station at Linwood was a playground of kids who got along most of the time. We rode our bikes, played kickball, 2-square, and chased the ice cream truck whenever we heard the music blaring. We were all varying hues of brown, but I don't recall any of us ever making a point of that fact.

Everywhere Mom and I went back in those days, there were white people –the grocery, department stores, banks, you name it. It doesn't sound noteworthy unless you lived in Detroit in the '80s, a decade when the only white people one would see were those who were lost or on their way to or from secure offices in the Fisher Building or General Motors Headquarters. There were very few businesses left—no grocery stores, no department stores. Before that, seeing white people was common when we went out, but not so much when we came home with the exception of our neighbors Mr. and Mrs. Painter.

St. Cecelia was a nice enough school, but I was a little ahead of the work and Mom began to look for something more challenging for me. Through her contacts at the hospital, she learned about the

Roeper City and Country School in Bloomfield Hills. Known as a school for the gifted, the admissions process required some aptitude tests. At St. Cecelia, Sister Margaret was very stern, but Sister Mary Jean and Mrs. Love were as warm and supportive as any parent or student could ask. I wasn't thrilled about leaving them, but once I saw the Roeper School, I was captivated. The campus is set on several rolling acres in the most affluent zip code in the Midwest, heavily treed with paved footpaths between the various buildings that housed upper, middle and lower schools. The k-2 lower school classrooms were in the Martin Luther King Jr. Domes. The domes are concrete half-spheres with whimsical eyebrow windows that create an atmosphere of cozy creativity and safety. The middle school classrooms were a short 50-yard walk from the domes and occupied converted single or double-wide mobile homes. High above the middle- and lower schools atop the "Big Hill" (there were many hills, but only one Big Hill), stood the upper school where junior and senior high school and administrative offices looked out and down upon the idyllic little village.

It wasn't so much at Roeper where I felt "different" as it was when I returned home. At Roeper 3rd grade was called Stage III. I'm still not sure how many years students remain in each stage as the stages did not correspond directly to traditional grades. In Stage III we called our teachers by their first names. There were Tom and Karen, a yellow submarine made of wood and I recall singing *Yellow Submarine* at assembly on at least a couple of occasions because I learned the words to the song and probably would not otherwise have done so at that age. I'm pretty sure I was the only kid on my block at home who knew them. At least I never heard any black kids at the parks around home singing it.

Roeper truly was diverse and integrated. There were black, white and Asian children learning together in a very unstructured environment. I used to walk from my grandmother's house on

Santa Rosa several blocks to St. Cecelia. Even in the snow and rain, we never took the bus. We always walked it. We usually walked down Livernois, a main artery that was wide, well-lit and heavily-traveled. In better weather and daylight hours, we'd walk down Santa Rosa, Stoepel or Monica—residential streets with tall trees and canopies of leaves in the early fall and spring. Once I started at Roeper; though, Bus 9 was the only way to go and it started early. In the winter, this meant before dawn. The bus picked up the Detroit kids first since we were the farthest from school and circled back toward the destination, picking up the suburbanites along the way.

The bus was nearly empty every morning when I got on. Most of the kids attending Roeper regardless of race were the children of professional people. Their parents were physicians, attorneys, accountants, judges, and politicians for the most part. They were largely pretty good kids. There's always a bully in every group, and there are cliques of common interest, but for the most part it was a pretty supportive place. There was the time I smelled something awful and it really turned my stomach. The nurse's office was all the way up in the administrative offices on the Big Hill. Mrs. Haisch asked Sheila Brodsky to walk with me to make sure I got there ok. I was so grateful to them both. I can't remember the diagnosis, or the treatment, but I remember their kindness that day.

It was back home while playing with neighbors that the dichotomy of my worlds was made starkly apparent to me. I don't recall the words I used or any details of the preceding conversation, but I do remember my younger neighbor Karen snorting, "You talk so white." Now, I had noticed the difference in the way kids at school talked—not just the white ones—all of them. It was different from the way most of the kids in my neighborhood spoke. Until then, however, I never assigned a color to the sounds, rhythms and patterns. Throughout my young life, I simply parroted what I saw and heard. I mirrored my environment. When I was with family, I spoke as they spoke. When I was with friends, I spoke the way they did. When I was at school, it wasn't difficult to speak the way my classmates did. For me, it was a choice, but not a very conscious choice. Until that moment, how I spoke and behaved had been largely shaped by a natural yet subconscious desire to fit in and to not be different.

Little Karen's announcement alerted me to a fact I would not otherwise have noticed—I slipped up. What had once been an effortless transition from one dialect to another until that time had all of the sudden become something that required deliberation. Forgetting where I was and to whom I was speaking could invite derision, bullying, marginalization, exclusion. From then on, I would pay attention before speaking. I would know where I was, to whom I was speaking and make sure that I was using the appropriate words, tone, inflection, and pronunciation. It wasn't at all complicated for someone who is truly fluent in two dialects, but it comes off as insincere and insulting when attempted by anyone else. I was already a polyglot—I simply needed to be a more mindful one. I thought, "When I want to, I can speak however I need to in order to fit in." I felt proud of this ability because I didn't think many of my Roeper friends could pull that off in my neighborhood or vice versa. I was confident this skill would serve me well and be one that I would never lose. I simply had to pay attention and use it to my advantage. That was 3rd grade.

# CHAPTER NINE

---〜๑๑〜---

## ON OUR WAY

The Roeper School is designed for gifted children, but not all academically accomplished children have the same gifts. In addition to being able to understand and contrast subjects considered advanced for their age, there is a psychological and social maturity that also contributes to their academic experience. Mom wanted me to be among the best qualified, most highly capable children of my age group. As much as I proved an academic eligibility, I did not have the intrinsic desire or curiosity to make the most of an environment as unstructured as Roeper. I felt that I had choices at Roeper. I could choose to go for a walk, exercise my creativity or imagination in any way I desired, and if that did not correspond to some academic schedule, the choice was all mine without consequences.

I didn't feel that I was learning much and Mom apparently agreed and began to look for something more fitting. Was I attuned and mature enough to know that I wasn't getting what I needed, yet not mature enough to exercise the initiative and responsibility on my own? I think this may have been the case, but I wasn't wise enough to recognize it then. Many of my friends at Roeper went on to very successful and rewarding professions, but one of the best lessons I learned was that they were not unique. Examples of success and failure in children attending public, parochial, and private schools abound. What I needed was structure and discipline. I needed people smarter than I was to tell me what to do, how to do it, and when to do it. When you consider the implications of that when critical reasoning and social justice are central topics, you inevitably consider Jesuit institutions of education.

As Roeper nurtured the curiosity and initiative of self-disciplined children, the University of Detroit Jesuit High School and Academy nurtured the Ignatian ideal, which is to help one conquer oneself and to regulate one's life in such a way that no decision is made under the influence of any inordinate attachment. More simply it is the spirituality of finding God's will for better decision making. It was exactly what I wanted, although I could not articulate it at the time, and it is into a system of education based on this spirituality that I immigrated in1975.

What drew me to this Jesuit ideal? I had it made at Roeper. There were no consequences that I could discern for mediocrity or failure. Why did I wish to subject myself to a system and culture that many considered strict, regimented, or even reactionary? I can only explain that I didn't fit at Roeper and Mom encouraged and allowed me to talk to her about it. It seemed great for many other kids, but I knew that I was supposed to be learning, but what I was learning didn't seem "right" for me at the time. I was learning about diversity, acceptance, sociology, and many other disciplines in the way that subjects learn about their experimenters. I am now certain that the Ignatian characteristics were signposts placed in my life to draw me closer to God through Jesus Christ whom I had accepted only a few years earlier in Granddad's church.

In my early years, I went to church often with Mom and Granddad. When she didn't go, he'd pick me up and I'd ride with him in his green Buick to Greater Ephesian Baptist Church on Oakland Avenue in Detroit, only a mile north of Grand Boulevard. Granddad's Buick had a bench seat in the front and the fabric wasn't quite cloth and it wasn't anything like leather. It was more synthetic or nylon and it made a noise like fingers sliding down guitar strings when you scooted your backside across it. My head was just enough above the dashboard that I could see out of the windshield and the passenger window pretty well—maybe not the ground beneath us, but the buildings ahead and on either side of us were clear.

Oakland was a bustling avenue back then. Barber shops, dry cleaners, King Cole grocery, Parks Old Style Bar-B-Q, banks, and many other businesses stretched from Clairmont to Pingree and Grand Boulevard. Most of my memories of church with Granddad were hot, hot summer days in a hot car in a hot church with a tight collar and a clip-on tie. But they were beautifully colorful, loving memories, too. The church was a converted former bank building. Following the Rebellion, the bank was deserted and the building was easy pickings for Granddad to establish his church. The windows of the bank had been stained red, green, and blue, which lent the interior a reverential and loving warmth. There were no more than 10 pews on each side of a center aisle and two or three rows of chairs on either side of the pulpit yielding a total capacity of not more than 150 people. In the basement, the ceiling height was exactly 6 feet; there was a concrete block baptismal pool, a small kitchen, a nursery where a crib and sofa were kept, and heating and plumbing pipes were ever-present but easily navigable obstacles for children, adults of smaller stature, and anyone who missed them once or twice.

The choir processional began in the basement and as the organ played *We Are On Our Way*, they arose and coursed down the center aisle and into the stands flanking the pulpit. Even at the age of 6 or 7 I loved seeing and hearing them sing. The colored light from the stained glass danced among the folds of their robes as they swayed from left to right. The songs, my grandfather's preaching and God's presence among us often caused me to forget that my collar was tight, that there was no air conditioning, and that I was a small person. Being a child or grandchild of a pastor can be a challenge and does affect different people in different ways throughout their lives. Granddad was my idol, my example, my love. He cherished me and I him. He was the barber who cut my hair and the teacher who showed me God at work on Earth. His faithfulness to his congregation, his devotion and service to them, and his sacrifice for my mother was all the more special because it never seemed like a sacrifice. He never complained and it never seemed to trouble him when we were in need or when anyone else was. He always helped, always encouraged, and always loved us all. The man who never lost his southern dialect, the fair-skinned man who could have "passed" but never tried, and the one who bounced me on his knee was the one who welcomed me into the church when I accepted Christ as my savior at the age of 7.

The sermon was typical for Granddad in that it was heartfelt, well-practiced, spirit-led and authoritatively delivered, but there was nothing else about it that caused me to stir that Sunday in 1971. Mom was not there, so I sat next to one of our church mothers, Mrs. Mary Silas. At the end of every sermon, I noticed that folding chairs were placed in front of the congregation and the deacons stood, extending their hands in some sort of invitation. I knew that on these occasions, people would proceed down the aisle and sit in one of the chairs. Granddad would say some words, but until this day, it was not clear to me why they were sitting or what he was saying to them. This day when the legs of the folding wooden chairs were spread and the seat bottoms slid easily down the well-worn rails into their resting place with a quick *thwack…thwack…thwack*, I asked Mrs. Silas, "Why do we put the chairs out after every sermon?" She explained that people who believed in Jesus sat in the chairs in order to join the church. I said, "I believe that. Can I join? Is it ok if I sit in the chair?" She nodded.

I was only about 7 years old, but I knew what I was doing, I knew what I felt, and I had no fear or hesitation. I knew I was in a place of love and acceptance, and I felt it was so easy and obvious to say something I already believed. Well, if you've never been to a Baptist church, when people accept Jesus Christ as their savior, it's a joyous occasion. If you've never been to a Baptist church when a pastor's grandson accepts Jesus Christ, you might mistake the reaction of the congregation as common to all who confess their belief the first time. There is always joy and exuberance, but their love for my Grandfather (their Pastor) and by extension for me intensified the experience 10-fold. I mean church elders *caught the spirit*, got happy, fell out, wigs came off, tears flowed like rivers, and it was quite a spectacle from my little-person point of view. It didn't frighten me because I had seen bits and pieces of it on other occasions, but in today's terms it's a bit like going from standard definition to high definition or mono sound to Dolby Digital Surround IMAX. It's turned up several notches when you're the pastor's child or grandchild. That is to say, it is love, it is goodness and there's never too much of either, but if you don't know it's coming, I imagine it can be quite a lot. I wish everyone could experience it exactly as I did.

Protestants believe that upon acceptance of Christ through belief and profession of faith, they are imbued with the holy spirit of God which guides them forever more. In my experience, this is precisely the reason I left Roeper to attend the U of D Jesuit Academy and High School in 1975. I was unfulfilled, unsatisfied, and unprepared while at Roeper. Not through any fault of the faculty, administration, or my mother. I was simply not in the right place at the right time. I tested at U of D and entered 7th grade in September of 1975 at the age of 10. I was on track to graduate high school at the age of 16. The ambiguity of grade levels and unorthodox learning methods of Roeper were not ineffectual even on a reluctant student. One might ask what a 10 year old can possibly know about being *unfulfilled* or *unprepared* for academic instruction. That is not only an understandable reaction, it is one I have asked myself. The only answer I can offer is that I did not know—God knew. God knew and set in motion the events that made my transfer possible. The test scores, the words of my mouth, my mother's deliberations, the financial obligations of parochial education… all of these things had to align in order for me to attend, and they did.

# CHAPTER TEN

───────── ༄ ༄ ༄ ─────────

## KEEPING HOUSE

M om was the very definition of fastidious in the appearance and cleanliness of our home. She enlisted me in the completion of chores with her as early as I can remember. Her ways were consistent and logical, and I never thought much about why they were that way until much later. Whether passing ingredients to her as she cooked, mixing ingredients as she added them to a bowl, or folding laundry, we did them together from the time I could stand and read. She had a system and process for everything. I'm not sure where she learned it, but her way of doing things worked well and she showed me the difference. She hated ironing and she found that being at the dryer before the cycle ended while the clothes were still tumbling, they could be removed and hung or folded quickly without wrinkling. She showed me how women's pants were folded along a vertical axis so that the creases were at the inside and outside leg seams, while men's pants were lined up at the seams so that the creases would be the front and back of the legs. We'd take the king and queen sheets out of the dryer, stand at opposite ends, pull them tight and bring the two adjacent corners together letting the slack gather in the middle in a long u-shape between us. Then we'd rotate the sheet 90 degrees and bring the opposite ends together. When we got into a rhythm it must have resembled an allemande left or a do-si-do more than a military ritual. All we were missing was the square dance music. In the end the clothes were creased, folded, hung, and put away looking as though they had been ironed, when in fact the iron was used only in emergencies at our house.

Cleaning dishes involved a certain unalterable order. After meals any food remaining on the plates that was not fit for leftovers was scraped into a plastic garbage liner in the days before electric garbage disposals. When we first moved into the Mediterranean on LaSalle, the kitchen was original equipment. Built about 1915, it was outfitted with an icebox. Before electric refrigerators, food was kept cold by using blocks of ice. This was the first item to be replaced in Ronald's pre-habitation remodeling. There was also a coal chute in the basement, but the furnace had been converted to natural gas before we moved in. Another modern innovation which was a first for me and mom was an electric dishwasher, but without a garbage disposal Mom's process required removing as much food as possible before soaking them in a sink full of hot soapy water. After rinsing them in the water so no visible evidence of food particles remained, the dishes were loaded. All plates and saucers faced the same direction. It didn't matter if they were facing left or right, as long as they were all in agreement. Forks and knives were loaded with handles pointing up, and cups and bowls fit in the most efficient method in the remaining space on the upper rack. Large pots and roasters were washed by hand along with any other pieces that didn't fit nicely and neatly with the rest of the load. The hand-washed dishes were allowed to dry in a rack only until the last item had been washed.

Then they were finished with a dry towel and put away in the cabinets. When the items in the dishwasher were cool enough, they were put away as well. Rarely were dishes allowed to spend the night away from their home in the cupboards.

Vacuuming, sweeping and mopping were also precision tasks. Mom showed me how to sweep carefully and quickly, controlling and directing the debris rather than spreading it further. When I swept outside, I used a push broom or an angle broom: the goal was usually to clear a path. The strategy indoors was to collect the debris and remove it entirely. Sweeping too fast or forcefully only moved the dirt from one place to another, she explained. I developed pride in these techniques as I learned how effectively they could be performed and the difference they made in comparison to alternative methods. Vacuuming the thick, plush green carpeting in our living and dining rooms was done after the wood and tiled floors were swept and all counters and surfaces were dusted or washed. Any dust or dirt that escaped the expert sweeping and dusting was sucked up in the vacuum—a high-end Kirby model with its very own high-beam headlight presumably for all the times one would need to vacuum in complete darkness. That marvel had all the bells and whistles. It had a slightly bulging rubber bumper around its base to prevent scuffs and other damage to furniture legs and molding. It had a heavy cloth bag that housed the replaceable paper filler bag and it came with all manner of hoses and attachments.

In the days when vacuum cleaner salesmen went door to door and we lived in the tiny house on Doris, that machine may have been the most expensive thing we owned other than the automobiles. Given Ronald's hustles, however, it was more likely acquired secondhand for a song at a grieving family's estate sale. Over the years, the model changed once or twice, but the method remained the same. All furniture was moved so that every square inch of the floor could be vacuumed. Sofas, dining tables, chairs, end tables, coffee tables, credenzas, heavy, light, big, small... every stick was moved once to vacuum underneath and then moved back to its starting position. The direction of the vacuuming was important, too. The dense pile of green carpet appeared darker or lighter depending on the direction in which the machine brushed the nap. It wasn't possible to vacuum such large rooms without leaving brush marks, so the trick was to create them in the most aesthetically pleasing pattern, which was lengthwise in a *V* or herringbone pattern. The movement was straight forward and back followed by angled forward and back, from the marble-tiled fireplace at the head of the 20-foot-long living room to the 14-foot-wide cherry wood French doors at the other end.

Mopping, whether in the heavily trafficked foyer and hallways or the tight spaces of the Pewabic-tiled powder room, included a hands and knees sponging of the perimeter and baseboards. The Spic and Span antibacterial cleaner was preferred, but Lysol, Mr. Clean, Lestoil and Murphy's Oil Soap all performed their share of duties. The abrasive Comet Cleaner bleach powder was the only designated hitter in the lineup and it was assigned to all things porcelain. Inside and outside of toilet bowls, tubs, and sinks, I wet the surface and sprinkled the magic powder which turned to paste as it made contact and I began to scrub. The bristles of the toilet brush stabbed the paste beneath the rim and the sponge kneaded in and around every handle, drain, appurtenance and obstacle. When every inch of every white surface was covered, the sponge was rinsed clean and the wiping and rinsing cycle proceeded until there was no residue of the paste and the surfaces shone like the sun in the middle of August—white bright.

I never thought this process was particularly onerous, but I can't say that I looked forward to it either, especially as I grew into adolescence and other "priorities" insinuated themselves into my life. Rather it was part of our routine, our square dance, our do-si-do. Many, many years later when I handed my son a broom for first time, I took for granted all of the training and practice I received: I stammered, "Wait, let me show you!" as he fumbled about slapping at the floors as if trying to frighten the dirt away from his violent attack. We think the way we do things is natural, but they are only so because we learned them early and practice them that way often. I learned one autumn evening in Detroit that there are other ways in which things become natural—through terror.

Mom always made large meals on the weekends so that we could have leftovers during the week when work schedules were less predictable. She'd make enough ham, black eyed peas, greens and cornbread to feed a family of eight and we three would eat that for at least three to four days before she'd make another big meal. On a crisp Saturday in October we performed our usual cleaning ritual early. Ronald had not come home the previous night, which I learned not to question, and by the time I was six or seven I actually preferred his absences. He was never violent with me, but the air stilled when he entered a room. Dark clouds followed him above, below and roundabout. Anything good or pleasing held its breath within earshot or spitting distance of Ronald.

Before heading out on our errands, Mom made a huge pot of spaghetti with another pot of green beans which she seasoned with salt pork, pepper and quartered small white potatoes. Mom's sauce was a mixture of canned tomatoes, tomato paste and I believe she added a jar of store-bought sauce and always a pound or two of seasoned ground beef. We didn't do meat balls (maybe because that was the childhood nickname Ronald so despised), but her spaghetti with ground beef was fantastic, and she mixed the sauce and the noodles in the pot and let it mingle a while before serving. The first time I saw sauce served separately from the pasta, I thought, "These folks are really missing out on something." Mom even made a loaf of garlic cheese bread and had it all ready for serving when we left for our weekly shopping run.

When we returned a few hours later, Ronald's car was parked in the driveway. There was always a gulp, a hard swallow, when arriving at home after him. When we were already home and he entered, I felt more in control of my options. When he was on the scene first, I was never quite sure what to expect upon opening the front door. We carried our packages up the concrete steps of the porch and I held the aluminum screen door as Mom unlocked the heavy, paneled main door. We entered the foyer quietly, not quite tipping, but also not speaking. We listened and hearing nothing, we proceeded through the hallway, past the paneled library into the kitchen where we froze agape. The spaghetti was still on the stove, but it was also on the floor, on the walls, on the ceiling, the refrigerator, and the cupboards. There was a moment when I wondered if he had fallen and thrown the pot into the air to free his hands. But the pasta was everywhere. Clearly he had very deliberately in a drunken rage flung the meal everywhere but into his mouth. I never knew what set him off, but I would learn over time that there didn't have to be a trigger event and it didn't matter anyway. He did what he did because he was an alcoholic, a mean drunk, and an abusive, unrepentant bully in spite of the loving mother and siblings who raised him.

This was the first time I thought to myself, I might have been better off if my birth parents hadn't placed me for adoption. Surely their life wasn't lived on eggshells as ours was whenever Ronald was present. They had children who looked forward to seeing their father come home from work and to having a gaggle of siblings gather around a table for noisy nightly suppers and arguing over the last slice of dessert. It wasn't the indifference of Ronald toward me, it wasn't the disciplined work and patience I learned from my mother, it wasn't the structured lessons and requirements of private secondary education, it was the sinister, angry perpetual self-loathing and psychological bullying of the man that forced me to consider the possibilities. I never wanted a different mother, but at times such as this I did want a different life. I wanted peace and civility. I wanted Mom to be loved and appreciated by everyone as much as I loved and appreciated her. Until this night, I knew Ronald was unpleasant, mean, full of nasty curses and threats, but I don't think I really believed he would be physically violent toward either of us.

Unless you had the distinct misfortune of knowing Ronald personally or professionally, our lives may have appeared normal and even quite blessed. We lived in a beautiful home with more bedrooms than occupants, a large swimming pool, a recreation room with a pool table and an early model projection television, and a fridge that dispensed crushed and cubed ice with the press of a button. It didn't matter if you were an immediate family member, employee, business associate or customer, to know Ronald was to be on the receiving end of a string of "got dams" and "muthafuckas" as often as the sun rose and set. This must have been where I first learned to fear his disposition—not when it was directed at me, but when I witnessed it turned upon others. From an early age I heard the rage and invectives—words I never heard from anyone else and of which I had no understanding—unleashed on the telephone.

Whether he was berating an employee or collecting a debt from a client, I knew I did not want to be the person on the other end of that phone ever. Mom never spoke critically of him when I was young. She'd say, "Daddy's not mad at you. He's handling business." When she knew he was settling in for a work-from-home session, she'd find something for us to do away from home. She would plan shopping trips and visits to her father or mother-in-law's house. Any time she could avoid his soul-sucking torment, she did. She felt safest when she was at work where she was surrounded by friends and colleagues who all worked together for the good of their patients and one another. They were a second family in many ways, and I believe she took call as much to be away from home and in a setting that she controlled as it was to earn more money. In the operating room, she was more than competent. She knew what was expected, she anticipated, she taught, and she was appreciated and loved. One might think it inconvenient to drag a 10- or 11-year-old to work every time an emergency surgery was scheduled, but it was much preferable to remaining in a dungeon of Ronald's odious presence.

Soon after if not immediately upon moving into the LaSalle home, Ronald and Mom settled in separate bedrooms. Upstairs a long hallway divided a loft which we called *the sitting area* with a beautiful bay window overlooking the tree-lined street in front of our house and two-story leaded and stained glass window flanking the stairway leading from the first floor. To the left of the hallway were two bedrooms, the master being at the end on the left. Straight ahead at the end of the hallway was my bedroom with a double-hung window overlooking the backyard.

When the pool lights were on in the summer evenings I opened the wide double-hung window to smell and hear the night and watch the shimmering blue battle the dark green shadows of the oak and maple trees or see giant raindrops drum the surface of the water and surrounding concrete deck. My bedroom and the master were adjacent but not adjoining. They each had a six-panel solid mahogany door that opened onto an enclosed porch we called the *sun room*. Six-inch square ceramic tiles of fern green blended subtly with burnt umber and taupe adorned the 150-square-foot floor. Accordion-style windows, each with eight panes of glass filled the east, south and west perimeter walls from waist to the ceiling. A near duplicate of this room was directly below, end-capping the formal living room and dining room. The house had many curious and exquisite features, not the least of which was a plaster relief of Roman or Greek inspiration presiding over the Carrera marble fireplace and its ornate andiron sentinels.

The first week of our residence was full of discovery. The crystal chandelier was a focal point of an elegant formal dining room with shoulder-height recessed panel wainscoting perfected in white semi-gloss and capped by linen wallpaper of 19th century scenes. The built-in buffet was recessed, with glass doors and a mirrored backsplash centered by more leaded stained glass above. As Mom and I stood in the dining room that first day surveying our blessings and planning the décor, the doorbell rang. She went through the living room to answer it, but no one was there. This happened several more times in ensuing days, and we worried that troublesome kids were pranking us until we realized that there was a pressure switch beneath the carpet that allowed the original owners to call for servants to attend to their needs.

We laughed at the indulgence of such a contrivance once the shock subsided. We who were used to shouting from one room into the next for any large or small concern found it quite silly that anyone would need to ring a bell to summon help which was likely to be in the adjoining kitchen or pantry whenever the dining room was in use.

Yes, there were concrete blocks with iron rings for tethering horses in the backyard. Yes, there was a gardener's apartment above the detached carriage house that we called a garage. Yes, there was a maids quarters with an adjoining full bath and hidden staircase leading from the kitchen. As beautiful and well-appointed as the home was; however, it was no sprawling palace. The biggest rooms were the living room and the recreation room below it in the basement. Each was 20 feet in length by 15 feet in width. The walls were lath and plaster and the building materials of their time certainly insulated sound and temperature to an extent, but the sound made by summoning the "help" was identical to that of the doorbell. We never quite understood how the servants or owners could have distinguished the two. When the doorbell rang, did they run to the dining room or to the front door? Not employing servants and having the utility of our own vocal chords, we disconnected the switch permanently.

On the right side of the upstairs hallway was a large bathroom almost fully tiled. The walls were decked with rectangular subway tiles bull nosed at shoulder height and painted from there with a satin finish to the ceiling. The custom porcelain bathtub was set flush into the floor—not the more typical clawfoot style which was the design in the maid's quarters. The floor was hexagonal white porcelain and a spacious enclosed shower abutted the tub. A built-in medicine cabinet with drawers flanked the entry to the room and topped a clothes chute that delivered dirty laundry to the basement level.

Entering the master bath, a porcelain toilet was to the left, and directly in front lay a generous porcelain sink with widespread polished chrome faucets with engraved porcelain handles labelled *hot* and *cold* in black letters. On either side of the sink was a double hung window offering plenty of light during the day and polished chrome wall sconces with vintage frosted glass diffusers framing a large mirror with a marble shelf for essential items. To the right of the entrance were the tub, shower, and built in towel bars. The master bath was as big as either of the two secondary bedrooms. The last stop on the clockwise tour of the second story was the maid's quarters. The sitting area was at the 7 o'clock position, the first bedroom at 9, the master at 11, the sunroom at 12, my bedroom at 1 the master bathroom at 3 directly opposite the first bedroom.

The maid's quarters was at 5 o'clock. Making an immediate right at the top of the main staircase one passed the built-in linen closet and opened a door onto a landing that revealed a private staircase to the left leading down to the kitchen, another door and staircase directly ahead leading up to the attic, and a third to the right, which was the maid's bedroom. This is the bedroom that Ronald chose to inhabit. Secluded, isolated and nearly self-sufficient, it had everything except a kitchen, but it had direct and exclusive access to that just one floor below.

The one modern amenity the historic house never enjoyed was central air conditioning. Detroit summers were often sweltering and we were used to it. We didn't have air conditioning in the much smaller house on Doris, either. We put fans in windows and pointed them in or out depending on which side had the cooler air. Usually this meant pointing them outward during the day, and inward at night. On Doris, Mom and Ronald had an electric air conditioning unit in their bedroom windows.

When it was unbearably hot and Ronald wasn't home, Mom and I holed up in there for naps or at bedtime. No one approved of putting window units on the front side of houses on LaSalle, but the maid's quarters was the smallest of all the bedrooms and on the back corner of the house. Ronald had the air-conditioned bedroom. We also put one in the paneled library off the main floor foyer. The doors to these rooms were kept closed when the units were in operation. The selfishness and thoughtlessness of the arrangement wasn't unnoticed by an 11-year old, but I spent so much more time in air-conditioned cars, the more temperate recreation room in the basement or elsewhere that the heat was the least of my concerns. It may have been hot, but rarely was it Mississippi-hot.

Keeping the house clean, decorating it nicely, having meals prepared and clean clothes ready to wear were things I thought Mom did because she wanted to. I thought she did them because they pleased her, because she took pride in our well-being and our appearance, and she wanted me to develop the same sense. While these were all true, there was also an unspoken reason. She worked incredibly hard to remove any possible excuse for Ronald to become foul. I never asked her, but once in a while she'd say, "Shovel the snow from the driveway before your dad gets home," or "Take this tray up to your dad's room," not because she was concerned for him, but because she wanted to remove any molehill he would seize upon to build his mountain of fury. When she had done all she could, she hid, shrunk, cried, or prayed.

I recall one moonless winter night after bedtime when the blue glow of the mercury vapor streetlights in the alley filtered through the sheer curtain panels in my room. I wasn't yet asleep and Mom asked me to come into her room. This rarely happened since we moved from Doris, but when it did it was usually to monitor my breathing during or after colds or flu symptoms, or so I thought.  On this night, I wasn't recovering from any illness. Perhaps I thought she was nervous, worried and just needed my presence to reassure her. I fell asleep on the side of the queen bed closest the windows overlooking the street. She slept on the side of the bed closest to the hallway—between me and the door. I don't remember the door being locked or closed when I climbed into bed, but I shot upright when I heard banging. The heavy door was closed and the crystal door knob rattled left and right vigorously as the slurred voice shouted. "Come outta dere!" "He don't need...[bang, bang]...innair!" I was wide-eyed with fear as Mom pushed a chair against the door and shouted, "Go away, Ron! Leave...[bang]...alone!"

The banging of fists, knees and shoulders against the door was loud but lacked the focus and coordination to break through. "[bang, bang, bang]...dat GOT dam room right dam now!" Mom's tears frightened me as much as the constant banging and screaming of the stupefied man she'd married. I didn't understand how anything one drank could cause this kind of behavior, but as he eventually tired and stumbled back to the maid's quarters, "...muthafuckas, got dam bedroom...mah howse, mutha..." and as Mom's trembling and crying subsided, I fell asleep with the beginnings of resentment toward the people who placed me for adoption leading to this horribly unfair childhood. Years later I came to understand that she wasn't protecting me from Ronald that night, she was protecting herself from him with me as a shield.

# CHAPTER ELEVEN

---

## IMMACULATE INDISCRETION

When I first imagined the circumstances of my birth and the identities of my biological parents the vision was highly romanticized. In every vision my mother was white and my father was black. In the seventies interracial dating was not widely accepted, but the couples I saw were usually a black male and white female. Now I wonder if this was really the case or if my awareness was skewed by my own racial identification. Perhaps it's a little like buying a new car. When you first see it in the showroom, it's novel and you've never seen another like it. As soon as you hit the streets, though, every other car is the same make, model and color as the one you just bought. Similarly, when we are single, we rarely notice pregnant women or couples, but when we are expecting our own child, suddenly it seems that every woman we meet is in her last trimester.

I counted 16 years backward from my own birth and estimated by mother's birth year to be about 1945. In the 1950s Detroit was one of largest most densely populated cities in America and white flight to the suburbs was only a trickle. I decided that my mother and father lived in the same neighborhood—a few blocks between them—but within walking distance. They attended the same high school, but there was little interaction between them or their respective racial cohorts until the bell rang. I could see her face, a little foggy, but certain features were discernable. A narrow nose, sandy brown hair, and gray eyes were all I could make out. My birth father was an unassuming young man. He was the last guy anyone would suspect of bucking norms or making waves. He was not more than 6 feet tall with copper skin, a square jaw and exceptionally large ears. They saw each other frequently—not daily—but often on the walk home from school. She on one side of the street with a friend or two. He on the other, a few steps behind, with a sibling or friend. Her parents were angling to move to the suburbs. New freeways were making it easy to get to jobs and businesses in the city which was bursting at the seams with unskilled labor and every manner of vice to satisfy any yearning or obscure any defect.

His family had recently moved into the neighborhood, professionals happy to find themselves in hot pursuit of the American Dream. They noticed one another from a distance. She found him attractive and was flattered by his poorly concealed glances, but she would never risk the humiliation of being seen with him or talking to him. She never spoke of him to her friends and they never knew of their mutual interest in one another, but at least one of his friends warned him to avoid her—advice that he heeded until one frigid January night.

School was in recess for Christmas break and one of the white boys on the basketball team invited a few friends over for a party. His parents were out for the evening and weren't expected back until early the following morning. The gathering turned out to be much larger than intended and kids of both races were packed into the small basement of the bungalow. The Cascades, Chiffons, Surfaris, Bobby Vinton, and Elvis were a few of the artists whose tunes were played. Booze was shared discreetly but freely. Bumping into bodies in the dark hallway, he caught a glimpse of her through an open bathroom door as she was fixing her hair and makeup. The blue glow from the street lights shone through the narrow transom window and illuminated her smile.

He quickly closed the door behind him so that no one would see them. What the tiny bathroom lacked in comfort, it made up for in privacy. They couldn't be gone long or someone would notice and come looking for them. They made out and stopped short of actual intercourse, however, not short enough. They were never found out by their friends and she never spoke to him again—not even after realizing that she was pregnant. She tearfully confided in her mother. The family did not condone abortions for any reason—not even this one. They had to tell her father who demanded to know the name of the boy, but mother refused to divulge that. Together they devised a plan to conceal her condition until exams and then reported her as ill from school when it could no longer be hidden. She mailed in her exams, and graduated in absentia. Four months after graduation her father drove her to a hospital, dropped her at the front door and came back to get her two days later. She left me there in the hospital without ever providing her real name, and I became a ward of the state, eligible for adoption, and I never saw her again.

# Chapter Twelve

⸞ ⸙ ⸝

## Flipping the Switch

Lest one think that every day of our lives was insufferable, there were myriad wonderful blessings also. Grandfather, grandmother, uncles, cousins, and friends who knew or suspected were never able to prevail upon Mom to leave her abusive relationship, but they were all a constant source of love, encouragement and fun. Mom believed that she kept his abuse secret and forbade me from discussing it with anyone, but those who experienced him in any capacity other than passing must have been desperately aware of her plight and of the futility of any attempt at intervention. She relied on Ronald to pay the bills, which consisted of utilities, property taxes and any loans for the pre-habitation renovations and upgrades. All of the food, clothing, furnishings and decorations, tuition and extracurricular fees came out of mom's earnings. She used to say if Ronald didn't do what he did, she wouldn't have enough to do all the things she did for us. I never felt that was a fair trade, but it was her decision.

In spite of the episodic domestic terror, we persisted to live *normal* lives whenever normal was within reach. Those first two years on LaSalle were 1974 – 1976 and coincided with my transfer from the Roeper School to the University of Detroit Jesuit Academy. New school, new bus, new neighborhood, new friends. An October birthday meant that I was only 10 years old when I started 7th grade in the Academy. I was a couple of years younger than most of my cohorts who came in all shapes, sizes, and colors. There were some boys smaller than I, some bigger and taller, but most of them were at least a little stronger and more physically developed. Two years is quite a gap at that stage, but no one attributed it to immaturity. To my classmates I wasn't the fastest or strongest because I hadn't played organized sports in my prior school as many of them had, or I simply lacked the talent. Both of those things may have been true, but the physical and emotional immaturity were plain as day to anyone who knew the truth. I was welcomed onto the Academy Track and Field team where Mr. John Zybard coached and encouraged us all greatly. He spoke often to my mom about my development, and she truly appreciated his candor and kindness.

By end of 8th grade I wasn't coming in last in every race. In the 440 sprint, I took 3rd place in a meet at our home track. I'm not sure how many runners there were, but there were at least 4 because I wasn't last and that was cause for a Burger King celebration. A Whopper with cheese, fries, onion rings and a strawberry milkshake from the restaurant on McNichols Road owned by the first black franchisee, NFL all-pro defensive back, Brady Keys, thank you very much! You'd have thought I won a gold medal at the summer Olympics in Montreal.

Academy football was not quite the "success" of track, but I gave it a shot. At lunch and recess, we junior high schoolers would head outdoors in any weather except rain to play touch football or handball. When it rained, we headed to the gym for basketball, but even in the snow there were enough of us interested in football to brave the elements and pretend to be our favorite players—Lynn Swann, Fran Tarkington, Mean Joe Green, Terry Bradshaw and at the very pinnacle of his popularity, the Juice, O.J. Simpson. My hands were just big enough to throw a decent spiral accurately 15 – 20 yards. The QB position was hotly contested for each team, but in the interest of using our time for playing rather than arguing, concessions were usually made quickly, often as we were putting on our coats and heading out the door.

Although we played touch, touching "hard" as in body checking and pushing was not only allowed, it was celebrated. The oohs, aahs and hoots when a classmate was stiff-armed into a snow bank were every bit as exhilarating as the "long bomb" touchdown passes to a sprinting receiver cutting around a big tree in the "end zone" of our small field. The fun of lunchtime football didn't quite translate to organized competitive Academy football for me, however. That's where the real football players ruled. Some of the boys playing at recess or intramurals also played on the competitive teams, but they were much more serious in pads and helmets, let me tell you. I learned quickly that I knew next to nothing about the game. Even at the ages of 12 and 13, many of these boys had already been playing organized ball for 4 or 5 years. Subtract 2 years of muscle maturity, and 5 years of practice and game experience and you got—me. Swimming seemed like a much less painful alternative.

Although I didn't learn to swim until the age of 10 in our backyard pool, I took to it quickly. I loved the solitude and weightlessness of it. The hot summers without air-conditioning found me in or around that pool cleaning the filters, vacuuming the bottom, putting on and taking off the cover after each use, perfecting the pH and chlorination levels, and swimming... and swimming. An only child seeking further solitude was surely a sign of environmental stress, but that correlation hadn't formed in my mind by grade 9. Summers for children of families of means, I gathered, included summer camps, travel abroad, and weekend excursions to theme parks and monuments. A couple of the black girls in my class at Roeper returned to school after spring break and they looked so different—I had never seen skin that color. It wasn't just darker than their usual cinnamon shade, it was redder, deeper, and unlike anyone's in my neighborhood. When I learned that their unusual glow was a tan from the Bahamas, I could only wonder if everyone in the Bahamas looked like that all of the time. I spent hours riding bicycles and playing in the Detroit sun every summer, and I never achieved anything close to that rich, exotic look. Our summer trips were much more pedestrian. I recall a bus trip with our church to Washington, D.C., which included a tour of the White House, but the only other traveling we did were occasional road trips to Ontario or once to Mansfield, Ohio to visit maternal cousins.

The summer of my 10th year introduced me to the National Youth Sports Program at Wayne State University in midtown. The NYSP was founded in 1968 to provide positive outlets for young people following the urban rebellions like the one in Detroit. NYSP is a partnership between the National Collegiate Athletic Association, the United States Department of Health and Human Services, the Office of Community Services and other sponsoring institutions. NYSP participants attend a five-week summer program at one of over 170 colleges and universities. NYSP's programs combine sports instruction with the teaching of vital life skills, such as personal health, job responsibilities, nutrition, alcohol and other-drug prevention activities. Expert instruction is provided to participants before they engage in numerous sports activities, including swimming, basketball, football, golf, soccer, tennis, and track and field.[3]

I was 3 months shy of the 10-year minimum age when I began participating. Wayne State was perfectly located for me—within a short bus ride or leisurely 2-mile walk from home. On the first day, Mom brought me early to ensure that I didn't miss the opportunity. Free physicals were conducted to ensure we kids were healthy enough, and ID cards were issued. Each year in June or July when registration time came, I arrived two hours early for two reasons. First, because ID cards were issued numerically and I wanted to be number 1, and second because I had nothing more pressing to do at that age than sit in the blazing heat bouncing a tennis ball off a wall, reading a book or smack-talking with friends and learning how to talk to girls. For 5 of the 6 years I participated, I was ID number 1. To beat me, you had to be willing to get there more than 2 hours before registration was scheduled to begin.

In the first years, the schedule of the southbound bus headed down 12th Street, winding its way along the Edsel Ford service drive to the Matthei Physical Education Center, was pretty dependable. The pickup at my stop may have varied by 10-15 minutes depending on factors to me completely unknown and unpredictable, but the 5-minute ride got me there in plenty of time to beat the rest of the kids. I don't remember who got in line before me one summer, but I blamed the buses that didn't show up at all. I adjusted the following year by assuming I'd have to walk the entire 2-mile route and leaving home earlier for that eventuality.

As the years progressed, the reliability of the buses declined rapidly and I developed friendships with other neighborhood kids who also participated in the program. We could walk there in

---

about 20 minutes, so waiting 15 minutes for a bus to show up was a waste of time and quarters. We knew the distance between each bus stop along the route. If the bus didn't come within several minutes, we'd start walking the route looking over our shoulders occasionally to see if we could spot one heading toward us. If we did, we'd sprint ahead to the next or back to previous one, whichever was closer.

In the latter years, if a bus hadn't come within sight by the time we were half-way, we'd just walk the remainder out of spite refusing to give our quarters to public service that neglected and despised us even if it passed us and beat us to our destination. This was another ding for those who abandoned Detroit while continuing to call it their home as far as I was concerned. No one cared that people who relied on public transportation found it entirely unreliable. Employers didn't care, politicians didn't care, suburban non-residents certainly didn't care, but I cared. Those of us who remained cared.

The most important thing about registration was getting into the instructional classes you wanted. The sooner you completed registration, the more likely you were to get the classes you wanted in the order you wanted them. Everyone had to take swimming, which I preferred to enjoy at the end of my day after all the sweatiness and outdoor activities were wrapped up. Optional classes including basketball, racquet ball, tennis, squash, weight training, golf and football. I always chose squash as one of my classes and for my second session I alternated basketball, tennis, and weightlifting from one year to the next. The first four weeks of the program were filled with instruction and personal development. The last week or two included tournament-style competitions. In swimming and squash, I won or took 2nd place in everything by my second year in the program.

I developed a real love for squash. It's much like racquetball on a smaller court with a lifeless ball and quicker movements. We played with balls that bounced once when dropped. If your racquet didn't return the ball between the boundary lines on the front wall before it bounced a second time, you lost a point. The athletic ways we found to keep those balls in play were as exciting to watch as they were to perform. By year 3 shots behind the back and between the legs were attempted with confidence and often successfully. Volleys of a dozen or more shots were not uncommon in championship rounds, but we'd dispatch beginners with practiced overhand bank serves quickly in the preliminary rounds.

The indoor natatorium had a 15-foot deep diving pool with 2 1-meter boards, 2 3-meter boards and 1 5-meter diving platform. The Olympic size pool had 8 25-meter lanes. With scores of kids in attendance, the swimming period was divided into groups according to ability. Those who could swim a length above water using any stroke and below the surface on a single breath were placed into one of two competitive swimming groups in the left 3 lanes of the pool. The others we placed in learn-to-swim groups and occupied the right 3 lanes. The advanced swimmers ready for life-saving and CPR training were assigned to the diving pool.

By age 13 I was in the diving pool treading water for 30 minutes, practicing with improvised floatation devices by disrobing underwater and blowing air into pants and shirts, and doing compressions and breaths on CPR mannequins. Susie, our advanced swim instructor, was also a synchronized swimming athlete. She and Ed Moten and so many of the instructors and coaches were amazingly talented professionals and they were nothing short of amazing with children—mostly African-American, economically underprivileged—but all eager to learn and improve. *Underprivileged* was a relative word for me.

I recognized even then that I enjoyed privileges many of the kids in my neighborhood and those participating in the program did not. I attended a private school, lived in a big house with my own pool, and my parents were both employed. From that perspective, I was certainly privileged. We did not, however, have the extra money to pay for summer camps or expensive equipment and team fees. It was all mom could do working overtime and taking call to keep up with tuition and her bills. Ronald never pitched a dime into that pot, so a 12-dollar speedo was ironically a cheap way for a black kid to play a white sport as I would later learn swimming was known. I never saw black athletes swimming in the Olympics. I didn't know of any champion divers who were black.

My summertime idols were Mark Spitz and Greg Louganis. Spitz won an incredible 7 gold medals at the '72 Olympics and his face was everywhere, not just on the Wheaties boxes. Louganis was only 4 years older than I and was already well-known in the sport for the perfect 10 he scored on a dive in the 1971 Junior Olympics—when he was 10 years old! As he rose in prominence, I would learn that we had more in common than a love for the sport and being born in the same decade. Teased for his darker, not-quite-white skin, he was also the son of an abusive father.

I assume Mom understated her income on the application and omitted Ronald's altogether. However she managed it, I had a secure, positive place to be for several weeks in the summer that kept me off the streets and out of trouble. Did I take a spot that should have gone to a more economically disadvantaged child? I doubt it. I never heard of anyone being turned away from registration. Somehow they accommodated everyone and I hope that program had as profound an effect on the other kids as it did on me. It's where I learned the basics of sportsmanship, fair competition, and proper preparation and practice. It was my introduction to organized sports. As far as I could tell everyone in the program was there because they wanted to be and even if our family had been wealthy, there's no place I would rather have spent my summers. I still have most of the trophies I won in those swimming and squash competitions. I even took first place for the fastest mile-run in the weight training class one year. When you're 13 or 14 and you're used to competing against 15 and 16 year-olds the improvement is more evident as you return to your own age group.

At the age of 12 I was a freshman on our school's competitive swim team. Far weaker than the 17- and 18-year-old men who led our senior class, weaker than most of the 14-year-old freshmen, and far less practiced than all of them, I dove in and learned the strokes most of them had been practicing since they were toddlers. Our coaches were pretty patient and very persistent in perfecting our techniques. They emphasized the extension of the arm, rotation of the shoulders, and the pull-through of the arm and hand of the freestyle. "Kick, *kick*," we heard as some relied more heavily on the strength of their arms and neglected the core and lower body movements that added so much speed to any stroke. My event was the 50-meter freestyle, and I was pitiful but proud to be a part of the team. As much as I loved being in the pool, I also wanted to improve.

We practiced at the Northwest Activity Center, a community recreation building not more than a mile from our school on 7 Mile Road. It was used by many organizations other than U of D Jesuit. Local seniors rented it for aquacise, other school teams rented it, and a local Amateur Athletic Union team practiced there during the summer months. Mom dropped me off on her way to work at 6:00 a.m. every day during the school week. Some mornings the water was crystal clear and perfect, other days it was frigid and once in a while it was thick, green and hot. One might think pea soup would be a welcome feel on a mid-winter sub-zero morning, but the heat sapped our strength and the near-zero visibility even with goggles made sharing lanes a bi-directional hazard as we collided with teammates swimming in the opposite direction.

We swam clockwise within each lane, 4 or 5 swimmers to a lane. The leader swam lengthwise on the right using the black lane marker on the bottom of the pool as a visual guide. He flip-turned at the wall, bending at the hips, jackknifing his legs out of the water and bending at the knees as the remaining momentum of the stroke planted his feet on the wall. Pushing off with both legs, twisting 180 degrees from a face up position while executing two or three dolphin kicks and surfacing to resume the stroke in the opposite direction on the left side of the lane as the rest of the swimmers repeated the feat in succession. When the water was comfortable, I concentrated on my stroke, conjugated verbs in Spanish, recited biology definitions for Mr. Coyne's class, or thought of what I would do all day at school or when I got home.

In order to improve, I needed to be in the water more and begged Mom to let me join the AAU team so that I could continue swimming after our high school season ended. My racial awakening really began with my participation on this team, the Dolphins. Until then I moved in relatively homogenous socio-economic spheres. They weren't racially homogenous, but most of the kids in my classes at Roeper were from middle to upper income households and those who weren't got on the bus first, so no one knew otherwise unless we told them. Although purely and entirely in the city of Detroit, the enrollment at U of D Jesuit High School in the 1970s was approximately 70% White, 28% Black, and 2% Asian. There were a couple of black teachers, a couple of white female teachers, one Latino, and the rest were white males, a few of whom were clerics. The Academy 7th and 8th grades didn't present any overtly racial issues, but the critical thinking and social awareness of the Ignatian Jesuit experience led us to look outward and observe the world and our communities and to look inward and examine our place in that macrocosm. Discussions of the behaviors of one toward others and the impact and effect of personal, spiritual and political decisions were not limited to theology and sociology classes. Literature, science, language and other subjects integrated as much of this critical thinking as possible. By the time I reached 9th grade, the antennae were up, reception was good, and filters were only beginning to bud.

I began to question why things were the way they appeared. Why were nearly all of the boys on my high school swimming team white and why were most of the kids on my AAU team black? We lived a few blocks from Hitsville, the original studio of Motown Records. It was a very short ride from there to the Historic Boston Edison District where my best friend Tony lived. Mom would drop me off at his house early and we'd watch a little TV and chew the fat until it was time to walk across Hamilton Road to catch the Dexter bus at the corner of Boston Blvd. Also on that corner was the home of Berry Gordy and the pool house where Diana Ross first brought the Jackson 5 to audition several years earlier. The public transportation system was reliable enough at that time to transport us 4.5 miles to our final destination, and it was on these 20-25 minute rides that I contemplated justice, racism and the delicious honey buns that awaited me in the vending machine in our cafeteria. Fifty cents and 10 seconds in a microwave was a small price for few delectable minutes of sugary heaven to start the day.

As the kids from the public schools on the route boarded, we might nod or eavesdrop on their conversations, but there wasn't a lot of fraternizing. Henry Ford, Mumford and U of D were on the same line. Mumford and U of D's varsity lettermen jackets were similar with maroon woolen torsos, but Mumford had powder blue leather sleeves and U of D had white, although some Varsity Club members had recently begun electing maroon leather sleeves in favor of a more uniform, maintenance-free look. The white sleeves looked worn and dirty faster. The big public schools were perennial powers in football and basketball. Cass Technical High School was always among the leaders in public school academics and sports, but they were closer to downtown and not on our daily line.

None of the students or adults on the Detroit Street Railway (DSR) as the public bus system was known were white. The bustle of Detroit in my early years had noticeably begun to subside. The disdainful, dismissive, and indifferent looks I remembered from the faces of white adults at Hudson's and shops on Wyoming and Livernois were much fewer and further between. There were still quite a few businesses with white owners and staff, but the number of days when the only white faces I saw were at school was definitely starting to increase. I wasn't sure, but it seemed that other things were starting to disappear also. Mr. Williams was no longer at the gas station on Linwood and Doris where I was traumatically bike-jacked. The A&P grocery store on West Grand was falling into disrepair. The conveyor belts on the checkout were broken and groceries had to be advanced manually. Light bulbs that burned out were not replaced. Things were starting to change. U of D High began discussions about relocating to the suburbs and although I would have followed, we all hoped it would not come to that.

White flight to the suburbs made an unmistakable sucking sound. Once thriving businesses that catered to and relied heavily upon white patronage were the first to leave. Big ticket retailers were next and private schools were hanging by a thread. Detroit Catholic Central and U of D Jesuit were perennial adversaries in everything. U of D usually edged CC in National Merit Scholarship awards, CC more often exchanged athletic championships with Birmingham Brother Rice, but the 2 remaining Detroit Catholic secondary schools for young men were seeing enrollments fall more and more every year. Suburban students whose parents left everything in their haste to flee the rebellion of '68 were now sharing the same bus into Detroit to be deposited on Outer Drive and Hubble for CC or 7 Mile and Cambridge for U of D.

Many of us native Detroiters rode the iron pimp to school, but no matter our mode of transportation or points of origin, we were all aware of the controversy surrounding the fate of our respective schools. A growing number of parents and educators believed that schools could not survive financially if they remained in Detroit. In fact, the 7th and 8th grade classes were added in 1973 in response to the vacuum created by the relocation of so many other private schools to the suburbs. The parochial feeder schools were leaving, businesses were leaving, it seemed only a matter of time before all of them would be gone. There was a popular saying in Detroit at the time, "Will the last one out turn off the lights?"

Catholic Central succumbed in 1976 as they moved to Redford, and we rejoiced when U of D announced its decision to stay put after much prayer and examination of the Jesuit mission. To their great credit, they remained committed to providing the finest college preparatory education to as many students as possible. After two years of junior high at U of D, Mom and I talked about the possibility of moving to a different school. I had friends at Cass Tech. There was a wait list, but we had faith I could get in and the notion of a quality education sans tuition was certainly at top of mind. But I felt I was in the right place at U of D. I was learning a lot and quickly.

Classes were very demanding, the workload was greater than anything I had ever experienced, and I was still younger than my classmates, but now there were boys my age starting 7th and 8th grade. I wasn't the lowest man on the totem pole, and frankly I was proud of my school. I loved being a Detroiter and I loved that U of D chose to stay. The floor of the breezeway connecting the Jesuit residence and administrative offices to the school is tiled and inlaid with the crest and founding year of the school—1877. As I stood and looked into that tile 100 years after the school's founding, I felt a part of something much greater than myself. If they could do that, then I wanted to stay and to be a part it, too.

In spite of my Baptist beginnings, my Catholic education, and my Ignatian awakenings, I was pretty resentful of everyone that was leaving Detroit. I felt that it was their fault that basic city services like waste management, safety and infrastructure maintenance were being neglected. The tax dollars they siphoned from the city left the remaining residents, many of whom were underemployed or undereducated as a result of redlining and other artifacts of systemic racism enacted by the very people leaving it, holding a bag they had no means to open.

If you wanted to start an argument with me, let me hear you say you were from Detroit knowing that you lived in Southfield, Farmington, Grosse Pointe, Redford, or Roseville. If you can't stay in Detroit, don't say you're from Detroit, I reasoned. Suburbanites often replied to inquiries about their hometown with an understanding that most out-of-staters had never heard of their little boondocks. Staying in Detroit was a statement. It said "We remember. We believe!" Staying at U of D was my statement, "I remember, I believe!" We remembered our history, our mission and the greatness of Detroit. We remembered what we are capable of when we work together in spite of our differences, and we believed we could do it again. We believed it wasn't over until it was over. We weren't ready to throw in the towel yet, and we were not alone.

The two events which had the greatest impact on my racial identity and burgeoning animus occurred in the context of competitive swimming. And how could it not, considering I spent all of my time at pools when I wasn't commuting, eating, sleeping or studying? In the summer, our AAU Dolphins swam at outdoor pools often. We practiced at Palmer Park and I vividly remember swimming breast stroke laps while watching the lifeguards and their friends dancing to the Hustle by Van McCoy. The bigger the boom box, the more speakers and equalizer settings, the better, and their box was envied by all. Two woofers, 4 tweeters, 2 midrange, 10 faders, and dual cassette players—that's what we called portable bliss.

The breast stroke is the combination of a kick with the legs while reaching forward, straightening the arms and body followed by a pull downward and retraction of the feet to the buttocks causing the head and ears to break the surface of the water. Each time I pulled, I'd hear of few words of the song followed by bubbles as I kicked and thrust forward. "Do the Hustle"....[bubbles]...."Do It".....[bubbles]...it's mostly an instrumental song, but they made the dance look like so much fun, I wanted to hop out of the pool and learn it then and there. This and the Northwest Activity center were our home pools. There were a couple of white kids on the team but we were a team and race was never an issue until we went to meets at other pools. The looks, the epithets, you know when you're not wanted and parents can only protect your eyes and ears from so much. Although our U of D team was almost entirely white, we had 3 black members.

When we arrived at meets and all of these black kids and their coach strode toward the pool, the stares really cut through me. There must have been some welcoming faces in the crowds. Surely there were some who appreciated diversity and competition in all forms, but if there were any welcoming smiles or nods, they were outshone by icy glares. Words weren't necessary to convey the displeasure some of these people felt. Once or twice, I actually surveyed the crowds to see if any parents removed their swimmers from the competition to avoid having to swim in the same water as black children. You know that look when you know you shouldn't feel a certain way, but you can't help that you do....you know it's not worth the commotion it would cause to say what's really on your mind, so you grit your teeth and bear it? That was the look on more than a few faces on several occasions as we prepared for our heats and stepped up to the starting blocks. We talked about it as a team and determined that we were there to do a job. We were there to do our best, to show what we could do, and we let our talent and effort speak for us. We had some really strong swimmers and we surprised quite a few spectators.

While there were no clear divisions or cliques within my AAU team, The U of D team was stratified along the lines of seniority. Freshmen got a little ribbing, and if you were a smack-talker like I was, you got a little extra. Rolling towels and snapping them like whips could really sting and even leave a mark. Although the image elicits unmistakable racial implications, in the context of a team of nearly all white kids who did it to one another, it was anything but that. No one was above getting snapped, either. If you were brave enough, strong enough, or could run fast enough to escape, you could snap an upperclassman, The penalty was a pounding, getting stuffed into a locker, or headfirst into a trash can full of orange peels and snot rags. That's the kind of stuff that passed for fun in all boy's school when no one was looking. How much more mature we all behaved publicly, especially around parents...and girls. The racial aggression with the U of D team was similar to that experienced on the AAU team; it came from outside—not within.

When our only diver graduated in my sophomore year, our coach held an informal tryout. Everyone who wanted to was allowed to demonstrate his best dive. It was very evident that the broad shoulders and strong backs of the butterfly swimmers were not particularly helpful in the graceful execution of a forward one-and-one-half somersault in pike position. The snaps of the towels were nothing compared to various pain we all experienced watching the belly-smackers and back-splats of many comedic attempts. In the end, the swimmers who managed to enter the water with some semblance of composure and spatial orientation were conscripted. It so happened they were both black. My teammate continued to swim and dive, but I transitioned to diving

Ronald G. Levi Jr.

exclusively. As I enjoyed the solitude and peace of swimming, I enjoyed the same qualities in diving. When preparing for a dive, the concentration can be very intense verging on hypnosis: so much so that other noises become muted. There is a quiet peace in this state as well that is more mental than the out of body peace that comes with putting one's muscles on autopilot for 20 laps.

Our swimming coach was a novice to the sport of diving. He was great at helping us resolve issues with our strokes, but he didn't have the experience to judge or teach diving. One of our team moms dove in high school or college and she had a membership at a Grosse Pointe country club. One of the first commuter suburbs to its immediate neighbor Detroit, the Pointes are composed of Grosse Pointe Farms, Park, Shores, and Woods. Since the 1880s the Pointes have been home to some of Detroit's wealthiest residents including Fords and Firestones. The Shores is home to the Grosse Pointe Yacht Club, and the 93% white enclave has used its wealth and influence for many decades to stay that way.

Our team mom was a resident of the Pointes and as college-educated, liberal-minded as she was, it never occurred to her that bringing black boys to practice diving at an exclusive club would be objectionable. She certainly didn't bring us there to humiliate us, and to their credit, no one confronted us divers directly, but we never went back to that club even though it was more convenient for her to coach us there and even though she was a resident. Ashamed by her association with such a community, she confided to Mom that the manager of the pool told her directly that we were not welcome there and asked her not to bring us again.

These incidents, the aftermath of the rebellion, the coming of age in the era of civil rights and becoming conscious of global, national and local struggles with racial identity ultimately led me to the conclusion that there were two types of people: well-intentioned

88

and ill-intentioned ones. It was as easy for me to count the names and faces of many white people who were kind and decent as it was to recall those who were hurtful, antagonistic, or hostile. Many of the adults and kids in my neighborhood did not have so broad a perspective, however. And this certainly had something to do with the color of my skin and theirs. It had to do with how we dressed and talked.

As sure as I knew there existed white people who lynched black men, I also knew there were white people who died for our freedom and dignity. It wasn't the people I despised; it was the habit that people lazily fall into of distilling the essence of any into a single label. I especially despised it when I felt people were doing it to me, but it wasn't always as easy to see myself perpetrating the same offense.

# CHAPTER THIRTEEN

## BAD BOYS

Mom thrived at Martin Place Hospital. After completing her certification, she became active in the Association of Operating Room Technicians which evolved into the Association of Surgical Technologists. When she attended annual conferences in other states, I stayed with Grandfather or Grandmother for a few days. She assumed leadership roles in planning the annual AORT dinner dances in the metro Detroit area. She ordered and picked up hundreds of tickets from Mays Printing, a black-owned business that had a huge Linotype machine. Before the days of computers, they entered text on a keyboard that mechanically assembled molds for lines of text called slugs. The contraption looked like an old weaving loom married a dentist's chair, and bolted on a vacuum cleaner and a belt driven sewing machine for good measure. I marveled as the operator put it through its paces while my mother placed her order with the owner. Mom doled out those glossy-colored card stock tickets with contrasting ink to AORT members for sale at their respective hospitals. Health professionals, administrators and staff from every department attended in their finest gowns and suits. The venue, menu and live entertainment were chosen by committee, but it seemed to me that Mom did much of the heavy lifting. On top of keeping our house running, my schedule, and flying under Ronald's radar, she did an amazing job with those functions.

Finding the right ensemble each year was a long day for us both. Marty Fuerst on the Livernois Avenue of Fashion was one of her favorite stores for gowns and shoes. If the shoe color didn't perfectly match the primary or accent color of the gown she picked, she'd have them died. There were so many clothes at Marty's, and it seemed we were always there for hours. I took a book or did homework as I sat beneath a rack of blouses or on one of the pedestals reserved for fittings and viewing if one was not in use. The time spent was worth it, because she always looked spectacular on the night of the big event. Everyone knew Mom and as far as I could tell, she knew all of them. These relationships never seemed forced. They were genuinely friendly or at least it appeared that way to me. The nurses and docs had witnessed me grow from a toddler. They were used to seeing me sleeping in the nurses' lounge when Mom was called in for emergency surgeries, and they all treated me wonderfully always.

Although I wasn't much of a basketball player, I was thrilled when Mom told me that Dr. Paolucci asked her if I would be interested in becoming a ball boy for the Detroit Pistons. I didn't ask how much money they paid or what the job entailed, I just said "Sure!" Not only was Benjamin Paolucci a doctor of osteopathic medicine and surgeon at Martin Place Hospital, he was also the team physician for the Pistons and our friend.

I had only seen professional basketball on television. I had never attended a game in person. I was familiar with some of the

Ronald G. Levi Jr.

players' names from television, newspapers, magazines and conversations among the boys at school, but my first impression upon seeing the players at training camp was how tall they were. Ronald and his brothers were all 6-footers and when I started working as a ball boy I was about 5'7." Staring up at players a foot or more taller than I was unusual at first, but I got used to it quickly. Forward George Trapp asked me to fetch him a newspaper, Bob "The Dobber" Lanier liked to mix orange juice and Vernors ginger ale.

Howard Porter was a jazz aficionado like no other. Each of the players had a nickname and style all his own. Some were more approachable and gregarious while others were all business and rarely acknowledged us. By the time camp ended and the season began the captain, Dave Bing, had been traded to the Washington Bullets where he won the league's Most Valuable Player award in his first season there. In 1976 the Pistons played at Cobo Hall built in 1960 and named after the late Mayor Albert Cobo. It was a fun place to work, and I enjoyed watching it come to life in the evenings after school an hour or so before game time.

The ball boys were a team of six reporting to Locker Room Manager, Jerry Dziedzic. Had I known then that Jerry's alter ego was the mascot, Magic Cylinder, it would have been much harder to take him seriously. In the locker room and at Cobo, there was no joking around with Jerry. He'd let a colorful word fly now and then to get your attention if you weren't pulling your weight, but that was rare because the more senior ball boys kept the rookies in line for him. We divvied up the work in three teams of two. Two under the baskets—one at each end of the court, two on the home bench, and two on the visitors' bench.

We made Gatorade in five-gallon batches, scooping the flavored powder into coolers and filling them with a rubber hose attached to a spigot in the shower. We left room for 4 to 5 hefty scoops of ice that melted just enough by game time to give the batch the

92

perfect amount of sweetness without diluting it too much. We made Ben Gay sandwiches, at least that's what I called the slathering of balm on rectangular pads of gauze that trainer Mike Abdenaur peeled apart, applied to each Achilles' tendon, arch and instep before wrapping each player's foot in athletic tape in their pre-game preparations. Twelve players, twenty-four feet, six sandwiches per foot, every game. When the players arrived, clean uniforms and sweatsuits hung in their stalls. Once they were taped and suited up, we hit the court with them for warmups.

We all shared the same locker room duties—pre-game prep, errand running, and post-game cleanup. The courtside duties of a ball boy fell into one of four categories. The first was shagging balls. During warmups we wheeled an aluminum rack of twenty-four basketballs out to center court. The stands were just beginning to fill, concessions were up and running, and the players came out to warm up by shooting, practicing a few moves or rehearsing their pregame rituals. Two ball boys stood at center court with their backs to one another facing the opposing baskets. Two stood under each basket facing the players as shots rained down from every angle. Catching the balls and returning them quickly to the shooter is called *shagging* the balls and was probably my favorite time of the game. It was time we interacted directly with the players—even the less talkative ones. I never had a conversation with the Ice Man, George Gervin or Dr. J., Julius Irving, but I did shag balls for them.

There were some players who indulged us further. Phil Sellers would humor us once in a while by letting one of us defend against him during warmups as he took a jump shot or drove around us for a lay-up. That's the closest any of us ever got to playing professional basketball, but it was a thrill, nonetheless. We played at least for a few seconds on an NBA court in an arena filling with fans against a bona-fide professional athlete, and we knew that boys our age all over the city envied us. It gave us a little "cred" on the street. I imagine I would have had much more cred if I had any athletic talent whatsoever, but I took what I could get and it was pretty heady for a kid who was always a little physically behind his peer group.

Another pre-game courtside duty was running errands for players and coaches. Pistons who had friends or family attending the night's game would often ask us to run tickets upstairs to Will Call. Imagine being in the lowest bowels of an arena and having to run halfway up and nearly as far out from the center to a ticket window. We were young and healthy, but that was a bit of a workout, and I don't remember ever seeing one of us walking it. I never received a tip from a player for taking tickets to will-call, but we always looked forward to a chance to work the visitor's bench and get a big tip for an extracurricular diversion. Visiting players often stayed at the Hotel Ponchartrain directly across the street from Cobo Arena. They brought their gear with them and once in while one would forget something in his hotel room. He'd give us a key, we'd throw a coat on over our red, white and blue uniform with our first name emblazoned across the back, and we'd run like the wind across Jefferson Avenue in 15-20 degree sleet storms, up to the room, grab the sneakers or whatever item prompted the diversion and always arrived back in the locker room out of breath. The faster we retrieved the item and the more out of breath we were, the bigger the tip we received. The most I ever got for the two-way run was $10 but the Philadelphia 76ers were good tippers and one of the boys swore he received a $20 bill once.

Another duty of the bench crews was to manage the warmups. The players had personalized warmups that could be torn away with a quick tug as they left the bench to go into the game. The metal snaps popped in succession from the waist downward along the outside of the legs like a long fuse of firecrackers, and whoosh, the pants dropped to the floor for our retrieval, the jacket only seconds behind. We'd see the coach signal a substitution and one of us would grab the discarded warmup while the other would ready the neatly folded suit of the panting player coming off the court.

The trick to getting this done quickly was writing the player's number in permanent marker in the tags of the jacket collar and pants waistband. When they checked into the game, we folded the garments so that the number was easily visible, jacket on top, and then stacked each pair in a staggered fashion on the floor in front of us. At any given time, 5 players were on the floor and 5 tags were visible to us on the bench. When #21 came out of the game, we were already standing behind him with Gatorade or water, a dry towel and his jacket.

The final duty of the ball boy was that of mopping the court after warmups were completed, when players fell, or whenever the referees noticed a wet spot from sweat or blood. The mop heads were 24-inch wide wire frames wrapped with white towels that were secured to the frame with cloth athletic tape. The entire court was mopped to remove any debris and sweat so that the floor would be safe and ready for play at tip-off. After warmups, the players returned to the locker room for their private pre-game meeting. Ball boys were not allowed in the locker room for these sessions or the corollary post-game debriefings. These 10- to 15-minute stints were about the only downtime we had. Each team had 2 ball boys assigned to its locker room and one ball boy worked under each basket for the entire game.

When we worked the home bench, we were not paid. When we worked the visiting bench, we received whatever the visiting team trainer wanted to pay us, which was usually $10, but depended on his generosity as well as our performance. Philadelphia usually paid us $20 each and the others varied. When we worked the home team, our first question to our partners on the other side at the end of the game was, "How much did you make?" Truthfully, most of us would have done it for free hot dogs and Gatorade. As a matter of fact the Pistons' ticket stubs could be redeemed for a small order of French fries at the Red Barn hamburger joint on Woodward, which was nearly next door to a White Castle. We'd get our fries at Red Barn, our burgers at the W.C. Lounge and that was a great night any time. Mom always picked me up at 11:00 p.m. sharp.

Pre-game music in the locker room tended to be low-key soul, R&B, or jazz. Audiophile Howard Porter's stall was directly beneath the boombox, so that may have had something to do with the selections. When the right groove spilled into the room after a win, the volume would be turned up a notch or two. Love Ballad by L.T.D. was one of those songs. Porter and M.L. Carr swayed and sang backup to Jeffery Osborne's lead as they dressed for civilian life outside the arena. In 1977 the 8-episode television miniseries Roots transfixed the entire nation, and the Pistons' locker room was not exempt. I can't say that the players' minds weren't on the business of basketball, but I do recall at least one postgame when a television was brought into the locker room. The electronics industry hadn't yet agreed on common formats for video recorders so VCRs weren't common. America was largely still watching programmed broadcasts, so if you missed an episode, you'd have to wait a year or more to see the *rerun*.

Watching those men watching Roots was surreal. Huge, strong, wealthy, free men quietly hanging on every word and scene, doubtlessly thinking of the ancestors that made their current success possible, the survivors whose genes gave them the advantages they now enjoyed, and the suffering and sacrifice endured for their sakes. I wonder if any of them considered their genetic relationship to the men who enslaved their people. I did not. As I watched, I identified with Kunta Kinte, Kizzie, Chicken George and all of the other black and brown people. Even though Chicken George was the child of an enslaved woman, Kizzie, and her white owner, Tom Moore, the likelihood of a similar union in my own biology did not occur to me. A glance at my face in the mirror told an unmistakable tale of miscegenation, but I counted it only as a recent event—not a recurring theme through generations. It would be decades before I would awaken to a very different reality. This experience, watching the series at home and at work with the Pistons, planted a seed that grew into an obsession for me and hundreds of thousands of people world-wide. Alex Haley really started something incredible by sharing the story of his search.

We were a pretty good bunch of kids and didn't try to get away with a lot of mischief, but we had these large canvas carts with flat metal ribs and frame that was on wheels. We collected used towels from the visitors' locker room and wheeled them back over to the home side for laundry after every game. Cobo Arena had a few elevators and stairs, but it also had two very wide spiral ramps allowing large numbers of patrons easy ingress and egress. They also provided an irresistible temptation for boys to joy ride. On at least one occasion, we took a towel cart or two up to the top of one of those ramps. Never mind it was full of sweaty and wet towels, we jumped in and rode them down the ramp from one level to the next no worse for the wear.

On school nights by the time I made it home, about 10 miles from Cobo Arena, I could still get in 6 hours of sleep before waking the next morning for the drive to Grandmother's house. In 1978 the Pistons announced they too were abandoning the City. For me, that was the beginning of the end of the Detroit that I knew and loved. The Pontiac Silverdome was the sparkling new home of the "Detroit" Lions and it would swallow up the tiny basketball court as a whale would a single krill. The Pistons cordoned off a fraction of the arena with make-shift aluminum bleachers and tall blue curtains. It just wasn't the same, and the hour-long commute home was too much to entertain on school nights, so I had to say goodbye to the best job ever.  Most of the boys stayed on a while longer. Pete even remained with the Pistons for many years and went on to become Executive Vice President and Chief Communications Officer at the next home of the Pistons, the Palace of Auburn Hills.  I was there when Marvin "Bad News" Barnes stole a few headlines, but Pete was there years later when the real Bad Boys made the name stick.

# CHAPTER FOURTEEN

---

## STAYIN' ALIVE

It was written or said and repeated widely long before the advent of social media and viral posts that it was rare for young black men in Detroit to reach the age of 30. Drugs, prison, homicide, and suicide all took their toll on the African American male of the '70s and '80s. One hundred years after reconstruction, the American Dream eluded most and choked the snot out of many more. Although my limited life experience introduced me to many kind, loving, generous white and black people, I was keenly aware of and saddened by the plight of so many African-Americans. Junior and senior years of high school were an amazing period in my life. An explosion of the senses ushered in an awareness that coincided with long anticipated physical maturation. Simultaneously I experienced the illusion of omnipotence and the hopelessness of futility. All of the intelligence, strength and energy in the world couldn't save some of the young men I called neighbors. Dropping out of school, selling drugs, getting hooked themselves and giving in to the negative stereotypes seemed to have become an epidemic. The street on which we lived in the white stucco Mediterranean with the pool and barbed wire fence had been an oasis in a desert of deterioration. The side streets were becoming darker and more dangerous. As men fell victim to despair, more single women struggled to raise their children alone, keep the utilities on and food in the fridge. I had no explanation other than to blame a system of government and policies that were designed to empower some at the expense of others. I knew that every white person was not evil—they weren't all racists, but I was certain that those who were had much more power and position than the rest combined. From my vantage point, you bet we lived in a racist country and we had a long way to go before we could claim the Dream of which Martin spoke so poetically. I was looking for someone to blame, someone to convince, someone to change, someone to awaken. As I heard people in barbershops, playgrounds, television and radio bemoan the unfairness of racial profiling, redlining, and systematic microaggressions, I sympathized. I didn't want to die before reaching 30 years of age, but I don't think anyone who did die so early planned for or expected it. I didn't worry constantly about it, but I did feel an urge to experience life and to suck the marrow from it as quickly as possible—just in case.

Freshman and sophomore years coincided with the global phenomenon, Saturday Night Fever. Night clubs were popping up everywhere and the radio waves were filled with the sounds of Donna Summer, the Bee Gees, K.C. and the Sunshine Band and Chic. I may have been the only kid in my neighborhood who knew all the words to Rocky Mountain High and Calypso by John Denver, but everywhere I went kids were doing the Freak and not so secretly listening to a strange new girlish looking man in bikini bottoms, high-heels with a falsetto who, it was rumored, played all of the instruments on his album. He called himself Prince, and the first high school dance I attended featured a little tune he called *Soft & Wet.* I don't think the priests were ready for that one or *Le Freak* by Chic, but the girls from Immaculata, Mercy, Regina and elsewhere sure were. I didn't know much about things that were soft or wet at that age, but stirrings within left no doubt how important they would become. My initial reaction to Prince's look was one of suspicion. I didn't think he was masculine enough, that is until I saw girls' reaction to him. Not since Michael Jackson's solo album *Got to Be There*, which I played continually as very young child (2nd and 3rd grade), did an artist create sounds and images that captivated me so. Every year of high school he released a new album and they just kept getting better.

I played my collection of vinyl 45 rpm records on the "hi fidelity system" in our basement. I'd stack them up with the yellow plastic spindle adapters and let them play one after the other. Shalamar, the Whispers, the Gap Band, Kool and the Gang, Sister Sledge and the Isley Brothers were all represented. I sang and danced all by myself until the last record dropped, working on my *moves* for the weekend.

One evening after school my cousin Pebbles called. She was a student at nearby Northwestern High School. She participated in the modern dance program at her school and she informed me that a local television show was looking for dancers. She invited me to try out. Having no perception of what I looked like in any medium other than a mirror, I jumped at the chance. There were girls, disco music, dancing, and it was free! That's all I needed to hear. Apparently, they had enough excellent dancers already— and didn't need another one—so my ineptitude was no obstacle and I was accepted into Show Coordinator Ylet's group.

The Scene, as the show was dubbed, aired on UHF channel 62, WGPR, tag lined, "Where God's Presence Radiates." Before cable, over the air broadcasts were in VHF (very high frequency) and UHF (ultra-high frequency). VHF channels were fewer, but the signals were stronger and the TV antennas picked them up more clearly. ABC (7), CBS (2), NBC (4) and Canada's CBC (9) were the mainstays. UHF channels started at 20 and went up to at least 62, which was WGPR's number. In other words, we were no American Bandstand or Soul Train, but just about every house in Detroit could get that signal without fiddling too much with the rabbit ear antennae. Produced and hosted by Captain Geek, Nat Morris, The Scene recorded shows on the weekends and aired them during the week. We also did 1 or 2 live shows weekly. To accomplish this, they had two groups of dancers, each with its own coordinator. Ron led one group and Ylet led the other.

Anyone who has ever heard the raw sound of his or her recorded voice knows the feeling. "Is that what I *really* sound like?" That feeling of horror and helpless pity is what I felt every time I watched myself dancing on television. Sometimes I actually had to look away, I was so embarrassed, but not so embarrassed as to quit. I couldn't stop myself from going to the tapings and live broadcasts. It was just too much fun. Before I could drive, Mom would take me down to the studio on Jefferson Avenue, drop me off and pick me up a couple of hours later. Almost all of the dancers were high school students, although a few more mature dancers joined in from time to time. We waited in the lobby until the studio was ready for us and then we walked 50 or so feet down a hallway, through a curtained opening and took our places.

Incredibly, I actually got better at dancing over time. I never became a great dancer, but I eventually found the beat and was for a time known as "a regular." I received a few letters of admiration, which was a huge surprise. Also surprising was that the guys at school didn't make fun of me nearly as much as I thought they would. It wouldn't have changed my mind about doing it, but it turned out that some of them wanted to be on the show, too, and I was happy to invite them on.

Uncle Buddy used to tease me about it, but his imitation of our dancing was so funny my feelings were never hurt. His eyes rolled widely back and forth as his hands and fingers swayed to an imaginary beat and his lips parted from ear to ear revealing a chasm of a smile that filled Grandmother's dining room. Anyone who saw it had to laugh, and it tickled me senseless every time. He looked more like the Hi-De-Ho Man, Cab Callaway, than a Scene dancer. I would love to have pulled him out there in front of the cameras! He would have been an *overnight sensation*, to borrow a song title from Jerry Knight. I don't know how executive producer Nat Morris made the decision to let people on camera. Maybe he left it up to the coordinators, or maybe he was personally involved to some extent. It wasn't always about physical appearance or dancing ability. Sometimes, I think they just wanted to fill up the studio with bodies. I rarely saw them turn anyone away, but it did happen once to a friend and that's the last time I danced on television.

In the winter, it was school, studying, swimming and dancing on the weekends. In the summer it was working, swimming, dancing on the Scene and at discotheques, chasing girls, having picnics, and going to house parties. Clubs like Taboo in the Riverfront district had selective admissions policies. New York's Studio 54 was notorious for such snobbery. It was a nasty way of generating interest, which presumed that the more exclusive a club was, the more popular it would become and the more money it could charge. People went to see and be seen. Taboo admitted 18 year-olds, but wasn't supposed to serve alcohol without ID. When I was 16, at 5'11" I could pass for 18 if I put on my "tough" face. I actually made my own fake ID just in case, and it worked on a number of occasions. Apparently, lamination of any handwritten form that fit in one's wallet was sufficient at many places in those days. I couldn't pass for 21, but I didn't drink alcohol yet, and I was there to dance.

I was also there for the lights, music and phone numbers. Tony and I always had a pen and paper ready. We made a game of who could get the most phone numbers, and we were pretty honest about it. We weren't asking every girl in the place for her number, or trying to break any hearts, but it was more of a barometer of whether we would go back to a place a second or third time. If there were more than a couple of pretty girls and the music was good, we got to know the place better. Tone and I were tight in those years. We did everything together. We rode the bus to school together since 9th grade. We walked or rode to the summer sports program together, and we hung out pretty much every weekend. Before we made plans with anyone else, we'd always check with each other first to see if he or I wanted to hang. We were 16 going on 20 in the "me" era. The narcissism and focus on self-fulfillment was rampant. Our parents had been children of the depression, stuck on the treadmill of scarcity, rationing and fear. Some of us wanted off of that wheel, and I was one of many young black men who had a feeling that we might not be around long enough to enjoy life if we didn't grab it by the short hairs then and there.

Getting my first car was the beginning of a particularly self-indulgent period for me. I could not wait to go to the Mumford High School Drivers Education School on Wyoming Road. The Detroit public high school popularized by Eddie Murphy in his Beverly Hills Cops movies five years later is a real school, and it had its very own closed driving course complete with traffic lights and signs. Although I attended a different school for academics, the driving school was open to the public. Montgomery Ward was a department store that also offered drivers' education. One ride with Mom in the passenger seat after taking that class was all it took for her to pay Mumford to "fix" me. Money was suddenly no object. I'm not sure why either of us thought learning to drive from a store that sold back-to-school clothes and ladies' intimates was a good idea, but Mumford certainly was a better option for me.

I had a friendly rivalry with Kevin, a neighborhood friend who signed up for the same class. Our competition was not on the driving course but in the classroom. We worked to see who could get the highest score on every exam. I really did want to be a good driver—good enough so that Mom would trust me with the car alone. Once I completed the class, the search was on for "cheap, reliable" transportation. *Trading Times* and other publications were distributed weekly for free at newsstands. The pictures and information were more informative than the classified ads of the News or Free Press. I was looking for used Mustangs from the '60s. I made a lot of phone calls, scheduled appointments, and Mom took me for many a test drive. The first break came from her workplace, however. Dr. Simonian was selling his brown 4-door Oldsmobile Delta 88 with a beige vinyl landau roof. Not my first choice, but that car had everything: air, power seats, power windows, power door locks, and an 8-track tape player! I could have fit at least 10 people in that car, although I never tried.

Around this time I also completed lifeguard training in the NYSP summer program I had been attending since age 10 at Wayne State University. I applied for a job with the program and was hired. Suddenly I was guarding and coaching kids I had been playing with the year before. There's nothing like making money doing something you love, I thought. No more waiting for the bus that never came, no more walking two miles in the rain or blazing sun. I swung the big cruiser up to Chicago Boulevard, picked up my friends Anthony, April and Timithe, and we arrived at the Matthei Sports Center and pulled into our very own parking space. Not surprisingly, the wheels also came in handy for partying.

Ronald had transformed our basement recreation room into something of a medieval tavern. He covered the hardwood floors of the 30-foot-long room with red and black game room carpeting, installed a black wood-paneled bar with 4 high-back swivel stools, a fully stocked liquor counter, popcorn maker, pool table, and projection television. At the foot of the room was the original cobblestone fireplace that was uniquely magnificent and blissfully ignorant of the gaudy surroundings thrust upon it. It would have been a great party spot if anyone had ever been allowed to visit. I don't recall him ever bringing guests over and

Ronald G. Levi Jr.

Mom and I were too afraid of the embarrassment we would experience if he arrived in a certain state while we were entertaining. I did have close friends over once in a while. When we were most certain that he would not be coming home or that he had been in a sensible mood for a while, I'd have a few people over. We'd shoot pool, play music or work on some dance routines for the show.

Transitioning from the staircase down into the basement, a faux arch separated a 10 x 10 space with mirrors on one wall—the perfect place for rehearsing dance routines—from the rest of the recreation room. The façade of the arch was adorned with framed pictures of Ronald with people I didn't recognize. They were not family members. They appeared to be service personnel and perhaps the pictures were taken while he was stationed in Europe. Three black men sat smiling in what appeared to be a pub with two white women. I never asked him or my mom who the people were or where the photo was taken. I sensed the answer would be a lie, an embarrassment or another excuse for a foul-mouthed diatribe. I wondered if one of the women might have been my birth mother, but I brushed the idea off as quickly as it came. They were in Europe and I was born in Detroit. Other pictures on the arch did include some of Ronald's family.

The Alex Haley fever found its way even to Ronald's dark and desolate psyche. He'd curse any family member over the slightest perceived offense or for no reason at all, so it was especially peculiar to see any evidence that he cared for anyone. In fact, to those who knew him best—Mom and me—the photos weren't evidence of anything more than pretense of a man utterly isolated by his own self-loathing. He framed and displayed the photos to prove to himself, if not others, that he had family and friends. He displayed them as trophies rather than as personal mementos and genuine sentiment. I'm sure his mother loved him, but I never actually heard anyone utter the words to him or about him. If we ever said them to one another, it was a time before my memories formed and certainly long before I had any understanding of their meaning. That leaves a sliver of time between learning to talk and forming the words to tell Mom I loved her, so I'm pretty sure it never happened with him.

Mom and I sang a song to one another as early as I can remember. I thought she made it up just for me, but I discovered years later that it was sung by Doris Day in the Broadway show, "Guys and Dolls." The name of the song is "A Bushel and a Peck."

Those pictures got me wondering about our family, however. I knew Grandmother was from Canada. I met her brother Jim and I heard that we had relatives in Ontario, but we never visited anyone there. Beyond my grandparents, I didn't know much about our ancestry then. I had never seen a picture of a family tree or any written list of family members. I knew Ronald's siblings and parents, and I knew Mom's siblings and parents. Her grandmother came from Mississippi to live with us for a while; however, she died when I was in 1st or 2nd grade. We visited her cousins in Mansfield, Ohio once or twice, but both sides of my adoptive tree were generationally limited. I also wondered about my own biological parents. I wondered if they were living in Detroit and what they looked like. I resigned I'd never have pictures of them that I could hang on a wall like Ronald. I wouldn't even know where to begin looking.

The summers of 1980 and 1981 were composed of many firsts. I finally found a Mustang. The first was a $600, 1968 convertible with a sagging frame and doors that needed extra "persuasion" to close. Once closed and locked, they remained that way reliably, but if I tried to swing the driver's door closed casually as with most newer cars, it would simply bounce back at me. I had to lift the door up while simultaneously pushing it closed in order for the mechanisms to catch. This was much easier to do from the outside of the car, and was no inconvenience at all for a 15 year old in summer who watched too many episodes of Batman and Robin on television. I'd close the door, jump over and into the seat in a single fluid motion. We tried strengthening the sagging frame, which my back-alley hook-up mechanics assured me was possible, but it didn't do much good. So, I painted it black, mounted louvered flood lights under the front bumper and replaced the ragged black drop top with a white version that had a folding rear window. Although the doors never closed properly, and there were a couple of rusted spots in the floorboard of the passenger's side through which the road was visible, when I was cruising down Woodward, Jefferson or Grand Boulevard, only the most astute enthusiasts could ever have noticed what a piece of junk it was. And I had my Mustang—I was beyond thrilled.

Cruising was a big deal long before the days of the now famous Woodward Dream Cruise. You cleaned and waxed your ride, and then you took her out to be seen and admired. My spots were Palmer Park, Greektown, and Belle Isle. In the late '70s and early '80s, the parking lot near the public pool at Palmer Park, which was on the periphery of the Detroit Golf Club and within walking distance of the exclusive Palmer Woods and Sherwood Forest neighborhoods, was a hit or miss spot. If I saw someone I knew, it was a hit, if not, I gave everyone a look-see and kept it moving on to the next spot. I pulled through slowly with top down, music playing loud enough, but not too loud, sunglasses posed, left arm on the driver's door, right hand at 12 o'clock and attitude naturally well-adjusted. The lot was filled with all kinds of vehicles: some were new models, others were classics, and most were just average daily-use vehicles people used to get to and from their obligations. Many were probably held together by little more than a song and a prayer, but they shone brightly in the setting sun, basked amicably in the twilight, and we were all one for a while.

I didn't smoke marijuana in high school, I had never had a drink of alcohol or beer until senior year, so I was quite clear-headed as I poured down the Lodge Freeway, under Cobo Hall and into Greektown. Each weekend in the summer Detroit celebrated

"Ethnic Festivals" at Hart Plaza, an open-air amphitheater on the River at the foot of Woodward Avenue and home of the famed Noguchi Fountain. One weekend was the Country Western Festival, another was the Polish Festival, the German Festival, and so on. Every Friday and Saturday night, cars with their music blaring crept through Greektown. Injected into the veins of Brush or Beaubian, I pulsed through the artery of Monroe Street. Two or three cars ahead of me, I could hear strains of Journey. When I passed Second Baptist Church on my left, I heard REO Speedwagon on my right.

To hell with this, I thought. This is Detroit. This is my city—these people left. They don't live here. They lay waste to my home every weekend, piss in my streets, litter my highways, clog the freeways for stupid hockey games (what a ridiculous sport), running across freeways on foot to get to Joe Louis Arena, and they have taken the tax base necessary to sustain basic services. Because of them, traffic on the weekends was impossible. Because of them, the Fox Theater was in shambles, because of them people couldn't get jobs, gas prices were sky rocketing, and we were headed for war somewhere soon. They have shat all over us true Detroiters and taken the toilet paper with them, I thought.

One Nation Under a Groove began to play, the white convertible top was down and the graphic equalizer was perfectly set for Parliament Funkadelic to whoop some Journey and REO Speedwagon ass. Fuck the Stones! Fuck Springsteen, Black Sabbath, Deff Lepperd. Marylin Manson, and fuck Rod Stewart!

Perhaps the open convertible amplified the already amplified sound of the new stereo system installed in the old Mustang. Not only did it drown out the "foreign," traitorous music that incited my revolt, it also attracted the attention of a white Detroit police officer. Now, in a congested artery flowing with the life blood of Detroit and constricted fatally by the plaque of years of institutionalized racism, there was nowhere for a *carpuscle* to escape. We all crept forward at a speed that rendered me easily apprehendable by anyone with a heartbeat and one good leg to hop on. The officer simply walked up to my car and said, "Turn it down!" I was naturally offended.

When a black family in my neighborhood was assaulted, it took hours for police to respond. When my lawnmower was stolen, I didn't bother filing a report because I knew I'd never see it again. Insurance rates continued to rise, and I can't play my radio in the city where I lived my entire life, but other people who do not live here can play whatever they want as loud as they want without repercussions! I was incensed and indignant, but not crazy. I turned my music down as ordered. As I pulled forward and left the officer in my rearview mirror, I turned left on St. Antoine to leave Greektown and I turned the music right back up to where I had it—this was eight years before NWA played their historic concert at Joe Louis Arena. I was ahead of my time.

Cruising Belle Isle was fun, not so much for who one might see, but for the views of Detroit from the River. As a child I enjoyed visiting the zoo and the aquarium there. By 1981, those attractions and many others were closed. Families still frequented the island for picnics on weekends, but after dark it was largely a no-man's-land of drugs, alcohol, and drag racing. I cruised it for the beauty of the island in the night as well as the day. Circling the island in a convertible is the closest a landlubber gets to the exhilaration of yachting.

A couple of weeks after my personal Rosa Parks revolution in Greektown, I swung back from Belle Isle west on Jefferson back to Brush and north up to Monroe, then hung a right into Greektown. Just as I passed Beaubian, home base of Detroit Police Headquarters, the lights flashed and now I was more pissed than ever before. My windows were up, the top was secure, all lights and equipment were in working order, I'd made no moving violations, I was not under the influence of any substances, and these mugs were hassling me in *my* city for driving while black. I pulled over west bound on Macomb Street literally in the shadow of Detroit Police Headquarters. There were untold numbers of squad cars and resources surrounding me. It was like a "guess who's coming to dinner" at the chief's house. I rolled down my window and waited for this shit-head to give me grief, but I was ready.

I knew my rights. I wasn't some punk he could frighten. I'd been to some of the finest schools in the city, and I was ready to take his name and badge number and start calling everyone in my little black book, which was literally a little black book because iPhones hadn't been invented yet. Truthfully, I was a little afraid and my pulse was racing, but I'd had enough of this crappy treatment by interlopers, carpetbaggers, people who only cared when their friends and families were involved. It had to stop and maybe, just maybe, I was meant to be a small cog in that wheel. I saw the officer approach in the side mirror and I lowered the window, roll, roll, roll, roll (it's a 1968 car, remember?).

The officer didn't ask me for ID; he put his hand on the door frame near the lock and leaned in. Very calmly, almost casually, he said, "Last time I asked you to turn your music down, you waited until you got to the end of the block and then you blasted it." Wow, same darn guy I saw a few weeks ago. I said, "I know, officer, but I feel you guys always let everyone else (white kids) play whatever they want as loud as they want, and you don't say anything. I live here and I'm the one who has to be inconvenienced for their sake. If a young black man has a decent car, he's singled out, but given the same car and the same circumstances, a white kid is never hassled." He said, "I can't speak for anyone other than me, but I treat everybody the same. If it's too loud, it's too loud." I believed him—I was disarmed.

I knew in my heart that this man was not picking on me because of my skin color. He didn't pull me over because I was a black kid driving a "nice" '68 Mustang convertible, he pulled me over because it was a unique and unmistakable vehicle with which he'd had an interaction only a week or two previously. He wanted to explain to me why he chose the actions he did, and I had to respect that—and I still do. He didn't beat me, shoot me, threaten me or abuse me in any way. Every interaction was professional, personal and appropriate—and it showed me that I was the one who was in need of an attitude adjustment.

Death trap that it was, I continued looking for a better Mustang and in my senior year of high school, I came up upon a 1967 coupe, aqua blue with a white vinyl top, turn signal indicators in the hood and a brushed aluminum center console with T handle gear shifter. It had relatively low mileage for a 14-year-old car and had been kept in the garage of an elderly lady who didn't drive anymore. I sold the convertible junker easily and bought the coupe. I took her to Mickey Shore on Woodward for an audio upgrade. I put in a new Jensen radio with an under the dash 7-band graphic equalizer and 4 new speakers. That's all she needed. No new paint, and no major repairs. Not quite as sexy as the convertible, but a very cool ride and a definite steal for the price of $800. In retrospect, I should have put this car away and invested in its care and preservation. Instead, I took it to college and drove it to death, but it sure was fun while it lasted.

# CHAPTER FIFTEEN

## WINTER WONDER

The maple and elm leaves inevitably left dark stains on the concrete deck of the pool each year in the late fall. The first order of business in the spring after removing the cover was a good scrubbing of the entire deck with muriatic acid sold by the gallon in pool supply stores. I first wet the deck with a hose and then splashed few ounces of acid at a time onto the surface, scrubbed vigorously with a nylon brush at the end of a 4- to 5-foot wooden handle and repeated that process over the entire deck. I covered every inch and no one ever acknowledged the effort, but it looked great to me and was worth every bead of sweat and every second of time I put into it. I couldn't really begin to enjoy my summer until the pool was completely clean and free of any distracting blemishes. After a few laps when the sun was high directly above, I stretched out on a folding aluminum chaise lounge with nylon basket weave and pondered my birth parents' relationship—how I came to be.

Maybe they weren't high school acquaintances caught up in a moment of indiscretion. Maybe my conception was something far less romantic. As fortunate as I was, I couldn't escape the feeling that nothing more than chance was the best explanation for my existence. My mother, I reasoned, was a runaway who escaped the cripplingly high expectations of her assembly-line father. He berated her constantly for what he called a lack of ambition and plain looks. If she didn't finish high school and get a job at the cosmetic counter of the Federal's Department Store on Grand River, she'd have to find a husband because he was finished with her willful disobedience and smart mouth. Her mother was powerless to intercede even when she wasn't three sheets to the wind, and my mother had enough of the whole scene. When the bell rang in May of her 11th grade year, she got on a bus, passed by home and kept on riding. She didn't say goodbye or leave a note for her parents, she knew her father would be relieved to be rid of her and her mother wouldn't even notice. At the bus station, she watched as well-dressed couples and singles streamed in and out for departures and arrivals. She saw a couple of dirty-faced drunks fishing the coin returns of the payphones be chased away by uniformed security guards. Cigarette and cigar smoke filled the waiting room as she pondered her next destination. She had enough money for a ticket to Chicago, but she didn't know anyone there. The uncertainty must have been evident in the furrows of her brow.

A young man and woman about her age, maybe a little older startled her. "Hey, you lost?" the woman asked. "No, just trying to decide. Where are you headed?" my mother answered. "We're just putting up signs for roommates. We have a place a couple of blocks away in Elton Park and need someone to share the rent and utilities or we're going to have to find another place." She showed the hand-written flyer to my mother who was wary, but realized this might be just the thing she needed to start living independently from her parents. She wasn't making enough money to pay for a place of her own, but if she could share the costs, she could save some and as she earned more or maybe when she got married, she could transition to a place of her own. The freedom of not having to answer to anyone else was exactly what she wanted and she didn't mind sacrificing creature comforts for that privilege.

She stayed with that couple for a while, came and went as she pleased, and dated whomever she wanted. That's what got her kicked out of a couple of places. The Hippie counter-culture was taking off and before the Summer of Love and Woodstock, she had her own Winter of Wonder in Detroit. She was attracted to dark men: Latin, Italian, Black...she sampled them all. If it got "too heavy" she simply found a new *pad* or a new partner. When she discovered she was pregnant it was too late to do anything about it, but she wasn't going to let it or anyone control her. She wasn't sure which of the men she had been with was the father, and she didn't bother trying to find out. She enjoyed being pregnant. She wasn't into the psychedelic scene, mushrooms or LSD, so the pregnancy didn't cramp her style too much until the final month.

When the time came, she delivered at home with a little help from her Bohemian housemates who went with her to the emergency room, which to their relief was a madhouse of activity with emergent cases rushing in. Two served as look-outs as she placed the bundle gently on an unattended gurney and they all walked out quietly, arm-in-arm, unnoticed, unencumbered, and unfazed.

# CHAPTER SIXTEEN

⁓⊃◌⊂⁓

## LASALLE BOULEVARD

From the time we moved in until the present day, there's been something special about the old Mediterranean stucco home on LaSalle. In my sophomore year of high school, before I could drive, Mom took me to parties, dances... well, she drove me everywhere, but house parties, dances, sock hops, and anywhere with music and girls were high on my list of priorities. In the summer of 1979, I had not yet reached the age to have a driving learner's permit, but all of my peers had, and I was doing my best to experience all of the things they were experiencing. Mom was really amazing about allowing me that latitude. On June 10th of 1980 I attended a house party on the west side and was ready for a shower and bed as we returned home south on LaSalle from the Chicago exit of the Lodge Freeway. As we rounded LaSalle Gardens Park, we saw flashing blue and red lights. The streets were barricaded. Only residents were being allowed through. Our next-door neighbor, Reverend C.L. Franklin, father of Aretha had been shot. Little information was available then or after, other than it was presumed to have been the result of an attempted robbery. Reverend Franklin never fully recovered and he died 5 years later.

On my 16th birthday in 1981, LaSalle Blvd., was also the place where Ronald was finally called to account for the years of abuse heaped upon his family and all who had the misfortune of making his acquaintance. Then a senior in high school, Mom and I returned home from a long day. When we arrived, Ronald was confrontational and drunk. There was some difference of opinion in a way that I had learned to dismiss or ignore. As always I assumed, he would soon be ensconced, stupefied in his private bedroom suite, and I began to head up the stairs from the foyer past the stained and leaded glass windows of the landing. Over my shoulder I heard Mom say, "Don't go," in a trembling voice I had never heard from her before that moment. It froze me. As I turned and saw tears flowing down her face, Ronald looked at me with a menace he would soon regret. He ordered me to "Go upstairs," but I was no longer a child. I was not quite the physical equal of many of my 18-year-old peers, but I was an athletic 6 foot tall, 16 year old in condition and position to defend his mother and unafraid of a drunken bully. When I hesitated upon his command, Ronald stepped toward me. Mom shrieked, "No!" perhaps the only time she ever mustered the courage to defy him and certainly the first time I witnessed such. Ronald had never laid a hand on me in anger, let alone love, in my entire life, and Mom had never let it be known to me or anyone that he physically harmed her, but we both sensed his intent at that moment and we set upon him like summer in the Sahara.

The only punches, slaps and kicks being thrown were upon him. Off balance, he fell into the leaded glass window on the right of the heavy wooden front door, breaking it before stumbling forward into the center of the foyer. Beneath the chandelier that had welcomed many guests over the decades, we kicked and pummeled him until we realized he was unable to resist or put up any defense. Within a short time, I realized that for so many years we had feared someone who was ultimately incapable of harming us. He was a pathetic, impotent bully, and I could take no pleasure in exacting any sort of revenge upon him. He was no challenge, no threat, of no import whatsoever. Any effort of any kind at his expense was wasted, I concluded. This miserable specimen of humanity who never attended a single event of my childhood, who I never heard use the word *love* to describe his feelings about anyone (least of all his son), who cursed and alienated everyone who ever called him friend or family, —the essence of this piece of human garbage was finally exposed as a weak, cowardly, vile excuse for a man.

In time this experience also revealed to me more about Mom. I loved and admired her because of her sacrifice for me and because of all she accomplished in spite of her modest beginnings. She endured the pain and humiliation of a relationship with Ronald for my sake. But I was angry that she put up with him for so long. How much better might our lives have been if she'd had the courage to accept help or to fight back sooner? I felt in some way responsible. If I had been more aware of what she was enduring, I could have done something. If it hadn't been for her desire to protect me, she could have left him. She tolerated his tantrums and as far as I knew, she never fought back. She was afraid of what he would do, but it turns out he did nothing. All those years of cowering, she could have gone upside his head with an iron skillet and our lives would have certainly been transformed for the better, I reasoned. He collected a few things and got the hell out of there that very night. The beating sobered him up enough to fear what might have happened if he'd fallen asleep there overnight.

That winter was cold and when the natural gas was turned off for non-payment, Ronald's only worth was revealed. Mom barely had enough money to pay for groceries, fuel for the car, tuition and electricity. That winter we piled on the blankets and kept a couple of rooms habitable with kerosene heaters while the windows in the rest of the rooms frosted over. This was the first time in my life that I truly envied my imaginary siblings. If my birth mother or father had kept me, none of this would be happening. They had heat, food, and were probably sitting on comfy couches in t-shirts and boxers while I was here in a freaking ice box in this God-forsaken crumbling city. Why did these two have to choose me? Why couldn't they have let some other couple adopt me? Someone who lived in a warm house!

We turned off the porch lights at night to discourage anyone from visiting and discovering the embarrassing truth of our frigid existence. I wasn't too concerned about it because we rarely if ever had unannounced guests, so I was suspicious when the doorbell rang one dark December evening. All of the lights in our house were turned off except for the television and the kerosene heater in the library, which couldn't be seen from the windows on either side of the front door. After a minute or so of knocking and bell-ringing, I tipped around the back of the house through the kitchen and dining room to get a side view of the porch without being seen myself. I was panic-stricken and my heart stopped.

It was my friend Jimmy from school and a couple of girls from another school with whom we were also friends. "What in the world are they doing here?" I hyperventilated. He had never shown up unannounced before and the girls had never been to my house. Of all the time I lived there, why now? Would it have killed him to stop at a payphone and call me first? What could I do? He wasn't leaving until I answered the door. I opened it just a crack praying that none of them could see the frost in the corners of the window panes of the living room. "Sorry it took so long to answer

119

the door. Mom and I are both feeling really sick. Must have been something we ate. I can't invite you in now, but thanks for coming by. I've really gotta get to bed. I'm sorry." Jimmy wished us well and they returned to his vehicle.

I never regretted the whooping we put on Ronald. We never let on what an incredible strain that put on us, but we remained thankful that his torment was over. At least he was out of my life for good, I thought.

# CHAPTER SEVENTEEN

---᧞᧞---

## FOUNDLING FINDERS

P eople don't abandon babies for convenience or fun. They do so out of desperation and hopelessness. I knew that the answers would likely be a mixture of sadness and joy. I told myself that all I wanted were names and basic geographic information. Any additional information beyond that would be an overflow of blessings, I told myself.  It was too much to ask how my parents met, under what circumstances I came into being, where were they raised, and what were their families like.  No, it was too far-fetched to think I would ever know those things, but maybe I would find a picture of one or both of them. Wouldn't it be cool to see a resemblance of something more than my big ears?

I had heard of *Search Angels* but had no idea where to find them until my FamilyTree DNA match Emmilie told me about the Facebook groups, *DNA Detectives* and *Foundling Finders*. In order to join the closed groups, requesters must answer a few questions describing the circumstances of their birth and what they are hoping to accomplish. On September 16, 2015 at 5:34 p. m., my request to join Foundling Finders was approved by CeCe Moore with a welcome message to the group. That name didn't mean much to me then, but she was already well-known among members of the International Society of Genetic Genealogy. Today, she is much more widely known as a consultant for television shows like *Finding Your Roots* with Henry Louis Gates, and she very deservedly produces her own series on ABC, *The Genetic Detective*. Her personal interests have evolved from helping adoptees find birth families to helping law enforcement agencies solve cold cases using the science of DNA. In her wake, she created an army of search Angels, enthusiasts, hobbyists and sub-cultures all benefitting from her early work, commitment and compassion.

The Facebook groups are a trove of information and active expertise. In addition to Foundling Finders, which is exclusively for adults who were abandoned at birth, DNA Detectives provides support for any adoptee seeking assistance. I began following every piece of advice offered. Upload my yDNA results to ySearch. Cast a wider net: test with all 3 major service providers, Family Tree DNA, 23andMe and Ancestry. Write the State of Michigan requesting identifying information, and upload DNA results to GEDMatch. Check! GEDMatch is a clearing house that compares raw DNA results uploaded voluntarily and in most cases anonymously. The key benefit to uploading results to GEDMatch is that if a close relative tests with only one provider, you'll never know of the match if you tested with a different provider. If you both upload your respective files to GEDMatch, you'll see the connection within 24 hours—often sooner. There are detailed instructions for everything on YouTube as well as the Facebook Groups.

A search Angel contacted me. Understand, this was not a formulaic assignment. An experienced genetic genealogist caught wind of my posts in one or both of two private Facebook groups created by CeCe, and reached out to me. These are subject matter experts who spend many hours applying their considerable knowledge of DNA testing, results analysis and many evolving tools and services to the cause of helping adoptees and foundlings find their biological families without any remuneration whatsoever.

Having tested with 23andMe and Family Tree DNA, I was still sore at Ancestry for charging so much money for the Y-DNA test that was of little help several years prior. But my Angel Linny assured me that autosomal testing was different, and the biggest pond to fish in was Ancestry's. Another $100 roll of the dice and a teaspoon of spit were exchanged, and the 4 – 6 week wait for the results began. In an amazing 2-week turnaround, my results were posted, and they did not disappoint. The results from the Ancestry tests are 3-fold. First, I received an Ethnicity Estimate showing the approximate percentages DNA I inherited from each region or country of the planet. Second, I had a list of DNA matches— thousands of them! And third was something called ThruLines®, which is a nifty tool that uses trees created by its millions of users to suggest possible relationships with my DNA matches. A first cousin once removed, *A.S.,* and a second cousin, *FRANCESSTEPHENS140*, were among the thousands of matches listed.

"That's close enough," Linny said. "If they know who their grandparents and great grandparents are, we may be able to solve this." Linny explained how DNA matches compare segments of each set of chromosomes. We have 23 pairs: 1 set from each parent. The larger the number and length of the shared segments, the more closely related two people are. If the segments of 2 people overlap on the same paternal chromosome, that segment was inherited from the same shared common ancestor. Likewise on the maternal side. Distant relations are prone to false positive indications or should warrant more careful scrutiny, but the upper and middle ranges are extremely reliable. I learned that the hardest thing for many beginners to do is to identify which of their matches are paternal and which are maternal. Once that determination is made the fur begins to fly.

In my case, we knew from the early 2009 tests that my paternal side were largely African-American and the Ancestry results quickly revealed that my maternal ancestors were 100% Eastern European. Even before identifying which side any of my matches were on, the biggest shock was the ethnicity estimate. Linny asked, "Could your father have been bi-racial?" I was 71% white, 28% black and 1% Indigenous American. I had identified as an African-American all my life! I empathized with causes that positively affected and benefitted black families and in turn all families. In spite of my lighter complexion, I always thought of myself as 100% black on the inside and 50/50 on the outside.

While most African-Americans, I felt, correctly recognized my blackness, I was mildly offended when someone mistook me for a white person. In my early years of driving I received a couple of moving violations. After the officers concluded issuing the citations, I noticed in the box labelled *race* was written the word "White." I couldn't rightly use the excuse that they pulled me over *while driving black*. Surely I could fight the tickets in court on the basis of mistaken identity or at least poor observation techniques! An officer who couldn't distinguish the color of a person's skin could not reliably differentiate red, yellow and green, could he? The kids in my neighborhood who infuriated me by calling me *white boy* weren't so far off after all, I pondered. My wife laughed at the irony of my indignation. "You're so militant, progressive and liberal, but your little feelings are hurt now that you're whiter than you thought." It wasn't that I had a grudge with white people in general, rather I had a bone to pick with the institutionalized practices that hurt black people and any minority. I was fortunate to have many positive, trusting relationships with people of diverse origins. It's just that until that moment, I'd thought of myself as exclusively black and an example and ally of the underserved, underrepresented, undereducated and underemployed—terms that I did not associate with white Americans.

Intellectually I accepted that somewhere in America there were poor, disadvantaged white people, but I never saw them. I didn't see them on television, in my neighborhood, at school or even in movies. My earliest years seeing soldiers in the streets, riding the school buses to the suburbs and watching my family's behavior around white people, informed my opinion that I was not on the *white side*...I was on the *black side*. Was the one-drop rule evaporating before my eyes? Had I failed the paper bag test once too often? Was my black card on the verge of revocation? This was a shock for me if not for many in my periphery who saw the lack of pigmentation more clearly than I did.

Linny built "mirror trees" that involved identifying shared ancestors among my DNA matches. By identifying how they were related to one another, it became possible to identify how I might be related to them. There were only a few names in their trees, but it was enough for Linny to trace them back a couple of generations to common ancestors. A.S. (Annie) was the aunt of FRANCESSTEPHENS140 (Frances). The most recent common ancestor of Stacia, Annie and Frances were William Lowther and Amelia Harvard, Annie's grandparents and Frances's great grandparents. Annie and my father were first cousins, so her grandparents were my *great* grandparents. As second cousins, Frances's great grandparents were my great grandparents. The elegance and simplicity belied the effort, expense and time it took

Ronald G. Levi Jr.

to see these pieces fall into place. It sounds so much simpler than it felt when I was new to the scientific method.

# CHAPTER TWENTY-ONE

## HYPOCRITE HEAVEN

S pring brought glorious warmth and high school graduation with it. Savings were eventually enough to pay the past due amount and get the gas turned back on but not before a water pipe froze and burst in the wall of the downstairs sun porch. I knew enough about the workings of the house to turn off the water to that section, but the damage was done. Mom must not have carried property insurance because it stayed that way for years until I began working and was able to repair it myself. Mom still worked doggedly, but she was never happier or more fulfilled than when she was working at the hospital among her friends and colleagues. Occasionally the doctors might ask her to house-sit while they vacationed or to watch their children while they enjoyed a night out. They were her extended family, and a big part of her sanity.

I went away to college and drove home some weekends to see Mom, do laundry or just to get away from campus. It was a relief to know that she was safe and her "husband" was staying far away. It always chafed me to know that she continued to carry him on her medical insurance. She insisted that if anything ever happened to him, it would be her responsibility to care for him. I encouraged her to file for divorce and erase him from memory completely, but to my great chagrin, she never did. It never grated more than many years after I was married and had children of my own, Ronald suffered a series of strokes resulting in the inability to care for himself.

He lost the use of the right side of his body, his speech could be difficult to understand, but miraculously his foul belligerence remained undaunted. He bounced from nursing home to nursing home, cursing every "got dam muthafucka" who tried to help him. He fought with his "good" hand, slapping, punching, and throwing anything he could whenever he was displeased... which was often. The worst part of it was that Mom asked me to check on him from time to time... to take him clothes, new underwear, and personal items. She paid a provider to groom him biweekly, not that anything could improve such an ugly disposition. He was still an ogre albeit an ogre with a haircut. It was torturous for me, but if I didn't do it, she would have done it herself and I couldn't bear the thought of her having to be in his presence for any purpose.

I'm not proud to admit there was a small part of me that found comfort in the irony of this tragically proud man imprisoned in his own feebleness, relegated to the worst elder care imaginable by his own combative, evil nature. When I'd see him spinning his wheel chair in circles because he could only turn the left wheel, I half chuckled as I shook my head in pity. He started off in facilities that were fairly nice, but each time he attacked, insulted, and alienated the staff, he found himself in a new facility that was another step down in quality. In fairness, the last home he was in before he died was probably the best of them all because they seemed to provide reasonable care in spite of his disposition and behavior. They could somehow ignore the bullying and abuse that others would not suffer without any sort of retaliation. When others had enough, they ignored him, stayed away as much as possible. The last home did what they could no matter how many "muthafuckas" he slurred. I rarely spoke to him when I visited. If I had a new robe or pairs of boxers for him, I was overjoyed to find him asleep. I was grateful to put them in his hanging closet and leave without a word.

Grandfather was gone, but the baptism, lessons, and love he gave me never left. After several years of squeezing every bit of juice out of a life I was told would last no more than 30 years, I discovered that somehow, I was still breathing and I might actually make it that far. I survived a lot of things that could or should have killed me. Fist fights at Belle Isle, interceding in a knife attack against a young white couple in Hart Plaza, foolishly free climbing the face of Ford Auditorium, and speeding at 100 miles per hour southbound on the Lodge Freeway, to name a few. At 19 years of age I was far from saintly, but I knew that I'd had enough of the fast life and thrill-seeking. I prayed to the God I knew was always there for me—the God that I had been taking for granted—the God I knew was not just my heavenly father, but my only father.

Throughout my Baptist upbringing, Catholic primary school, and Jesuit secondary education, pieces of the Gospel got through to me, and more than anything I knew He was real and that He was forgiving and loving. He delivered me from a lot, and I wanted something special and specific. I wanted a wife. Not immediately, but I wanted one person with whom I could build a relationship that would at the right time result in marriage. I prayed that He would send someone beautiful that I could trust with everything, someone smart who knew some things that I didn't and who could manage the complexities of life independently. I asked for a woman who would be a great mother and who knew what a good family looked like. I tell you the truth that by the time I finished that prayer, the name and face of a young woman I already knew came instantly to my mind. How had I not realized this already? Maybe I dismissed her from consideration because she was still in high school and I was already in college. I can wait for her, were the words I heard within but did not speak. She was all of the things I prayed for and much more. I called to ask her out and we began seeing each other pretty regularly. A year later she was in college and I was visiting her every weekend. We continued dating and within 3 to 4 years she discovered what I had known since she was 17 and I was 19—that I was not going to let her get away.

After working at IBM for about 5 years, I paid my way through college and was able to fix some of the damage Ronald's neglect and imposed absence caused to our once beautiful home. Mom moved into a nice apartment that she loved and my new bride moved into the LaSalle home with me. Detroit of the late '80s was far from the memories of my youth, but I hadn't given up on her yet. I was a super-booster who believed better days were just around the corner. I had become accustomed to seeing broken glass bottles in the streets, streets and alleys darkened by broken, unreplaced lamps, and to the blight of burned out houses. My wife, however, had not become accustomed to such scenes. She was rightfully fearful about coming into the city after living in the suburbs for many years. I shrugged off her concerns and those of anyone who argued that Detroit was unsafe or to be avoided. Fear is what'll get you hurt, I maintained. Being aware of your environment and not doing "foolish" things like leaving your doors unlocked or walking alone down a side street were the keys to safety. If you act like a victim or look like a victim, you will become a victim, I believed.

One afternoon I was sitting in our back yard with our infant son watching and listening to the gurgling water in our pool, surrounded by the 12-foot-high chain link fence with barbed wire and I heard gunshots. They didn't startle me at all. I was used to hearing gunshots during the day as well as at night. It wasn't a constant occurrence, but it was frequent enough that I had begun to treat it very casually. It didn't change my opinion about my beloved city or its inhabitants until that moment with my son. Although it never occurred to me that I faced any real danger in my city, I suddenly understood the randomness of such acts and calculated the possibility of a shot fired in the air coming down and striking my son. I postulated the possibility of a poorly aimed shot fired a block away tearing through the orange canvas covering our fences and piercing my wife. The odds, no matter how small I wanted to make them, were not zero and that was far too great a risk to accept. The time had come for me to say goodbye.

The crack epidemic had people doing previously unimaginable things. One week a man dove through the picture window of my neighbor's family room. She retrieved her pistol and put him out of his misery.

Another afternoon following a day at the office, I was talking to my wife in the kitchen when she looked over my shoulder and said, "Someone's trying to steal our lawnmower!" Somehow this man climbed over a 12-foot-high fence with barbed wire, went into our garage, and pushed out our lawnmower without a plan for getting it over the same fence. I raced out to the back yard and grabbed the long pole I used to skim leaves from the water and cornered him. Meanwhile, my wife was standing frozen at the screen door, mouth agape in astonishment. I thought, Why is she not calling the police? "Call the police!" She snapped out of the trance and officers arrived within minutes, which was very unusual for our neighborhood at that time. The whole scenario could have gone so much worse. If the thief had been carrying a weapon, if the police had not come so quickly, my wife and I could have been seriously injured or killed. Yes, it was time to pack up and leave the home I had lived in since I was 10 years old. This was the home where I learned to swim, where Mom and I managed to create some very good memories in the gaps between Ronald's violent episodes and where we held our wedding reception. The craftsmanship was something I knew I'd never find again—or be able to afford. It was a very distressing decision for me, but one I knew I had to make and did so without reservation. There is no lock, camera, security system or weapon that can effectively combat utter chaos and depravity 24/7, and locking ourselves in a prison of our own making was not an option.

Having a child opened my eyes and changed my priorities. The blessings of marriage and children led me to reflect much more on my faith and to strengthen my relationship with God. Having saved me from so many perils, I couldn't help but wonder, "To what purpose?" As Ronald stubbornly clung to his abhorrent existence, I asked myself if perhaps God was allowing him to hang on so that he could be evangelized. If God could love anyone, he could certainly love the unlovable, and Ronald was a poster child for such as that.

So one day when I visited, I asked Ronald about his thoughts of God. He scowled. "I don't believe in that." I told him that I found comfort in the ministry of Jesus and asked why he refused the gift. He said, "It would make me a hypocrite." I said to God, well, I guess that's not what you're saving me for, so he's all yours. None of us can know the fate of another person. I know now that a change of heart and conversion can happen any time, and it's never too late until we've drawn our last breath. It's possible that God softened the old recalcitrant's heart and opened his eyes to the light before his time was up, but the message I took from that interaction, my last with Ronald still breathing, was that I'd rather be a hypocrite in the last row of Heaven than an unabashed apostate headed for a front row seat in Hell.

# CHAPTER EIGHTEEN

— ༄༅ ༄ —

## TRUTH OR DARE

Having children also gave me renewed interest in my genetic identity. When physicians asked, "Is there a history of heart disease in your family?" I had to shrug. "I don't know. I was adopted." I wanted to be able to give my children better answers someday, but with Mom's sensitivity to the subject, I preferred not to ask her directly about it. I sent a letter off to the State asking for any information and while I waited, I began learning more about my adoptive family. Computers, which Ronald and his brothers lacked when doing their research in the '70s were now commonplace. I began by creating an account on Ancestry.com to build a family tree. I started with my parents and their siblings and worked backwards from there. In 2007 working at it in my spare time I was able to piece together quite a bit from public records. I quickly ran into roadblocks on Mom's side, however. I found a military enlistment for her dad, but no other public records for anyone. No records of any kind for his parents or beyond. This was beyond frustrating—it was both infuriating and heartbreaking. Not because I was unable to find some evidence of things I already knew to be true, but the experience emphasized the effect of long-standing institutionalized racism on families.

As the absence of light is darkness, the absence of records documenting the existence of my mother's ancestors all but erased them from history if not our own aging minds. Willie Jamerson, Ethel Strong, John Wright and Clarissa Baker were Mom's grandparents. They existed whether the United States wanted them to or not. Jim Crow could hide them from the rest of the world, but not from us, their family. Because of their emigration to Canada, their return to Michigan, and their roots in New Jersey, Ronald's family was easier to trace at least until the birth of John Wesley Levi in 1809. Only the line of his paternal grandmother Emily Gould could be traced far beyond 1800. The unique circumstances and customs of Gouldtown, all that's been written about them and their own penchant for fastidious genealogy documentation, permitted me to trace the English Fenwick ancestors to their arrival in America aboard the Griffin in 1675 and beyond that to the 1400s in England. The first free black person I was able to find on that branch was Abijah Gould, "that black," as Elizabeth Fenwick's grandfather referred to him in his last will and testament.

I traced every descendant of John Wesley Levi and Ann Garrad, my paternal third great grandparents, forward to the present date. Ronald may have been a rotten apple, but these were the people of a grandmother, aunts, uncles and cousins who loved, taught and raised me. I am them and they are me. I was proud to be able to document how each of the branches were related to one another and to reconnect our American family to our family members who remained in Ontario. The descendants of the pioneers of the Queen's Bush still living in Canada celebrate our

Ronald G. Levi Jr.

heritage with the North Buxton Homecoming every year. The first Homecoming was initiated by the Sunshine Club of the British Methodist Episcopal Church and was held on Labour Day 1924 in the pasture fields of Reginald and Minnie Robbins.

> *"This event was intended to draw those former residents who relocated to various parts of Canada and the United States for a return visit to this community. Descendants of former slaves have made this weekend comparable to a pilgrimage "home" where memories are rekindled, ties and acquaintances are renewed. That one-day event has evolved to a full four-day celebration where people celebrate their heritage through music, conferences, and a variety of activities in the community. The entire community of North Buxton works to host a holiday weekend..."* [4]

I was amazed to discover that my second great grandparents Fredonia Burgess and Thomas Levi who died in 1921 and 1929 were not buried in Detroit. They were laid to rest in the Forest Hill Cemetery in Ann Arbor, which is steps away from the Mary Markley Dormitory where I lived while attending the University of Michigan and across the street from the Stockwell Dormitory where my future wife lived while she attended. I had no idea my past was so present when I was on "the Hill," as that section of campus has long been known.

The letter from Margaret Hamer, Probation Officer of the Wayne County Probate Court confirmed the assumption I always had that my birth mother was white and my birth father was black. It left many other questions unanswered.

> *Wayne County adoptees with adoption placement agencies must contact the agency for birth family*

---

[4] http://www.buxtonmuseum.com/hcoming/hc-event.html

*information. Your agency is Children's Aid Society and
your written inquiry would go to Ms. Lisa Dion...It is not
likely that Children's Aid Society has additional birth
family information since Children's Aid Society was not
involved in your case until 12/22/64 (mother left the
hospital 10/8/64). It would appear that you lived at the
second hospital from 10/9/64 until 12/22/64 as a
lodger, not for a medical problem.*

*Michigan law does provide a process for possible contact
between adoptee and birth parent(s). The decision for
contact is made by the persons most involved: you and
your birth mother. Each must file consent for contact.
Although it is clear that in 1964 your birth mother did
not want to be known, perhaps in the intervening years
she may have changed her mind. To find out if your birth
mother has filed consent, you must file the enclosed form,
DAA 1925 with Children's Aid Society.*

*Sincerely,
Margaret Hamer, Probation Officer*

The non-identifying information which followed was tantalizing
and the redactions even more so.

*At the time of the filing of the petition the child was at ...
Hospital having been transferred from Saratoga
Hospital, Detroit Michigan, where the child was born ...
The child subsequently was placed in boarding care,
Children's Aid Society, on December 22, 1964 at public
expense, following a Preliminary Hearing of October 19,
1964.
Inasmuch as the identity, status, and whereabouts of the
parents, Mr. John Doe and Mrs. Mary Doe, aka [name as
reported by birth mother but presumed not her real*

*name] were unknown, no information is available as to
the history of the child and/or the parents..... A petition
for neglect has been filed. ... The petition alleges that said
child is without proper custody or guardianship in this
...The mother gave birth to the child at Saratoga
Hospital, registering as .... age 22, single. She asked [an
adoption placement agency] to see her regarding
adoption plan. She advised the worker from [that
agency] that she was single and had been raped by a
colored man. The information given the agency worker
was found to be false. The mother left...(the) hospital ...
without the child. Her whereabouts is unknown."*

Wow, *raped?* Wait, which part was false? All of it? How could they
have known that the claim of rape or her marital status was false?
The charge was a gut punch but not entirely unexpected. I told
myself before starting the search it would be ok no matter what I
found. "Prepare for the worst and hope for the best," I said. People
give up children for many reasons and I assumed conflict of some
kind was at the heart of it. I was loved, successful, and things
turned out pretty well in spite of Ronald's shortcomings as a
human being. God had seen me through plenty worse than ink on
a page, so bring it on, I reasoned. As much as I still did not know, I
tried to imagine a worst case scenario. Maybe there was some
truth to the report. The first of many partial truths led to more
questions than I dared hope could be answered.

The report modified my earlier imaginings. My birth mother was
from a working class Catholic family on the west side. She was
about 30 years old, single and worked as a shift manager at a small
pizzeria in Detroit. She often locked up the store at closing time,
which was late on weekends. Two other employees closed with
her, saw her to her car and waved goodbye as she pulled out of
sight. On the way home she noticed that she was so low on gas
that she feared she'd run out before making it to her apartment

building on Cass Avenue. She pulled into the first gas station she found. As she rolled over the pneumatic hose, the pressure triggered a pin to strike a bell inside the station alerting the attendant to her arrival. As she looked through her driver's side window into the station she noticed a closed sign even though the lights inside were left on. She sighed, hopeful that she'd pass an open filling station soon, when the passenger door flung open and a young black man sank into the seat beside her. Before she could utter a sound, she saw a glint and felt the steel of a blade against her neck. "Drive," he ordered. Trembling, she pulled slowly into the street and he began giving specific directions. "Turn left. Don't speed or draw attention. If you honk your horn I will slit your throat and disappear." "Please," she begged, "you can have the car. Don't kill me. I'll do anything." "Turn right!"

She drove only for a few minutes, but it seemed hours and through tears, she became disoriented and could not tell what street she was on or what part of town she was in. She did understand, however, that she had just turned into a dark alley and terror filled her every sinew. Neither was wearing a seatbelt in the old Buick as he grabbed her right wrist and pulled her across the vehicle through the open passenger door as if she were a sack of groceries. The big man opened a door, whether to a house, a vacant building, or something other, she could not ascertain. It was too dark to see anything and she couldn't stifle a scream that rose reflexively. Her attacker swiftly pounded the handle of the knife into her head repeatedly.

She awoke to pain all over. Her arm, her everything throbbed. She couldn't remember getting into her car or why it was still there. How long had she been there? Her attacker must have fled without stealing her car. She looked in the back seat fearing he might still be there. Seeing he was not, she quickly locked all of the doors for fear he might return. She pulled out of the alley and drove a few blocks before coming to an intersection she recognized. She was only two blocks from her apartment. The shock, fear, and pain of the ordeal were tremendous and debilitating. It was days before she emerged from her apartment, and she felt brutalized even more weeks later when she discovered she was pregnant. Her Catholic faith would not allow her to consider abortion even under these extenuating circumstances. She carried me to term, simultaneously detesting me and fearing anyone she knew might discover that she had been raped by a black man. She was furious with herself for not locking her car doors and paying better attention to her surroundings when pulling into that closed gas station. She fumed that she had not been able to see his face well enough to identify him if she were to ever see him again, and she was consumed by regret that she had enough gas to make it all the way home after all.

She remembered the color of his dark, dirty hands but that was all. After delivering me and leaving the hospital, she lived in fear for many years that every black man she saw could be the one who raped her. She couldn't bear to remain in the same neighborhood, reminded daily of the violence and horror she endured so close to home. The experience ruined her. It made her fearful, distrustful and she blamed God for allowing it to happen to her. For forcing her to carry me and give birth to me. She was still out there somewhere, angry, hurting, and alone after all these years. Maybe that's how it really went down.

# CHAPTER NINETEEN

### ⁊ ᚱ ᚲ

## COUNT IT ALL JOY

Every lead I followed was a dead end. My genealogy research sat on the back burner as we raised our sons and made a life for ourselves in Colorado. That old John Denver album I used to listen to in the basement in Detroit found its way back into my adulthood as I headed West on Arapahoe Road with a minivan full of kids and hockey gear. The Front Range stretched out before us in all its white-capped glory and Rocky Mountain High as well as the R&B and disco tunes from my Scene days, which were the soundtrack of our travels. Watching them developing into the young men they would become, I couldn't help but wonder what other influences made them who they were. Sure, they were my biological sons, but there was a part of myself that I did not know and therefore there was something about my children that was hidden from me. The part of my own children that I didn't know was an irritant as a grain of sand in an oyster shell.

The ensuing years saw the continuous obligations of life, work, family and faith form layers of nacre over the irritant, smoothing and shaping it, making it tolerable if not forgettable. When I heard that DNA testing was becoming affordable and could be used to identify relatives, I knew I would give it a try. Mom would never have to know. I could find out my truth, and answer the questions that she, the courts, agencies and the rest of the world could not. Only my biological mother knew the full truth, I assumed, so I would have to find her in order to get the answers I needed. I had it in my head that my birth father had no knowledge of my existence, that my mother never told him or anyone of her pregnancy, and that meant the whole truth rested on the slim chance of finding her alive.

DNA testing was not quite in its infancy then, nor was it as powerful and reliable as it is today, however. The tools for interpreting data as well as the tests themselves have continued to evolve in breadth and precision. The tests I purchased in 2009 were Ancestry's Y-46 and mt-DNA. Y-DNA tests identify the male patrilineal or direct father's-line ancestry, and mitochondrial DNA (MtDNA) tests reveal the maternal line. I paid over one hundred dollars for each test and waited weeks for the results, hoping to learn something—anything specific about my parents' ethnic origins. I was tired of being an African-American—I wanted to know the exact country of my ancestors' origin. "Black" and "White" were far too broad. I hoped the test would tell me that my mother was French or Swedish and that my father was Nigerian or Kenyan, anything more specific than *black* or *white*.

When the results finally arrived, I anxiously read the report describing my ethnic heritage. It described haplogroups, a fancy word for lines of descent. My paternal report said that I belonged to Haplogroup E1b1a, *The Language People*, and a map of the continent of Africa with nearly every sub-Saharan country shaded as a possible place of origin. My maternal report identified

Haplogroup J, The European Travelers, and a map of all of Western Europe shaded. Underwhelmed, I thought, "Ok, maybe I overshot on this one. Maybe my expectations were a little too high." I could see that my mother was white and my father was black, which I already knew from court records and correctly suspected since I was 10 years old. What am I supposed to do with this shot in the dark?

I discovered much later that the Y-DNA results from Ancestry could be uploaded to another service provider, Family Tree DNA. In addition to the narrative report describing migration patterns and ancient ethnic origins, a file (spreadsheet), containing numeric values for each of the 26 markers tested was included. I carefully typed the value for each of those markers into the corresponding marker on Family Tree DNA and waited for the system to process.

I didn't get the photograph, life story and social security number of my father, but it did find a single match. The name Willie Bell Brantley stared at me and I at it. Willie Bell? That sounds like a woman's name—specifically a woman from the South. Charlie Mae, Willie May, Bobbie Lee... lots of southern girls are named after their fathers and given a softer middle name to feminize it. But this was a Y-DNA test, so Willie Bell had to be a male. My hands became a little moist as I clicked the little envelope icon beneath his name and Outlook opened to compose an electronic message.

*Dear Mr. Brantley, I'm just beginning to learn about DNA testing and I see that our results indicate a definite relationship. I don't know much about my extended family. Hoping to learn more from you soon.*
*Warm Regards,*
*Cousin Ron*

Weeks and months passed without a reply from Willie. My attention turned back to the daily ebbs and flows of life. As our sons matured and matriculated, Mom transitioned into retirement. She was diagnosed with end-stage renal failure and made the very conscious, informed decision to forego dialysis. Despite the improvement in quality of life and general well-being experienced by many who accept the treatment, Mom had also seen the difficulties associated with the regimen. At her advanced age, she did not want to spend 12 hours or more per week hooked to a machine, and she resisted all attempts to make her diet more kidney-friendly. None of her doctors could say how long she had to live, but she insisted that we abide by her wishes to preclude dialysis. She and her doctor signed and notarized a Do Not Resuscitate request. She continued living a sedentary, though mostly comfortable lifestyle.

I gradually realized that if I were to find my biological family, any information that Mom might have—no matter how unimportant she might consider it—could prove fruitful in my search. The only other lead regarding my adoption came from an older first cousin who once confided that she overhead someone say, "Well, Ronald got his son back," implying that I was his biological child after all by another woman. As intriguing as the possibility was, I hoped that it was not true. I didn't see the point in asking Mom, but I did ask Ronald upon one of my visits to his nursing home. I chose to believe his answer if only for the ease it brought my mind.

Six years after my first foray into DNA testing, the science had become more precise and the tools for analyzing and collaborating had evolved in parallel. I ordered an Ancestry DNA test in 2015 for $99, hoping the new autosomal test would fill in some of the blanks the Y-DNA and mtDNA tests I took several years earlier did not. There were thousands of matches! Interpreting them and figuring out how I was related to any of them was beyond daunting, however. I contacted one of my matches, a young lady named Emmilie, and asked if she had any idea how we might be related. She knew her maternal family, and was searching for her paternal relations. She told me about two wonderful Facebook groups. *Foundling Finders* and *DNA Detectives*. I'd been on Facebook since 2008. I joined it to keep in touch with my adoptive cousins and used it to help us plan a family reunion in 2009; however, I never considered the value of using it as a reference for identifying and contacting genetic family members until Emmilie showed me the ropes. Foundling Finders is a private group created by genetic genealogist CeCe Moore in 2015 to support adults who were abandoned as babies or young children with no identifying information. Not only was there a name for people like me, there is an entire subculture! One month later CeCe created the *DNA Detectives Group* which focuses on using DNA to find biological family for adoptees, foundlings, donor-conceived individuals, unknown paternity and all other types of unknown parentage cases. Everyone is welcome in this group, not just adoptees. As I read the stories of foundlings who joined the group daily, my heart sank to my feet and soared high on the roller coaster of posts as if they were my own:

> *I found my birthmother in November 2015. We had a beautiful reunion for about a year, and then she pulled back and we have become estranged. Last night I was informed she is in the hospital, and doesn't have much time left. I am numb today, and fighting back the scream that is lodged in my heart. It has all been so unfair. – Michelle*

> *I was an abandoned baby, left in a car in a mall parking lot, with my umbilical cord tied with a string. Through DNA testing, we have now identified BOTH of my biological parents. I will be traveling 12 hours on Friday night to see my BM. She doesn't know that I have found her, so this will be a "surprise attack". She may also have*

*family around her that may or may not know I ever
existed. My thoughts and emotions are all over the place
as I try to sort out how to approach her and what to say.
I am BLANK. I'm trying to write a letter to give her, in
case I can't speak, or if the opportunity is just better for
that. I am BLANK. I'm asking God to fill my heart with
words and to help me write something she needs to
hear.... please help me pray that I hear His voice.... and
that her heart will be open and willing to accept what is
headed her way. – Stacey*

*I am 44 and have 3 kids and being adopted has affected
my entire life (big surprise) but in my 40's I have been
experiencing a more severe longing and deep sadness
over my adoption. I desperately want to find my bio
family and at the very least just 'KNOW'. I am sure every
person who is reading this can 100% identify with what I
mean. Thank you to all who are running this page - I am
delighted to have found it today- I need a page I can
come undone. – Lily*

*Hello everyone, if posting this pic is inappropriate please
forgive me. So my son is on the left and a man who is
believed to be my brother is on the right. What do you
think? I am not 100% sure but supposedly his mother
was shot and killed at her cantina near a hospital in
Nicaragua a few years back and according to an update I
was able to confirm that my biological mother was shot
and killed a few years back at her cantina near the same
hospital and she had 2 sons. Her spouse, possibly my
father, sold the place, packed up and left with his sons.
Could we be related? – Karla*

*I was abandoned December 1971 in Yuba City, Ca. This week I am an emotional wreck. The results for a suspected Maternal cousin should be in... This week, according to Ftdna. There has been some dispute if this is the correct side of this DNA cousin's tree (his grandfathers are brothers, parents are... Yep, first cousins). I have been somewhat assured we are on the right path. I'm nervous, grumpy, (from waiting so long for slow holiday dna testing), and I'm scared. I have found a paternal uncle and one of his brothers, out of 5 brothers, who I believe to be my bio dad agreed to test. Due to 23andme test kits being on back order, he just got his kit last week- 3 weeks after I ordered it. I'm trying to be patient, but It isn't easy. To know that I could be close to discovering my biological mom is both overwhelming and a miracle. – Jen*

*So, she died at age 28. That's unusual enough that I figured hey, I'll Google this and see if anything pops up. It did. She was the victim of a high-profile murder in 1982.... So I'm reading this article and first of all, more pictures pop up and they all remind me of myself as a teen too. But she lived - and died - in New York. I was abandoned in Chicago. BUT as I'm reading through, I see where she ran away as a teen and I'm thinking, could she have run to Chicago? Could she have had a baby? I contact the match, and we talk back and forth for a bit, he knows from the high DNA match that I'm clearly a close relative, and I tell him given the circumstances of my birth, I'm sure I'm a surprise to him and finally I just out with it - given the options of our match and that picture on your tree, I think I'm Gail's daughter. He says he agrees it's possible but wants to talk to his sister (which would be my bio grandmother). They also talk to*

147

*Gail's younger sister, who would have been just 12 at the time of my birth but who was very close to Gail, wondering if maybe she had confided to her at some point. That sister confirmed that Gail told her that when she ran away, she went to Chicago, and she had a baby. Aunt had apparently never told anyone before, maybe at Gail's request. So I went from nothing, to finding a birth mother, in just a few hours. This is surreal.... Apparently I have a half sister too, but from the article, after the murder she went with her dad since no one could prove he was the killer, and hasn't talked to her mom's side since...which I found out in an interview with bio-grandma on another link. This is gonna take some time to process. – Heather*

*I am one of at least eight children. My bio parents kept five children and sprinkled the rest of us around the south side of Chicago like garbage. I've had contact with one them. She was discovered near a dumpster a year before I was found. We have spoken often since finding each other and I hope we will continue to get to know each other. The other sibling has not reached out but we do know his name. It has been a strange, exhilarating and sometimes bewildering experience but I am glad I did it and I am eternally grateful for this group. It has given me hope, shown me that there are others feeling the way I am feeling and provided some really great advice  – Ann*

*Hello everyone! My name is Mary and I have been on the search for my birth parents for about 4 years now. I was born on November 25th 1987 in Calgary Alberta Canada. I was put in a garbage bag (head out) and left in a parking lot. Luckily I was found by two boys walking home from school. I was adopted and have lived a very good life. I little part of me thou has always felt lost. I have a lot of questions about who I am and where I come from. I am not angry or hold a grudge towards my birth parents, I just want to know where I came from. I now have a daughter of my own and feel part of her is missing too. – Mary*

*Hi Everyone! Thank you all for the warm welcomes, I appreciate it. My name is Shawna, I am 27 years old and a mother of 2. I was abandoned in the trash at birth by my teen mother in October 1988. I'm lucky to have survived because I wasn't found until 4 days later. I grew up in group homes and foster homes all over LA County CA until I was officially adopted at 10 years old. Adoption in my opinion is supposed to be an opportunity to be a part of a loving family kind of like your 2nd chance but I didn't get so lucky. My adopted family was very abusive and CPS ended up removing me from the home at 17. I went back into the system until I emancipated at 18 and have been on my own ever since. Once I turned 18 I started my search for my bio family but hit a lot of dead ends. A friend of mine recently told me about CeCe Moore and she amazingly has helped uncover so much information in one day verses my almost 10-year search. I'm hoping the information will lead to the answers I need. – Shawna*

*Feeling emotional ... I dropped of two letters at the door of my birth mothers house after knocking 4 different times in two days .. I'm in my hometown till Monday , trying to get answers .. After one of her daughter's called me twice yelling at me to stop knocking and leaving notes then she called .... I asked her who this was she said*

Ronald G. Levi Jr.

> *it's your mother .. My birth mother said she doesn't have*
> *time for me she's busy tonight, tomorrow and Sunday*
> *and doesn't have time for any of this and she said I could*
> *blame my father for all of this and hung up on me . –*
> *Jaclyn 2016*

Reading tale after tale of heartbreak and tragedy steeled me to the likelihood that my own truth would be no less brutal. There were some beautiful stories of tearful reunions and heartfelt reconciliation as well, but I needed to prepare myself for the worst, I felt. Although I had not attended church regularly since the mid- 90s when we lived in Columbus, Ohio, the fellowship and instruction I gained during that time were crucial nourishment for the rest of my life.  As I read the accounts of foundlings, I considered the circumstances that led to their discontent, and I recalled a couple of sermons preached by Rev. Jefferey Johnson of the Rising Star Baptist Church of Indiana, which he delivered as a guest minister during Vacation Bible School at New Salem Missionary Baptist Church in Columbus. In the sermon entitled *Count It All Joy*, Pastor Johnson brought to life the first chapter of the book of James in which he highlighted the unusual exhortation when we

> [5]*"2...fall into divers temptations, [3]knowing this: that the*
> *trying of your faith worketh patience. [4]But let patience*
> *have her perfect work, that ye may be perfect and entire,*
> *lacking nothing."*

The pastor explained that those who are in Christ have joy, but sometimes, it's not *all* joy. He recognized the incongruity of experiencing joy in the midst of trials and tribulations. To help us understand why and how James expected us to do so, he used an analogy from his own childhood. His mother was a single parent

---

[5] James 1:203 (King James Version)

working multiple jobs to make ends meet and she had to prioritize things. On some occasions she had to improvise. On one such occasion she served a big plate of French fries to her children for which ketchup is a highly valued commodity. She didn't have enough money to buy a whole new bottle of ketchup and there was a little left in the bottle which she withdrew from the fridge. She went to the sink, added a little water, gave it a shake, and voilà—ketchup! But it wasn't *all* ketchup, it wasn't *pure* ketchup. It was mixed with something else.

I hung on every word because I thought he was talking about me and my mom! Apparently, hundreds of others did as well. We all identified intimately with his analogy and his own personal experience. Pastor said this is how many Christians experience joy. It is mixed with complaining, grumbling, and gossiping. The lesson I learned from this powerful sermon was that the road would not always be easy and I would experience challenges, but I needed to understand that those challenges and disappointments were opportunities to grow, to become stronger, wiser and closer to God. I recalled scriptures such as John 4:4, "Ye are of God, little children, and have overcome them: because greater is he that is in you, than he that is in the world."

After all I'd been through as a child, I knew that I'd come through many battles—not because I was perfect or superior in any way, but because God was in me and with me. I prayed for the foundlings who were unable to find joy in their discoveries. I prayed that the love of God who is the Holy Spirit would be with them and comfort them and give them peace of mind. I prayed that all of us would see the wonder and greatness of God in our lives no matter what the outcome of interactions with others and that someone might find that same joy in our testimony.

Parents who never considered the necessity of warning their pubescent children not to experiment with one another learn that they have a double grandchild. Sperm banks allowing many donations in the same community create large numbers of half-sibling marriages and a migraine-in-the-making for hundreds of descendants. These are not hypotheses, they are true and verifiable occurrences. The term *non-paternity event* was new to me. When someone who is presumed to be a person's father is proven otherwise, it's called an N.P.E. Sperm donations, undisclosed adoptions, intercourse with multiple partners in close succession, non-consensual sex, and medical mistakes such as mix-ups during in vitro fertilization and artificial insemination are all examples of non-paternity events. According to Wikipedia the incidence of misattributed paternity ranges from about 2% to 12%. As I dove deeper into the science and sub-culture of genetic genealogy, however, it sure felt like that number could be much higher. A lot of people have detailed family trees that don't jibe with the DNA results and there's a saying that has become popular in recent years—"DNA don't lie."

I hadn't considered the possibility that I could have been the product of a sperm donation...that I might have dozens or hundreds of half siblings running around. How strange that would be, not bad or good...but a very unusual adjustment for anyone, especially an only child. No, I needed to prepare for something truly awful, so I prayed. I prayed that I would find my truth, and that whatever it was, my opinion of myself and my family's opinion of me (and themselves) would not be affected and that the lives I would touch would be open, accepting, and civil if not welcoming. And if they were not, I prayed that I would find the patience and lovingkindness to allow them to process truth more fully.

# PART II

*Figure 2 Biological Paternal Family – 6 Generations (1756 - 1992)*

# CHAPTER TWENTY

———✦✦✦———

## THE BRANTLEY CONNECTION

Checking for new matches and getting updates from my Angel Linny reminded me of the feeling I had as an adolescent when I hurried home from school to make a grilled cheese sandwich and watch the After-School Special on television, which was something like Son of Godzilla or War of the Gargantuas. Not that my genealogy research was scary or involving monsters, but because I looked forward to coming home from work each day to get to my computer and begin stitching together the day's discoveries from Linny, Emmilie and correspondence with my other matches.

"This is the best new hobby!" I gushed. "It's like Christmas every day. A new match, a new lead, a new branch." Adding source documents such as marriage licenses, death certificates, deeds of sale and census records to the names of people to whom I was related genetically was exhilarating. I was being introduced to them in a virtual, digital world that transcended time and location. To me, they were brand new and alive with promise. White, black, it didn't matter...they were me and I was them. I witnessed their births and mourned the deaths of children and unnamed stillborns. I agonized over their complicity in the brutality of slavery and cheered the fortitude of their passage to and survival in the new world. For someone who wasn't physically present for any of these occasions, I experienced a temporal bond with them as I traced their migrations from census to census and county to county. Knowing that I was related to them was uplifting, and establishing exactly how we were related became my new obsession.

Linny quietly went about her meticulous and incisive analysis. I was always a million steps behind her pronouncements, but I learned from every methodical step she took. Two other matches, *M.J.* and *britt1608* had public trees attached to their DNA results. Although they were more distantly related to me than Annie and Frances, they were still in the range of second to third cousins and their tree was well done. Many public trees have names and dates as remembered or recorded secondhand, but source citations are the key to reliable genealogy. Brittany's tree, as well as those of Harvie and Frances were well documented and sourced. Brittany was the daughter of Marcia who was the daughter of Eva Brantley. Linny recognized that surname from my long-ago Y-DNA test with Willie Bell Brantley. This was the first indication that Marcia and Brittany were on my father's father's branch. This allowed Linny to build out that section of my tree to 3 generations and to begin looking for an intersection of Brittany's Brantleys with the ancestors of Staciob, the Lowthers and Harvards of Laurens County, Georgia who were my father's maternal ancestors.

Having established my paternal great grandparents as those of my second cousin Frances, finding which of their children was my grandparent was simple. Since my father was a Brantley, we needed to find the daughter of William and Amelia Lowther who married a Brantley, and thankfully there were only two. When siblings in one family marry siblings in another family, it takes a little extra effort to sort out. Sisters Clara and Gertrude Lowther married brothers Moses and Jenia (J. B.) Brantley respectively. Frances already knew and had documented her family so well from firsthand accounts, she knew with certainty that I could only have been a descendant of J. B. and Gertrude. Gertrude Lowther married Jenia Brantley (J. B.) on September 27, 1908. These were determined definitely to be my biological paternal grandparents born in 1886 and 1887. Wow, my paternal grandparents were the children or grandchildren of slaves! That's a lot closer than I thought it would be. I thought of slavery as ancient history, ending 100 years before my birth. I was becoming quickly disabused of that notion.

Although we couldn't see living people in the Ancestry trees, Linny and Emmilie used other subscription services to identify the children of J. B. and Gertrude. In order to verify them and to find someone to test, I'd have to make direct contact. I Googled the names again and saw a familiar result. The message board I discovered years ago with Willie Bell's email address also had one for an Agnes Brantley. On November 21, 2015, I sent a message to her:

> *Hi, Agnes. I hope all's well with you. I'm doing research on the Lowther and Brantley families from Michigan and Georgia. I'm trying to figure out where you and Willie are in the tree. Do you have a tree on Ancestry.com or would you mind telling me the names of your parents and grandparents? I have a tree going all the way back to Amelia Harvard, but I haven't filled in every branch yet. Thanks so much for helping me out.*
> *Sincerely,*

*Ron*

She replied:

> *Willie has passed away. My parents are Malton Brantley*
> *Sr. (Born 1919 – died 1988) and Hazel Bell Walls*
> *Brantley (Born 1925 – died 1959). My grandparents are*
> *Shyfer Brantley (Born 1885 – died 1948) and Agnes*
> *Elizabeth Francis Jane Thomas Brantley (Born 1890 died*
> *1982). Willie was one of the Brantley family historians*
> *working along with Harvie.*

This was a goldmine of information. The default setting for Ancestry trees is to show deceased persons only in order to protect the privacy of the living. Other than obituaries, public records such as enumerations are made available 72 years after they are created. In 2015, the most recently publicized census was 1940. The 1950 census will be available in April of 2022. I didn't know at the time that her grandfather Shyfer would turn out to be the brother of my grandfather.

I contacted the family historian Agnes recommended and told him of my DNA matches. Harvie was kind and generous with his knowledge of our family. His warmth was almost surprising, but exactly what I had hoped and imagined. I expected people to be guarded and hesitant to share information with a stranger claiming to be related to them. Though not yet in the throes of identity theft and fake news, our nation was becoming wary of online scams and dubious motives. Harvie told me of the years-long effort that he, Willie Bell, Agnes and Dr. Wayne invested in documenting and validating their pedigree.

As Harvie spoke, I did my best to transcribe connections and references. I connected names as he said them to names and dates in the tree that Linny and I were building, all the while looking for the rip cord—the string I could pull that would lead to my safe

Ronald G. Levi Jr.

descent into the tent of our shared ancestors. Willie Bell tested on 23andMe, but he was deceased. I told Harvie of my other matches and he recognized Frances Stephens. Some families are fortunate to have an individual who is consumed by and dedicated to the discovery and propagation of their genealogy. Edgar Leroy Smith and I were those people for the Levi family. Harvie and Agnes were those persons for the Brantley family. Frances Stephens was that person for the Lowther and Harvard families.

According to Harvie, Frances was a frequent traveler, a road warrior of the first order, who plied the highways without hesitation when the need arose. And the need arose often for her. A travel services professional, she was the family member who led the planning of reunions. Accommodations and transportation were only the tip of the iceberg for her. More importantly, Frances Lillian Smith Stephens zealously guarded the treasures, secrets and trust of her family and ancestors. She was the one to whom all family members deferred for verification and validation of any claims. If anyone had questions about their family or heritage, they called Frances. Like Harvie and Agnes, Frances earned this right and respect through years of meticulous, arduous and expensive research and documentation the old-fashioned way—shoe leather. Before Ancestry and the Internet, Frances visited libraries, museums, courthouses and crisscrossed the country from Michigan to New Jersey, Pennsylvania and Georgia meeting with family members, writing down their stories, and copying their pictures. If I wanted to know about Harvard and Lowther genealogy, Frances was going to be my gateway. If I wanted to know about Brantley genealogy, Harvie was my primary source.

When my AncestryDNA results came on November 15th, Frances was travelling. She was not receiving or responding to emails. By Nov 21st, Linny's magic located Brantleys in Michigan who were descendants of the same Brantleys related to Marcia (M. J.) and her daughter Brittany. Census records showed that Gertrude and J. B. had 3 sons: Joseph, David and Willie, born 1915, 1917 and 1919 respectively. Within a week of seeing my DNA results, Linny, Emmilie and I had figured out on paper the identities of my maternal and paternal grandparents, great grandparents and second great grandparents. Although I had not yet made contact, we narrowed the list of possible candidates to only 3 women – sisters born between 1939 and 1943 in Detroit. We were all amazed at how quickly it came into focus, especially since I started at absolute zero. Now all I had to do was figure out which of the descendants of J. B. and Gertrude was my father. Was it one of their sons (all deceased) or one of their grandsons (all still living)?

As Agnes suggested, I contacted Harvie and explained as much as I knew. I was a Brantley, Harvard and Lowther all in one. I had matches with A. S. and FrancesStephens140. He knew that name and he had a phone number for her. He also had a phone number for his cousin Claudia Council who was also a Brantley, Lowther and Harvard living in Michigan. Claudia answered. Her first question to me was, "What is your complexion?" She wanted to know my skin tone and appearance. Well, the whole point of my inquiry is truth, and my truth was being updated by the hour. I told her that I was biracial, light skinned and we began to delve deeper from there. I told her about the DNA matches with the Brantleys. I told her about the matches with Annie and Frances.

As I explained that my DNA matches were both Brantley and Lowther and that the only connection I had found was the marriage of Gertrude Lowther and Jenia Brantley, Claudia revealed that they were her parents. J. B. and Gertrude were born in 1887 and 1886 respectively. They were the children of enslaved parents who were each the child of a white slave owner and an enslaved female. My father was a son or grandson of J. B. and Gertrude. He was either one of Claudia's brothers or nephews.

Claudia was much younger than her brothers who were born 1917 and 1919. Joseph and David passed on in the early '90s and Willie died in 2014—one year before my first contact with Claudia. She assured me that they would be in touch with me as soon as Frances returned from her travels in November.

I sent a message to Frances November 21, 2015:

> *Hi, Frances. Via a first cousin match to Annie Smith (A. S.), a second cousin match to you, a third cousin match to a Wynn (staciob), a third cousin match to a Marcia Shivers (Eva Brantley's daughter), and a Y-DNA match to a Willie Bell Brantley, I'm pretty sure that I am a descendant of Gertrude and Jenia Brantley. I had very pleasant chats with Claudia and she referred me to you as the family genealogy expert. I would love to compare notes with you at your convenience.... Please be assured that I am not seeking anything from your family other than the knowledge of my biological identity and heritage. I certainly do not wish to impose or disrupt any relationships. Ideally, I'd love to open and extend my family further inviting all of you in. I hope that you and they are willing to give it a try....*
> *Sincerely,*
> *Cousin Ron*

Five excruciating days later, Frances was back on the grid and replied to my message.

> *Let me share this with you: Amelia is the mother of Gertrude Lowther Brantley. Amelia Harvard was married to William Lowther (My Great Grandparents) I knew Amelia. Vera is Gertrude's younger sister. Gertrude and Jenie were the parents of 3 sons. Only one of which had children. Those 3 children have children. I would rule out Gertrude and J.B. I know the names of Amelia's siblings*

*and whom they married. The same for Williams's
siblings. You probably know that Amelia and William
were both born as slaves, not on the same plantation.
And yes I know about the family that owned each one.
8:30 is fine. You should write your questions down. My
email is ... if you would like me to answer some of them
now.*

I was ecstatic to finally be speaking with the person everyone told
me would have the answers. I may have been the son of one of
these men, but Frances had been in their family all of their lives.
They all knew one another's parents and grandparents. The
children of Joseph trusted their cousin Frances and Aunt Claudia
completely. If I passed their sniff test, I had a chance at taking the
next step. This was a living chess game, and I was about to put two
kings in check simultaneously. The science of DNA on one hand,
and the facts of their lives and those of their ancestors on the
other would leave them no move other than admission and
acceptance. They were such warm people; I was very thankful and
happy to know I was related to them in any manner.

I was certain my father was Douglas or Michael, sons of Joseph
Brantley. I found it funny that Frances believed I must be the
grandchild of one of their mother Gertrude's siblings because
Frances was certain that all of Gertrude and J. B.'s descendants
were known and accounted for. "Willie and David never had
children," she said. As far you know, I thought to myself. The
matches and genetic distances had by this time already proven to
me that this was the only branch on which I could hang, but my
paternal cousins would need to process it in their own time and
manner.

Frances and I scheduled a meeting at the Southfield Public Library
on Evergreen Road a week later to review the evidence and meet
my biological paternal relatives face to face for the first time. In

the age of Facebook and Google, we'd already seen each other's photos online, but seeing them walk toward me in the library was more joyful than I imagined. I was not anxious in the least about meeting them—I felt I already knew them. I knew they were not as convinced as I, so before they arrived I taped a family tree on the walls of the private room I reserved for our meeting, showing all of our shared ancestors as I understood them. I prepared and printed a PowerPoint presentation showing all of my DNA matches with known relationships to them verified through public records.

Instead of the typical tree showing all siblings, my block chart showed only direct line ancestors of my DNA matches. It showed clearly how Frances, Stacia, and Annie were all descendants of William Lowther and Amelia Harvard. It showed how Willie Bell and Marcia were the descendants of Taylor Brantley, who was the brother of J.B. Brantley. Taylor, was Claudia's uncle. In this way they began to see the other squares of the chessboard fall away and Michael and Douglas began to wonder if it were possible they could have forgotten such an encounter with a white woman 51 years ago.

What a moment that was! Imagine two men walk into a conference room absolutely confident they know all of their children and are confronted with so much evidence that they actually begin to consider the possibility that someone might have escaped their memory. I felt a little bad for putting them in that position, but Michael was steadfast. Douglas was really searching every memory he could, and he was doing it so honestly that I fell in love with them both. Just honest men, willing to consider possibilities they'd never imagined. After all I'd read and heard regarding the horror stories of foundlings, this was an indescribably intimate moment. After searching his past briefly, Michael promised, "I know it couldn't have been me. I'd tell you if it were, and I'd be proud to call you my son, but I'm not the one."

Douglas was less certain than Michael. He confided there was a relationship about that time in the winter of 1963 with a "very light skinned black woman." Many may have thought she was white, but at least one of her parents was black, Doug said. He was no longer in contact with her, but worried if he took a DNA test that proved he was my father, it might somehow disrupt her life. I explained that I already knew who my mother was. That she was 100% Eastern European, and my own European ethnicity percentages were too high to allow for my mother to have been bi-racial. The only possibility is that my father was biracial and my mother was white.

Although I was still waiting for the results of a presumptive maternal half-sibling test, I explained to the Brantleys that I had already concluded the identify of my birth mother—a white woman born in 1939 who lived in Macomb County Michigan. Douglas shrugged, "Then I'm not the one." We were all being completely honest and I believed these men, but my checkmate had just turned into a stalemate...unless one of them would test. If either Douglas or Michael would test, the result would show that we were half-brothers if their father Joseph was my dad, or it would show that we were first cousins if one of their late uncles Willie or David were my dad.

I asked Cousin Frances for permission to hold her hand. Smiling, she acceded and I took her right hand in my left, palm facing up. I covered hers with my right hand and closed my eyes briefly. The warmth of her father William and her grandmother Vera emanated. The kindness and spirit of Amelia, William, and Louisa pulsed. This was the first time in 51 years that I touched the skin of a person to whom I was genetically related other than my own sons. Blood of my blood, flesh of my flesh. Frances offered, "If it makes you feel that good to hold one hand, go ahead and take the other." I gladly accepted.

Douglas and Michael asked for time to think it over. We chatted about the family resemblances, I told them about my mom and my upbringing, and we agreed to keep in touch. I resolved to follow up with them every few weeks just to see if they had any questions or if I could give them a kit to send in. As I waited, Cousin Frances patiently and so very considerately shared everything about my paternal family with me. It was a journey I never ever imagined I would have the pleasure and honor of knowing. Finding the identities of my birth parents was all I ever dared to hope for. The stories and proof of their ancestors, were among the most humbling, comforting experiences of my charmed life.

# CHAPTER TWENTY-TWO

~ ᏧᏩᏇ ~

## COUSINS' LUNCH

I never imagined I would be able to know the names of my enslaved ancestors or where they'd lived. My own experience with Mom's family in Mississippi illustrated how complete and permanent the erasure of personhood had been in our country before my birth. Surnames were not important for chattel. Males and females were counted and grouped by age and value, but nothing more. Even after slavery was abolished, in the small Mississippi city of Granddad's youth, his name does not appear in any public documents before 1940. The anger, sadness, and resentment had nowhere to rest, no target upon which to fix, and little hope of eventual justice.

Today the subject of reparations is a talking point in political races, but money, land, health care, tax relief, free tuition and student debt forgiveness, as reasonable as they are for the

Ronald G. Levi Jr.

descendants of slaves who are largely only beginning to see second generations graduate from post-secondary institutions of higher learning, are mere tokens in my estimation. Reparations for me is giving me back the names of my ancestors—giving me back that part of my culture and languages that were obliterated, beaten, starved, raped and lynched out of them. The argument that black people should "move on" is hollow to me. Am I to forget my own grandparents whose words are only now being revealed to me? I am hearing them for the first time in my life and there are those who prefer that I forget them already. They argue to erase them not once, but twice and for all time. After all they endured and overcame, our ancestors are examples of resilience and perseverance from whom we can all learn valuable lessons if only we have the courage to discuss them civilly as brother and sisters, all. Their sacrifice, stamina and intelligence allowed them to survive while millions did not. Moving forward? Yes. Moving on? Never.

Frances and I talked, texted, emailed several times per week if not every day. We were both early risers and looked for each other on Instant Messenger as we sipped our first pre-dawn cups of coffee. She told me about my great grandmother Amelia's parents, Master David Harvard and Louisa Session. She told me about the home that David built that was still standing in Montrose, Georgia and still known as Laurens Hill. I researched the property and its owners from its original construction until the present day. I learned from Frances the stories that were passed down to her by her mother Vera who was the 11th of 13 children born to Amelia and William Lowther. Vera was the little sister of my grandmother, Gertrude. All of the stories were supported by census, birth and death records and now they were beginning to be supported also by DNA.

I searched my DNA matches for the name *Harvard* and found *Carol*. Sharing 2 segments of 11.9 cM, she was a distant match, but definitely related. As I built out her tree a little further, I recognized the name Fish. This was the name of my second great grandfather's wife. David Harvard married Mary Ann Fish. Their children were the white half siblings of Louisa's children. In this match's tree, the name was Emily Eliza Fish. I clicked the little animated waving leaf indicating hints and quickly saw that her parents were William Washington Fish and... Sarah Jane *Harvard*, David's sister! Sarah was my third great aunt and Carol was my fourth cousin once removed.

Our most recent common ancestors were the parents of David and Sarah Jane, John Harvard and Elizabeth Drury. This was the first bit of genealogy on our family that I had that Frances did not. While there were post-war documents showing that Amelia and William's family lived in the vicinity of Laurens Hill, there were no public documents supporting the relatedness of Louisa's children to the man who purchased her in 1845. We are certain that everyone in the small community knew who their father was. Our grandparents actually lived with and knew Amelia, who was born into slavery and lived in the Laurens Hill big house. Amelia herself lived until 1952, only 12 years before my birth, and she told her children and grandchildren in her own words who her parents were. As a plantation mistress and wife of a wealthy South Carolina planter, Mary Boykin Chestnut wrote in her diary:

> *Under slavery, we live surrounded by prostitutes, yet an abandoned woman is sent out of any decent house. Who thinks any worse of a Negro or mulatto woman for being a thing we can't name? God, forgive us, but ours is a monstrous system, a wrong and an inequity! Like the patriarchs of old, our men live all in one house with their wives and their concubines; and the mulattos one sees in every family partly resemble the white children. Any lady is ready to tell you who is the father of all mulatto children in everybody's household but her own. Those,*

*she seems to think, drop from the clouds. My disgust*
*sometimes is boiling over. Thank God for my country*
*women, but alas for the men![6]*

There was no question in anyone's mind that David was the father of Amelia and her siblings, but this DNA connection to Carol was the first of many that proved the genetic connection that everyone had known and accepted for over 150 years. Although we did not know the maiden name of David's mother at the time I met Carol, I later discovered that he had a brother whose given name was Drury. It was not uncommon for children to be given their mother's maiden name as first or middle names. This hint led me to search my own DNA matches for that surname and sure enough, David's mother was Elizabeth Drury before she was Mrs. John Harvard. Such is the ability of DNA to fill in gaps in the paper trails and make verifiable connections otherwise obliterated by time, customs and personal sensibilities. The hushed secrets that families kept for generations were being laid bare at an astonishing clip by people like the DNA Detectives, Foundling Finders and the army of beneficiaries of their compassion and dedication.

As I excitedly shared the news with Frances, she told me that she had a Bible given to her by her mother that was purchased by her grandmother, our great grandmother Amelia in 1876. "No way!" I exclaimed. "Yes and it has their handwritten notes listing dates of birth, marriage and death. I bet you'd like to see that wouldn't you?" "Of course! Yes, please!" I stuttered. "We senior cousins have luncheons once or twice a year. Sometimes more often if we can. I was speaking with Claudia about our next one. Would you like to attend?" "I can't tell you what an honor that would be and how that makes me feel. I am overwhelmed," I managed as tears welled. I mean, this was nothing like anything I had ever read in

---

[6] Mary Boykin Chestnut, edited by C. Vann Woodward, *Mary Chestnut's Civil War* (New Haven: Yale University Press, 1981), 29.

any Foundling Finders or DNA Detectives posts. Sure people had connected and been welcomed, but my family was going totally open-kimono on me! They were not only revealing what they knew to be true, they were sharing the most valuable things imaginable—their time, their history, and their Bible. "I'll bring the bible, too. It will be at Claudia's home and Michael, Douglas and Pam will be there along with Katherine and a few others." "I'm so excited! Thank you so much. What can I bring?" "Nothing at all—just yourself."

As I arrived at Aunt Claudia and Uncle Robert's home, some of our cousins were already there. I was greeted with such genuine warmth that I felt I had known them for many years if not my entire life. If I felt at all unusual, it had nothing to do with their reaction to me. For a moment I thought, "I can't believe I am here sitting with all of these close biological relatives, and they're so wonderful! Is this really happening?" Seated around the dining room table, we chatted about our adventure and our first meeting in the library. We asked about one another's families, and I must have looked so silly smiling as wide as the Cheshire cat the entire time. Soon Frances announced that the moment had arrived. She reached into a bag and carefully lifted out a wrapped package. I knew this was the Bible, but I was completely unprepared for my reaction. As she delicately unwrapped the paper revealing a book with a well-worn, though still intact cover, wave after pummeling wave of sorrow, gratitude, and joy overtook me. Not wanting to stain the pages, I suppressed the tears that welled in my eyes as I realized this book had been seen and touched by my grandmother Gertrude and all of her siblings.

Not actually a Bible, *Hitchcock's New and Complete Analysis of the Holy Bible* was published in 1871 and the copy staring up at me had been purchased by our great grandmother Amelia in 1876. It was the prized possession of Frances's grandmother Vera. In the brown, worn cover and tan, creased pages with tattered edges, I saw the faces of my people. I felt the warmth of their calloused hands and power of their indomitable spirits. I saw the furrow of Quinn's brow and I felt the weight of Lola's little hand. I carefully and lightly ran my finger over the letters and numbers representing the marriage of Amelia and William.

My hand was in the place and in the position their hands had once been. I bit my lip as I meditated on how difficult their lives during Reconstruction must have been and how long they remained in virtual servitude after emancipation legally freed them. I heard Amelia's voice reading passages to her mother as Louisa passed away in 1917. I saw Vera cradling the book in her arms when her mother Amelia died in 1952. Now my cousins, aunt, uncle and I had the great fortune to experience this moment together as Louisa always intended—her family *together*. Learning the full story of my father's ancestors has involved the meticulous research of my cousins, the triangulation of thousands of DNA matches, and the color of first and second-hand accounts. The journey continues, but it always comes back to Louisa Sessions Harvard.

# CHAPTER TWENTY-THREE

—————— ᘐᖚᖆ ——————

## LOUISA SESSION

They said her long, straight black hair and brown skin was proof of her naissance in "the Indies." Whether this was India, Indonesia, or indigenous could not be determined upon her arrival, but arrive she did in Charleston with her parents William and Amelia shortly before the War of 1812. By the time Louisa arrived in Charleston, it had already become the epicenter of the antebellum South. In 1807 the Charleston Market was founded and soon became a hub for African-Americans. Slaves as well as free people of color manned its many stalls. The passage of the Fugitive Slave Act of 1793 narrowly preceded Louisa's birth. By the time she arrived in Charleston and her children were born 20 some years later, the practice of abducting free black persons as fugitives was routine and placed the burden of proof on the captives.

Louisa was very aware of the vulnerability she faced. Although not born in Africa and not enslaved, she knew well that the color of her skin made her nothing more than a few dollar signs to opportunists. She may not have come directly from Africa, but her skin was brown, and to most white people, she was a nigger—free or not. She took great care not to travel alone. She never let her children stray from her sight and she was almost always accompanied by Mr. Clifton whenever she visited the Charleston Market. The sights, sounds and smells of the market were overwhelming to some, but Louisa looked forward to trips there. She loved talking with the shopkeepers and bargaining for beef, fish, and produce.

The mornings at the Market were full of activity and vigor. The days were long and the summers hot with the glorious smells of the Atlantic, filling the senses of all. Louisa's last day of freedom was particularly sweet. She would forever savor the feelings of that day: the delight in the company of her mother and children, the sights, sounds and smells of freedom would not be easily forgotten. She felt love in the midst of unbearable sorrow when she and her family were set upon; she fought, howled, and cried until her voice became a whisper. It is not that she had forgotten her children; rather they were her only thought. She did not have the luxury of protecting them from the sight and sound of her violent emotions as she summoned every sinew to their defense. Although she had never experienced it, she knew well what awaited them. As her mother ran crying in desperation and grief behind the ox cart that carried her, Louisa protested wildly with all her might. Mr. Clifton's reflexive action was swiftly muted by a blow to his head.

Louisa screamed without making a sound as even her voice abandoned her, and her final sight of him was blurred by the stinging tears and sweat in her eyes. Wrists and ankles bound, the heavy iron shackles that had already torn her stockinged ankles cut into her flesh. She was unable to comfort her children who bounced in the cart alongside her. Would she ever see her love again? Would she ever know if he was killed or if he was also sold into bondage? She knew that if he lived, he would surely find her and she vowed silently that she would live to see that day. She blamed herself. How foolish she had been to allow herself to believe that her worldliness and ingenuity would keep her free among the throngs of Charleston! Her husband's success and their constant vigilance were rendered useless in an instant. While they attended church regularly, it wasn't until she lost sight of Mother Amelia in the dust and distance that she prayed as she never had before. She began praying in that wagon, and she continued praying every day for the rest of her years that her children would be free and that she would survive to see it become so.

She cursed the day she left home, she cursed the day she arrived on these shores and she cursed the day she was stolen from her husband and from Charleston. If it weren't for her children, she swore she would have jumped right out of that cart and off the first bridge they crossed. Louisa and her children changed hands more than once on the way south from Charleston. They passed many a caravan and chain gang marching to the eternity of their afflictions. Although the burden of her sorrow seemed too heavy to bear, the presence and well-being of her children stiffened her back and her lip. Until she could find a way to deliver them from this horror, she would will them to survive. Only 2 or 3 times per day did they stop for water or victuals. Sometimes her captors traded or paid for provisions. Other times one or more would go off and return with fresh game. The traders ordered Louisa to do the cooking and left only the least desirable remnants for their captives, but it was enough to sustain Louisa and her daughter and son in relative functional health. Sometimes they rode in the wagon and other times Louisa and the children walked.

They were forced to maintain a quick pace, not as a punishment or cruelty for its own sake, but to maintain an expected profit margin and to ensure their fitness upon delivery. Their considerable investment would be for naught if their buyer were not pleased with the merchandise upon inspection. When they rode, Louisa comforted the children, caressed them, sang softly to them. She kept them low and covered when the wagon stopped in a shaded grove outside Pooler on the outskirts of Savannah. As they approached, she could see dozens of white men on horseback, some in wagons and some seated in folding chairs surrounding a make-shift platform of fallen logs. She held her breath as she saw 3 black men in manacles being inspected. "They will not sell my children!" she breathed. She would kill them with her bare hands before she would let them be sold from her! As all attention was upon the men being inspected, Louisa's children slept at her side. The abject terror of her circumstance eclipsed every hope she had of life for her children. She could not imagine allowing her little daughter Elizabeth being left alone with these or any slavers. If she could remain with her children, she could hope to raise them. She could hope for a reunion with their father. She could hope to keep them from greater harm, she could hope to spare them the lash or sacrifice herself for their survival if necessary, but at this moment she could not bear the thought of living without them or of them living without her.

Sweat poured from her brow and she felt it dripping from the bottom of her neck to the base of her spine. With each drop she willed her hands to close around her sleeping daughter's neck. Why would her fingers not tighten? Her blood boiled and her head grew light as she concentrated on commanding her hands to squeeze, yet they remained resolute. She began to pant and spit with drool and snot falling from her chin onto her heaving chest when she heard a word. "No!" She snapped her head to look in the direction of the logs. Did one of the slavers yell out? One of her captors was still tending the horses as he waited for his partners.

Did he tell her to stop? Had she been seen by anyone? There was no mistaking that she heard the word spoken, but by whom? It was clear and distinct, but she saw no one looking at her or near enough to have seen what she was doing. Slowly the color returned to her fingers and then her hands. Her elbows unlocked. Her breathing slowed and a northern breeze caressed her softly. She unclasped her hands and fell back into the side board of the cart as her other captors returned and they resumed their westerly route.

Joseph gently shook his mama's shoulders to wake her. She was sleeping when he awoke and it felt like he himself had been awake for hours. He heard the traders talking about stopping for water soon, and he knew they would be yelling at Louisa and him to go fill their canteens and water the horses. Louisa woke easily and felt unusually well. Her ankles were beginning to heal from the cuts of the shackles that had been removed once they were clear of Charleston and there was nowhere for her to run. She gave Joseph's hand a squeeze to let him know that she was awake and before opening her eyes she thanked God silently for her renewed strength and for letting her wake to the company of her children once again.

The traders rarely spoke to her and her children unless they were ordering them in or out of the cart, to fetch, tend, lift or cook something. She heard one of them say they should reach Savannah by sundown if they only stopped once today. By her reckoning, they had been travelling for 5 days and nights. Today was the sixth. She had no inkling of where Savannah was, but she learned to read before her children were born and knew that they were in Georgia. She recalled stories her husband would read from the newspapers after suppertime around the fireplace back in Charleston about the conflicts between the Cherokee Indians and the state of Georgia. The Seminole and Cherokee tribes were being forced out of the state and into Oklahoma. Cotton was king in Georgia, and Louisa suspected she and her children would be headed to the fields for that purpose very soon. The importation of slaves from the South Carolina Lowcountry and Chesapeake Tidewater nearly doubled from 1820 to 1840. Louisa, Joseph and Elizabeth had become 3 of the 280,944 slaves in Georgia in 1840.

It was dusk when the caravan pulled into Savannah and the brokerage of Cohen & Hertz. Louisa and her children were ordered out of the wagon and into a building with stone floors. They were taken to a room with other captives and a trough of water and told to wash. Her humiliation was not yet complete as she undressed first her daughter and then herself to wash. The water was cold but a welcome respite after so many long days of travel. Joseph washed himself and they were given burlap tunics that were not clean but were far better than the filthy rags their own clothes had become on the journey to this sty. Louisa knew they were being prepared for presentation and inspection. She had read accounts of the vile process and steeled herself to be seen as an agreeable sort whose value would be heightened by keeping her family intact.

The captives were ushered into other rooms. Adult men went left and adult women went right. Children went with their mothers. Louisa held Joseph's hand tightly. Even though he was a child, at 12 years of age he may have been destined for field work and Louisa wanted to make sure she was in the same field if it came to that. Males were poked and shoved left, but there was no objection from the overseers as Louisa steered her son to the right with her and little Elizabeth. Louisa was keenly aware of the heightened attention she attracted. Her skin was brown, though not worn and weathered. Her hair was not styled as she had kept it in Charleston, but it was a different texture than that of other women in this room and the men in the next. Her appearance and that of her children drew great interest from the men who had traveled from Bulloch, Washington, Laurens and adjoining counties to increase their fortunes. Louisa fought to suppress the disgust that befell her like an avalanche of steaming manure as hands tugged at her hair, kneaded her breasts, and squeezed her arms, legs and buttocks. Her eyes welled with tears as a brute forced his calloused fingers into her mouth, sweeping her gums to inspect for decay. The only sound she made was a muted gasp as her tunic was raised without warning and hands spun her at the shoulders and all viewed her nakedness and the shame she felt for them. Every overseer and owner inspecting the chattel instantly knew that Louisa had never been a field hand. Her condition was pristine. There were no marks on her body at all save the healing bruises at her ankles. She appeared to have been well-fed and her small children were equally fit and suitable. The bidding was quiet. There was no carnival barking or spectacle. Although the voices were loud enough to hear, she was distracted by Elizabeth who had begun crying over the commotion surrounding her mother. Louisa spoke softly and closely to her daughter's ear... "It's ok, darlin'. Mama is ok and she will never leave you. You be a big girl now and show Mama how strong you can be. No more tears, ok?" Her knees weakened as she stood up realizing how unsure she was of what she had just told Elizabeth. She felt that as long as she could keep her children, she could endure anything. She saw the proprietor and a customer studying her as money changed hands. A bill of sale was exchanged, and she averted her eyes as the buyer approached. "I am Master David Harvard."

Louisa feared only for her children. She gave no thought whatsoever to her own safety and well-being other than to survive for their sake. She knew that they were destined for hardship and she would do whatever was necessary to ensure that she could be there for them and give them the will and wiles to endure. Master Harvard had not spoken to her for many miles it seemed. Moonlight flitted through the towering Georgia pines as the horses clopped beneath low branches. Dread consumed her entirely, belying the serenity of the mask she wore for her children's sake. The cart approached a large white house with boxwoods flanking a long pathway leading to a massive set of oak double doors. The porch was a red brick platform for six towering square white columns that sentineled the prominence of the man who caused their erection. Young cypress trees surrounding the house had already grown 15 feet since being planted a few years ago by the Mistress. In another 4 or 5 years, they would shade the roof line of the 9-room mansion known far and wide as Laurens Hill.

The cart came to a halt and 2 slaves hurried to attend Master and his cargo. "This here is Louiza," he said to the woman, Disey. "Get her and them little ones fed and tell her how we do here." He made no sound to the man. He knew the routine well after living with Master all of his 44 years.  In 1840 David Harvard lived with his wife Mary Fish, daughter Sarah, and sons Quintilian and William. The two slaves, Louisa and her children were counted in the 1840 census among the 10 persons on the Harvard farm, but only David's name was recorded.

Disey took the remnants of Louisa's family to one of two clapboard quarters downwind from the main house.  Lewis, Disey's husband, built these with his own hands in his 20th and 21st years. He had help with the first one. Master borrowed a slave with carpentry and brick laying experience from his sister Jane for Lewis to apprentice.  The first quarters had a brick chimney, 2 chest-high windows, a single door and a covered platform porch. This is where Lewis and Disey stayed. The second quarters was much the same, but it lacked a porch. While Lewis took care of the horses and tack, Disey tended to the children. Louisa watched, unsure of what to say. She thought it better to listen in order to gain as much information as possible about this place. Disey delighted in caring for her and the children and readily explained, "I ain't seen no women servants 'round here since last harvest. It's sho good to have some comp'ny. Lewis, he a good man, but it ain't like it be wit womens. Like wit sisters," she smiled. Joseph and Elizabeth warily ate the beans and cornbread. They were so hungry they didn't once complain or compare it to the memory of suppers in Charleston. As Disey went on about the rules of the farm and how strict the Harvards were, she added, "As long as we works and don't make no trouble, we get victuals and don't get whupped. Massa a Crischen man and he ain't one for drinkin' and beatin' on his slaves till they ain't no use like some folk say. We had some hands hired to hep las year and they backs was all tow-up like I never seen!" As she turned to ladle water from a bucket for the children to drink, Louisa glimpsed scars that looked as if they had been inflicted long ago, but they were unmistakable signs of the torture that Disey assured her would not occur at the Harvard farm—as long as they minded their place.

Disey was used to minding her place. She worked in the fields, the house, wherever she was told. She did nothing unless it was ordered and did anything that was ordered until told to stop. She asked for nothing and was given little but she said she'd, "rather have a little bit of nothing than a whole heap of Hell." One thing she did not have, however, was Louisa's flawless complexion. She was no stranger to hard work. Louisa's hands were strong, but she had never been beaten, never felt the lash, and never been branded or marked in any other way. This and her unusual features, bone structure, and hair prompted David Harvard to buy her and her children. He wanted Louisa for his own comfort and to produce more slaves for his growing farm. He could buy just about any slave to pick cotton, but one so exceptional as this was a rare find only possible by his relationship with broker Octavus Cohen. Hiring the slaves of his family and neighbors seasonally put more money in their pockets than his. He had no immediate use for Elizabeth, but saw potential in Joseph as a fast-growing boy who could become very useful in the field quickly if trained properly by himself and Lewis. Elizabeth was too young to be of much use to him other than as leverage with her mother. By keeping them together he hoped to lessen Louisa's resistance to his plans. It was not love he sought, but a vessel. Her children were proof of her fertility, and her pristine condition made the thought of using her curious and far more comforting than the rough, battered, broken wenches of his siblings' farms. He would treat her justly, he thought, as long as she obeyed without hesitation.

It wasn't more than a few weeks after arriving at the Harvard farm that Master Harvard ordered Louisa to come to him in the barn. There was no flirtation or wryness in his tone, there was no lewd or lascivious expression, no hesitation or shyness, there was only a command, "Come here!" There was no smiling, no asking, no coaxing. He spun her around deliberately and lifted her skirt in a single motion. Instinctively she stiffened and bit her lip as she felt his right hand jerk the length of her long single braid tightly around his fist. As he opened his pants with his left hand he leaned over her back pulling her head close to his face and breathed hotly into her ear, "As long as you live, you belong to me, and your children belong to me. If you ever so much as look at me wrong, I will take Elizabeth and drown her in that pond out back. Don't you ever pull away from me again." The fear should have paralyzed her, but the terror of his words elicited the intended response then and every time thereafter. In 1847, Amelia was the first of 5 children born to David Harvard and Louisa Session Clifton.

# CHAPTER TWENTY-FOUR

## SARAH LOWTHER

In about 1811 the inland village of Eboundja in the southern region of Cameroon, was raided and the young ones were bound and latched to barges that navigated the Dibamba River from the interior to a sharp bend nearest the village of Yapoma. From there, they were marched for days to the coastal village of Deido, which is now called Douala. Young Adji could scarcely believe the scale and breadth of the vista as the hostages cleared the bush and beheld hundreds upon hundreds of chained and yoked men, women and children being funneled into large holding areas on the shores of Deido. Tears she began crying on the day she was taken left her utterly desiccated by the time she was prodded aboard a ship. She had not seen her parents or siblings since their tribe was separated on the march from Yapoma. The dark clouds racing her from the shores of her homeland obscured any glimmer of hope, and they overtook her swiftly. Surely the weight of her sorrow would be far too great for the vessel to bear. As the heavens sobbed and wailed, she had not the slightest fear, for she prayed they would all be rolled into the abyss beneath them. The torrent continued until they arrived at the Island of Fernando Po.

The day was now late, but sufficient light remained in that gray post-torrential oppressive sky to marvel at the thousands of glistening ebony-skinned people and the pale, angry men pushing, beating, slapping, whipping, and kicking them. The most fearsome sight of all for Adji was that of the largest ship she had ever seen. Many times larger than the boat that brought her and 20 others from Deido to this island, the towering beast seemed little-moved by the rolling waves assaulting it only a hundred or so yards off shore. Adji froze in terror as she instinctively realized that the first boat was not to be her only conveyance. This island was merely a concentration point to gather as many captives as would fit in the belly of the yawning leviathan. Her legs and vision dissolved in unison.

Adji lost track of the number of her fellow Africans who perished during the six-week voyage. On the march from Yapoma to Deido, she saw many killed for resisting or for being unable to keep pace with the group. Vultures circled low in the sky from the time she left the Dibamba river until she was swallowed by the floating behemoth. Of the 600 or so humans who boarded in chains, Adji saw several thrown overboard every week when the women were allowed above deck, and she was certain as many men were discarded when the women were in the hold. Although she dreaded her future, she refused to give her captors the satisfaction of her death. As she lay on the fetid shelf of waste with iron rings binding her to a poor girl who expired in her own excrement, Adji seethed but determined that despite her current circumstance, she would live. She would see a better day, she would make life work for her and she would never be defeated.

She promised this for herself, for the family she would never see again, and for those yet to come.

The son of John Lowther and Mary Hagan was also named John. Born in Laurens County, Georgia in August of 1800. He had 1 son with his first wife Abigail Howard and 5 daughters with his second wife, Eliza Moore. He also fathered 5 sons and 1 daughter by his slave, Sarah, the name he gave to Adji upon purchasing her. Sarah was his prize wench. After the expected resistance had been decidedly broken, Master John used the offspring of his Sarah to improve her compliance as well as the profitability of his own enterprise. On one occasion Sarah, after twisting her ankle in the field, had difficulty walking for a few days and Master expressed his displeasure at her reduced productivity by hoisting baby William by the ankles, threatening to dash him against the water trough. Sarah fell at Master's feet begging for mercy and swearing she would do better. John carelessly dropped his son into Sarah's lap growling, "See that you do!" Sarah was quite healthy despite the poor to fair conditions of her existence, but no matter what ailed her, she never again let Master see any evidence of weakness.

# CHAPTER TWENTY-FIVE

## CONTRABAND

L aurens, Twiggs, Pulaski and Macon counties were among those in the Black Belt of Georgia, named for its dark, rich soil. In 1860 the slave population was 10 times greater in cotton-producing Black Belt counties across the South than in the coastal counties that produced rice and indigo. When war commenced, Sarah's son William Lowther and his family were among 463,000 slaves that comprised over 40 percent of the state's total population. William had no opportunity, knowledge or plan to escape to the North, but word passed from farm to farm that as Union armies advanced, able men were fleeing to join their ranks. William struck out and quickly found a camp set up near Union forces. Congress and the U. S. Army classified these escaped men as contraband and used them as laborers to support Union efforts.

William was among those who received wages of $10 per month, a full day's ration, and education in exchange for his commitment to the cause. The day he made his mark on the paper was the most hopeful in his sorrowful life, William thought. As much as he would miss the company of his mother Sarah and his brothers Edgar, Andrew and baby Telley, William A. Lowther declared his freedom, not on the day he left the Lowther Plantation, but on the day in May when he heard that an act of Congress prevented the return of escaped or captured slaves to the Confederacy. The wages and rations were not the impetus for his relief. It was the realization that the country of his birth stood with him and his family for the first time. He was supported and justified in caring for them and providing for them. He felt indescribably whole. He was a man equal to every other, even if they refused to acknowledge that inalienable fact. Until that moment, William struggled to reconcile the preachers' words and the politicians' speeches with his own experience.

Now it became clear to him. To be a man is to be independent, to be responsible, to develop and apply oneself to caring for others, to sustain oneself and one's family. At that moment, he was no longer dependent on Master's benevolence. He no longer relied on the scraps and refuse of the Lowther household. Now he fought against it. He built bridges, he dug trenches, he hunted, he skinned and cooked game, he dug graves, he scouted positions, he fetched, toted, and hauled. But he did it all for himself, for his family, for freedom and for a greater America. Contraband or not, he was a Union soldier and prouder of that fact than anything else in his 21 years. He was bringing freedom to his family.

After Lee surrendered and the Great Emancipator was laid to rest in 1865, those who had not already fled remained in a purgatory of servitude. Not having experienced the quickening of consciousness that William felt upon providing for himself, many continued to labor as they always had in exchange for lodging and rations. On October 10 Master David Harvard accepted an offer of pardon and amnesty by President Andrew Johnson with several conditions. Among them were:

*1st. This pardon is to be of no effect until the said David Harvard shall take the oath prescribed in the Proclamation of the President dated May 29th, 1865.*

*2nd. To be void and of no effect if the said David Harvard shall hereafter, at any time, acquire any property whatever in slaves, or make use of slave labor.*

Nineteen days after signing his name to this document, David Harvard died. Some said the downfall of the South crushed him. Some said it was poison that did him in. His will, written before the cessation of hostilities bequeathed his daughter Amelia to her half-sister, Mary "Missy" Harvard as a wedding present. Missy was engaged to John Barkwell, and they were married in November not more than a month after her father died. It was November 13th when the newly emancipated Amelia accepted her sister's offer to come live with them as their servant –not as a slave. There wasn't a better place to go at the time, and Amelia wanted to remain close to her mother and little siblings. They needed time to figure out how they were going to adjust to their newfound freedom. Where else was there to go? How would they get there? These were all things they could ponder together, she thought, as long as they were all free. Her Harvard half-brothers had other ideas.

Louisa's 72 years belied her vigor and acuity. The Harvard boys didn't fuss over Amelia leaving because she was still with Missy, but they were not keen on letting Louisa leave with Richard, Reuben, Tobe and Roxey. They didn't have to sign any pardons as their late daddy had, and whether or not these niggers were slaves, they still belonged to them. They were bound by blood and they told Louisa without mincing words to "Git! You best forget about these. They stayin' here." Louisa remembered the words Master Harvard hissed some 20 years prior. "As long as you live, you belong to me and your children belong to me."

She remembered the prayer she said in that wagon the last day she ever saw her mother and husband. She had indeed lived to see the day of her deliverance, and had come to accept that she would not see her beloved husband again, but sure as eggs is eggs she was going to keep her promise that her children were coming with her. For all she endured, every indignity, every heartbreak, every atrocity, these were her babies no matter that they came from Master Harvard. They were given to her by God, they were all she had, and she was not about to leave them behind in the hands of these sour men. Quinn and William laughed at Louisa as she shook her fist at them and stormed toward the road spitting, "You will give me my children! You will give me my babies!" David Jr. hurled stones the size of walnuts at her from afar as the boys doubled over at the old woman's temerity.

It wasn't that they despised Louisa—she was a non-person to them. But her children, they were the offspring of their father, and their half-sister Amelia was raised in the same house as they and their sister Missy. She was much like a favored pet to them. Mistress Mary Fish Harvard cast a long shadow and the illegitimate progeny of her husband kept a wide berth around her, but Amelia was tolerated in the house. David was fond of her because she resembled him so closely, her skin only a little darker than his own, and she was an ideal companion for her half-sister Missy who was born the same year. She wasn't treated like family in the presence of Mistress Mary, but her half-siblings were particularly protective of her. When Amelia accompanied Missy to town, big brother Quinn always attended them and once beat a boy unconscious for pushing Amelia out of his way and spitting at her. No one could mistake the Harvards for nigger-lovers, but no one dared to take liberty with any of their property either.

When Louisa arrived at Missy's home to plan her next actions with Amelia, she found her daughter surrounded by a cadre of Union soldiers. The occupying force was thick throughout the county and Louisa recognized one of them from a time she was loaned out to the Lowther plantation. He was older now, bigger and stronger looking, but she recognized William. "Ain't you Sarah's boy?" she asked. The smile that Amelia's attention had coaxed from him waned as he translated the anxiety in the furrows of Louisa's brow. "Yes, ma'am. You ok?" "What's wrong, Mama, where Roxey and the boys?" Amelia asked. "They ok? Please tell me they ok!" Louisa sat in the chair that her daughter relinquished for her. "They ok, but them boys won't let 'em go. I don't know what they gon' do, but we can't leave 'em there. Them my children. Them our family. If they ain't free, I ain't free," she moaned. William assured her and Amelia that this is precisely why they were stationed in Laurens County and throughout the South—to make sure that people "did right" by the law. At the quick step, the troops headed down Blackhear Ferry Road for Laurens Hill.

The Harvards were a large family with considerable holdings among their numbers, but David's farm was like many others in Georgia at that time, a little more prosperous than most, but he was no magnate unto himself. In 1860 there were 3,269 slaves in Laurens County. The U.S. Census Slave Schedule for the county includes 18 slaveholders who held 48. Eighteen men owned 42% of the enslaved persons. The remaining 58% were held among 209 slaveholders of which David Harvard was one. David had about 10 –15 slaves on average at any given time during his adult life. Half of those were Louisa and his children with her. Taking the remaining 4 of her children from the farm finally brought that number to zero at the point of a dozen rifles in 1865.

William and his mates had the weapons drawn and levelled before the Harvard men opened the door. William explained that the children would be leaving with their mother in compliance with the laws of the United States and troops would remain stationed in the county to ensure their continued safety. The Harvard men were quiet as their little brothers and sister left their farm. Richard (15), Reuben (10), Tobe (9) and Roxey (5) walked quickly behind their mother, and with each and every step, Louisa thanked God for answering the prayer she began 25 years prior without losing a single child to death or sale.

# CHAPTER TWENTY-SIX

KING ME

I was amazed by Frances's memory. Much of the information she documented had been committed to memory and she rattled it off as if I were capable of assimilating in minutes what took her years to construct. I did not complain. I did my best to keep up, and her patience knew no bounds. She explained how little was known of the origin of Sarah, William's mother. We knew that Sarah was a first generation African, but we didn't know the country of her origin, her language, customs or anything more.

Frances showed me photos of Lowther Hall in Jones County, GA. She explained that the home was destroyed by fire in 1942. I was saddened that I would never be able to visit, but thankful that pictures survived. The home was built by Samuel Lowther of Virginia who settled there with his wife Ann Sophia Pepper after their marriage in 1814. The photographs in the Library of Congress show a home with a graceful white winding staircase with cherry treads and railings. I imagined what life must have been like for William and his siblings as children of Samuel. Frances even had a picture of a white William, the son of Samuel and Ann Sophia, born in 1816 in Warren, Georgia.

I was captivated and conflicted by the thought that this William owned my second great grandmother Sarah from Africa and fathered her son, William A. Lowther. How did he acquire her? Was he unusually cruel to her? As I built out the Lowther DNA matches of Frances and my cousins; however, the name *Hagan* appeared with increasing frequency. Dozens of DNA matches were all converging on the names of John Lowther and Mary Hagan of Bulloch County, Georgia. Like a great ship emerging from the fog of generations on a sea of silence, it became clear that the father of William A. Lowther was not William the son of Samuel Lowther of Lowther Hall. The man who bought Sarah of Africa and fathered her children William, Edgar, Andrew, Telley, Richard, and Susan was John Lowther Jr., son of John Lowther and Mary Hagan who lived in Bulloch County. Once again, DNA was informing and correcting our understanding of ourselves. The photo we had of Samuel was that of our fifth cousin 4 times removed, it turned out. Months later, I would discover a new photo: the headstone of my true third great grandfather, John in the Old Dublin Cemetery of historic Laurens County.

As was typical in rural agricultural communities of the mid-19th century, large families intermarried, and certain names appeared together with greater frequency. This endogamy makes it difficult for researches to tease out individuals, especially when the given names are duplicated among cousins as often as the surnames. I began to notice these patterns as I followed the hints and reviewed the source citations of census, birth and marriage records. Lowther, Hagan and Townsend formed one pattern.

Harvard, Drury and Drake formed another. I was confounded by the lack of documentation for my African ancestors before 1850, but many of my European ancestors could be traced much further.

Countless hours passed carefully comparing dates, places and names. My earliest experience with genealogy taught me the folly of adding unsubstantiated information to my tree. The algorithms used by Ancestry to discover public records and facts are based on an assumption that the starting point is correct. Two individuals with the same name and state of birth can be easily confused, and inserting the wrong name into my tree would lead me down an arduous path of deleting names and relationships upon discovering the error. It is much wiser to use caution on the front end. I made it a rule to only add names that were verified in public records at first. The trees of other researches were also available for comparison, but these are often very subjective or speculative. The only way to know which information is correct is to corroborate it with multiple other sources, such as public records and DNA results.

Of all the Lowthers and Hagans of Bulloch County, only John and Mary also lived in Laurens County, Georgia, the birthplace of Sarah's son, William (my great grandfather). I confess that when I began resolving my DNA matches to determine which were maternal and which were paternal, I assumed that those with larger percentages of African ancestry were paternal and those who were European entirely or mostly were related to me by my mother. I was frequently reminded by their places of birth, however, that almost everyone with American pedigrees, especially from southern states, were my paternal family regardless of the color of their skin. It became easy to identify the Eastern Europeans from Germany, Slovakia, Ukraine and Poland as my maternal relatives. If they lived in America before 1860 or they sprang from the United Kingdom or the Nordic countries, they were the precursors of William Lowther or Amelia Harvard.

Many of my DNA matches who descended from John and Mary, came to me from their daughters Sarah Ann, Celity and Catherine, my third great aunts. My stomach knotted as I discovered the military service records of my own cousins among the ranks of insurrectionists who fought to dehumanize and brutalize their own flesh and blood. I saw John's migration in reverse from his death in Bulloch County in 1812 to his birth in Craven County, South Carolina in 1770. I saw his father Edward from South Carolina to Queen Ann, Maryland and his ancestors for 5 generations to Westmoreland England.

Sir Richard Lowther, John's fourth great grandfather (my tenth) was knighted and appointed High Sheriff of Cumberland in 1565. He received a letter from Queen Elizabeth's sister, Mary Queen of Scots requesting his assurance of her safety after her defeat at the battle of Langside. Although his answer was evasive, he informed her that if she were forced to enter England, he would protect her. On May 16 Mary came ashore in a fishing boat at Workington where she stayed the evening. The next night Sir Richard and Henry Curwen conveyed her to Carlisle Castle. Historians know well that from this night forward, Mary was suspected of conspiring against her sister, and was held captive in various English prisons for nearly 20 years until her conviction and execution on February 8, 1587. Sir Richard's great grandson, Edward was the first of their family to arrive in the New World, and in 1761 Edward's son Charles was the first of their line to be born in America.

John's mother, Mary Hagan, a fourth generation American born in Charles County, Maryland was the fourth great granddaughter of Thomas Hagan who was born in 1645 in County Tyrone, Ireland. The O'Hagans originated in the province of Ulster at Tullyhogue where the chief exercised the hereditary right of inaugurating "the O'Neill" as king. The inauguration consisted of the O'Cahan throwing a golden sandal over the new lord's head to signify good fortune and the O'Hagan would place the shoe on the O'Neill's foot and present him with a rod of office.

This British and Irish ancestry, though fascinating, sadly reminded me of just how much history and how many generations were forever stolen from me. The likelihood that I would ever identify a living relative on the continent of Africa seemed infinitely remote.

While the pedigree of Amelia's husband William led to the nobles of England and Ireland, Amelia herself turned out to be a direct descendant of Kings and Queens of Europe. I could not identify the parents of her mother Louisa who was sold into slavery in 1845, but establishing the ancestry of her white paternal grandmother Elizabeth Drury actually became easier the deeper I sank my shovel into the soil of centuries past. The daughter of Mills Nevel Drury and Delilah Duke has a paternal lineage to Margaret Basset, daughter of Sir Arthur Basset, a descendant of Kings Edward IV, Edward III, and King Phillip (the Bold) of France. The endogamy of Gouldtown, New Jersey and Bulloch County, Georgia in the 19th century had nothing on European royalty 500 – 700 years prior. Once you stumble into one royal family, you've stumbled into them all. I chuckled to accept that I was the descendant of slaves as well as the Kings and Queens of England, France, Spain, and Denmark. Half of Amelia's 15th to 17th great grandparents were Royals. The real pill-popper is the scientific certainty that a living person of any amount of European ancestry is a descendant of Holy Roman Emperor, Charlemagne. According to study by Joseph Yang in 1999.

*Chang was not a genealogist who had decided to make me his personal project. Instead, he is a statistician at Yale who likes to think of genealogy as a mathematical problem. When you draw your genealogy, you make two lines from yourself back to each of your parents. Then you have to draw two lines for each of them, back to your four grandparents. And then eight great-grandparents, sixteen great-great-grandparents, and so on (until) the time of Charlemagne, forty generations or so, you should get to a generation of a trillion ancestors. That's about two thousand times more people than existed on Earth when Charlemagne was alive...As you go back further in time, more of those lines cross as you encounter more common ancestors of the living population. And then something really interesting happens. There comes a point at which, Chang wrote, "all individuals who have any descendants among the present-day individuals are actually ancestors of all present-day individuals."[7]*

This odyssey, I mused, is the essence of privilege. The ability to search for and find one's origins with a reasonable level of specificity is a privilege that oppressed people can never fully enjoy. The Lowthers and Hagans are well-documented and quite prolific. My father's mother's side (at least the white ones) were the first to reveal their secrets. As I turned my sights on the more difficult Brantley side, Frances had begun planning a grand family reunion in Dublin, Georgia for the summer of 2017. I would get to meet family members who never left the state; I would get to see the sights and sounds of a vibrant but relatively small town about halfway between Macon and Savannah—the place my father, uncles and ancestors were born and raised. It occurred to me that I finally had an ancestral home, that I was not *just* a Detroit city boy with a healthy side of Mississippi flavor, I was a Georgian, too!

One afternoon I paid a visit to Cousin Douglas and his wife Jewell. I always felt so comfortable in their presence that I fretted about wearing out my welcome. My wife joined us that afternoon and we exchanged stories about my youth and Doug's memories of his

---

[7] Carl Zimmer, Charlemagne's DNA and Our Universal Royalty, National Geographic, 05/07/2013

parents and grandparents. As we chatted with Jewell, Douglas disappeared for a few minutes until I heard his footsteps climbing up from the basement. He had in his hands 3 framed pictures. The first was a beautiful color portrait of his parents, Rev. and Mrs. Joseph Brantley. My uncle was slim, standing erect, short gray hair receding or cleanly shaved from the forehead to the back of his crown and neatly cropped on the sides. Large square bifocals perched on a straight nose with a narrow bridge. A trimmed grey mustache and a darker soul patch softened his sharp eyes, thin lips and square chin. The light caramel tone of his skin beamed a faint tinge of red as if a mixture of Georgia clay and sweet potatoes.

The picture Claudia shared of her family was black and white and was taken in the early 1950s. It was easy to see my resemblance to David and Joseph. Nose, ears, forehead, eyes...all mine. The distance from the upper lip to the nose was a smidge more, but yes, this made perfect sense. The color photo of Joseph was delightful, but none of that prepared me for the moment that stopped my breath as well as my heart. Douglas produced two more black and white photos. The first was his parents' wedding portrait, which was nothing short of stunning. The bride in her gown cradling a beautiful bouquet and the groom standing over her right shoulder gently grasping her arm in his black tuxedo, smartly-starched white shirt and tie. I saw even more of a resemblance to myself in this younger photo, but Douglas saved the best for last. Young Joseph was standing, wearing a dark suit, white shirt and dark tie—younger than when he married, yet already a man.

He was born in 1915 in Georgia and arrived in Detroit in 1939. Perhaps this was the first photo taken after his arrival. It was like looking at myself 30 years younger. I saw my resemblance in Douglas, Michael, Pam, David and others, but this was that moment I always wondered about. Is there someone out there who bears more than a passing resemblance to me? If I were walking down the street, would I ever be frozen by the uncanniness of the moment? I flashed back to that day in the library when my cousins approached me and I took their hands. It didn't show on their faces, but surely they thought, "Oh, yes. He's one of us for sure." They knew Joseph and his brothers and they most certainly recognized them in my face. Maybe not at birth, maybe not at 50, but at about 30 or 40 years of age their father Joseph was the closest to a spitting image of me I had always imagined. Still hoping Douglas or Michael would be willing to test, I was now convinced that they were my half-brothers and that Joseph was my father.

# CHAPTER TWENTY-SEVEN

⌐ ୬ ୧ ୧ ୧ ⌐

## THE HUMAN TORCH

I had not heard from Douglas yet regarding his willingness to test, but I was in communication with his adult children, nieces and nephews via Facebook. I let Doug and Michael know that if any of their children tested, that might be enough to solve the mystery. If Doug's children tested, the result would identify them as my first cousins (if Doug were my uncle) or as my half-siblings (if he were my father). If Doug, Michael and Pam were my first cousins, then their children would be identified as my first cousins once removed indicating that my father was Willie or David (Joseph's brothers). Doug's daughter Bianca was the first to volunteer.

Weeks passed, more DNA matches came in and were connected in my tree, and Bianca's results finally arrived—547 cM across 28 segments. "Linny, they're in! The range says *1st–2nd Cousin*. What do you think?" "I don't know, Ron. That's awfully close. Could be a half first cousin or first cousin once removed. Could be that Michael's your dad or one of his uncles could be. Do you think Michael or Douglas will test?" Bianca's results were in that overlapping region between ranges. She was in the high end of one and the low end of the other. I should have been patient to wait for Douglas instead of giving the test to his daughter.

When I explained the results to everyone, the eldest of the siblings stepped forward. Michael said, "I'll test. I know I'm not your dad, but it would be alright with me if I was. Let's see what it says." What a blessing! You can't convince anyone to do anything they don't want to, but you can pray and then recognize God's hand at work. I knew full well that the story could have ended at Bianca's results without a definitive answer, but it did not. At this point, we all knew with more certainty than ever that neither Douglas nor Michael was my father and that Claudia was my aunt. The last remaining answerable question was whether my father was Joseph, the Reverend and father of Michael, Douglas and Pam, or if the honor belonged to one of his brothers, Willie or David.

Aunt Claudia led the consensus opinion that it was not Joseph. He was a minister of the gospel, devoted husband, and would never have been with another woman outside of his marriage. Frances remarked that his mother Gertrude, would roll in her grave if he were my father. "She would love you just the same, but she would roll," Frances quipped. Willie was married, but never had any children and was a pious veteran. Although no one could place a specific memory of David that would connect him to me, he was the only one of the 3 brothers who elicited a "maybe" vote. We had 2 thumbs down (for Joseph and Willie) and one sideways (David). Considering that these were Claudia's brothers and she grew up in the same home with the same parents, she knew them better than anyone alive.

I nursed the idea that I might be the child of a pastor, like my mom. The man I admired most in my life, my late grandfather Rev. Jamerson, was coincidentally born in the very same year as Rev. Brantley, 1915. The difference in ages between my mother and father did not escape my attention. I incorrectly assumed Michael or Douglas was my father because they were nearly the same ages as the 3 sisters Linny identified as my birth mother candidates. Their father Joseph and his brothers were at least 15 years older than she. They were all nearly old enough to be her father. As I stepped back a few paces to review, the picture I was painting shifted.

As we waited for the results from Michael's test, Douglas called me one evening to prepare me for a disturbing possibility. Whenever I received calls from my paternal family, I was excited and did so with a smile because I knew what warmth and acceptance was always on the other end. I had no idea when I saw Douglas's name on my caller ID that this was the call for which I had been praying since beginning my quest. When I prayed for strength and peace to accept the worst, this would be the test.

"Hey, Ron, if you haven't already discovered it, I wanted to let you know that David had some problems." I was still certain that Doug's father Rev. Brantley would prove to be my father, so I wasn't quite dialed into this discussion about David, but I was getting there. "David went to prison for a while. He killed a man." I did not interrupt. "A man hit him with a hammer. Accused him of being with his wife. It's all on the internet if you haven't searched for it. They said David set him on fire and he died. But before he died, the man named David, so he went away." As I pondered the words, I had no doubt of God's grace. If David turned out to be my father, that would actually make more sense than my idealized version of events. I didn't really want the human failing of an idolized pastor to be laid bare. I didn't want to be the child of a murderer either, but the world felt more normal and God felt more Godly if the inexplicable twists and turns of men's failures could be used for good as promised in Romans 8:28, "²⁸And we know that all things work together for good to them that love God, to them who are the called according to his purpose." There is never a bad time to become familiar with God's word, but the sooner it is within us, the sooner it can be brought to our defense.

November 18, 1949, Detroit News
Assailants Make Torch of Victim
*Toss Gas on Worker, Touch Match to Him*
*Leo Mack, 49 of 4506 Harding was turned into a human torch when two strangers tossed gasoline on him in a dark alley near his home and set him afire. Receiving Hospital doctors said there was little hope for his recovery. He suffered third degree burns of his entire body.*
*A Neighbor, Render Cleveland, 41 of 4512 Harding leaped from a second floor porch to snuff out the flames on the screaming victim. Mack told police he was approaching his garage when he heard a voice say, "Let it go." He then was doused with the fuel. Mack, a mechanic, blamed a neighborhood fight for the attack. Police said he accused David Brantley, 32 of 4006 Harding. Held for investigation, Brantley denied the charge. He admitted having had a fight with Mack Nov. 10, police said."*

*April 27, 1950, Detroit News*
Torch Killer Gets Long Prison Term
*David Brantley, 33 of 4006 Harding, convicted of second degree murder for the torch slaying of a neighbor, was sentenced to 25-40 years. Recorder's Judge Christopher E. Stein imposed sentence after a jury had found Brantley guilty. Brantley was charged with first-degree murder for the death of Leo Mack 49, of 4506 Harding. He admitted that he threw gasoline on Mack as he emerged from his*

*garage last Nov. 17, then set fire to the clothing. Mack*
*died in Receiving Hospital last Dec. 7. Brantley told police*
*he had become angry with Mack when the neighbor*
*struck him with a hammer."*

As much as I hoped Joseph would prove to be my father, I didn't
want Pastor Brantley's reputation to be tarnished in any way, I
didn't want his memory and legacy to be affected in the least, but
I wasn't too keen on accepting a convicted murderer as a father,
either. I considered how I would react if someone hit me in the
head with a hammer, and I could not rule out a reflexive innate
response. What David lacked was a good defense attorney. I mean,
if you get hit in the head with a hammer, there's more than a good
chance that you are at least temporarily diminished mentally,
right?

Weeks later Michael's results confirmed without doubt that he
and his siblings were my first cousins. This meant that their father
Joseph (Rev. Brantley) was my uncle, and that my father could
only be Willie or David. Since neither of them had any known
children, I had reached the end of the line. There was no one else
to test and we had all accepted that David was my father. Claudia
confided that she and Gertrude wrote letters and visited David.
They continued to believe that he was innocent and that he was
set up by the other defendant in exchange for false testimony.
Either way, I settled in with the knowledge that if not the whole
truth, I certainly knew much more about my paternal family than
I had ever imagined I would find. Thanks to Frances, Annie,
Agnes, Harvey, Wayne and everyone else who took DNA tests. The
relationships were rock solid, each one a brick in an ever-growing
wall of identity.

Frances continued to share everything she knew about our family
with me. She was thankful to have someone as interested and
dedicated to genealogy and family history as she was, and I was
thankful to have someone as accomplished, trusted and sharp as

she. Frances painstakingly shaped her tree, pruning the unproven relatives and making private all of the proven ones. When she finally allowed me to see her full tree, I immediately set about making corrections in my own. Other Ancestry members mistakenly attributed events and dates to our ancestors. They added similarly named, but unrelated people to members of our family in their trees, but Frances had long since disproven them. She felt that by keeping her tree private, others would not be able to bastardize the truth.

I disagreed with her on this point, though. I believed that the only way to eliminate errors in other trees is to share publicly a fully substantiated version. As others build their trees, they have a proper reference point. Without this, they're only guessing and propagating false information. Frances honors the requests of family members who don't want their personal information made public. My research—in fact my very presence in her life—proves that nothing is ever truly private and that everything is available to the public for a price. Closed adoptions are figments of fading memories. Privacy is as elusive as a fart in the wind. Frances' refusal to contribute to the digital cacophony has earned her the trust of her family, which is a valuable lesson in itself; however, it has not shielded any of them from detection by anyone with purpose, persistence, and a little bit of cash.

# CHAPTER TWENTY-EIGHT

## THE ROAD LEADS BACK TO YOU

Frances and I have much in common. We are of the same generation. We share a pair of great grandparents. We enjoy our early-morning coffee. We were genealogy-aholics for many years before ever meeting one another. My wife's name happens to be Frances also (Fran). Frances and I are also very different. In addition to being 23 years apart in age, Frances enjoys road trips. She finds a drive from Michigan to Georgia, Florida and any points in between, therapeutic and relaxing. I abhor long trips of any kind. If I can't get there in 4 or 5 hours, I'm going to need to break it up with an overnight stay, or a good, long stretch. For the 2017 Harvard Family reunion in Dublin, GA, my plan was to fly to Atlanta, rent a car and drive two hours to Dublin. Frances drove all the way from Michigan and would meet me there the next day.

The candor and honesty of my cousin Carol was disarming. My preconceptions of Southern attitudes about race were fixed in Jim Crow Mississippi, not in Jimmy Carter Georgia. We communicated via instant messages, email and phone several times upon discovering our genetic connection. It didn't take us very long to determine that Carol was a descendant of my David's sister, Sarah Jane Harvard. Our Harvard Family Reunion was an opportunity for me to meet anyone and everyone related regardless of skin color. I invited Carol to attend. She declined, but invited me to visit her on my way to Dublin.

I landed at Hartsfield International, picked up my rental vehicle and headed toward the movie-making capital of Georgia, sleepy little Senoia. Located 35 minutes south of Atlanta, the city nurtured a population of 4,213 in 2017 when I visited. The pretty town with its vibrant main street exuded a charm and unpretentiousness that easily balanced quaint traditions with modern convenience. One would never guess that *The Walking Dead*, *Footloose*, *Fried Green Tomatoes*, and *Pet Cemetery II* were among the dozens of movies filmed there.

As I turned into the residential neighborhood from the business district, the late morning sun seemed to shine a path to my fourth cousin's doorstep. Unfastening my seatbelt, I shook my head thinking, What in the world am I doing? This little white lady doesn't know me at all. We've only spoken on the phone a few times. Sure, we've exchanged several emails, and it seemed like a great idea to meet, but now that the moment has arrived...what if she's crazy? What if she has a gun or knife at the ready to dispose of me? Had I given my wife Carol's contact information and told her exactly when I expected to arrive? Oh stop it! I scolded myself. Maybe she's wondering the same thing at this very moment about you. No sooner had these thoughts flitted through my mind, than Carol answered the doorbell with a wide smile, and a "Welcome, cousin!" in that soul-warming Georgian drawl.

She led me through a beautifully appointed living room to her kitchen and dining area. She had a pot of coffee on, invited me to have a seat and offered me something to eat. I accepted the coffee and thought to postpone the food as I dissolved into the genuine hospitality for which Southerners are well-known. Short, tastefully cropped white hair framed a delicate face centered by a button nose like mine with slightly narrower nostrils. Although I think of my own ears as disproportionately large for my head, hers were fashioned very similarly but in better proportion, I thought. I successfully resisted the urge to ask her to sweep her hair back so I could scrutinize them more closely.

We fell into very easy conversation about how remarkable this DNA science is that we should ever have found one another. She asked about my children and wife, and I about her family. I felt the biases heaped up on me by stories and traditions of the past falling away from me like maple seeds spiraling down after a soaking rain. An adult black man in the home of a single white woman in the deep South, not something I'd ever imagined, but the contrast did occur to me. This wasn't the 1960s or even the 1980s. Carol certainly wasn't concerned about it, and that enabled me to banish the thought as quickly as it arose. She showed me pictures of her parents. We knew of my relatedness to her by Sarah Jane on her father's side. We later discovered that we are also related more distantly by the Hollingsworths of her maternal ancestors. With my defenses utterly defeated, I surrendered to the snacks and to her kindness. We concluded a really wonderful visit with a hug and a promise to stay in touch.

Passing Macon I thought of what the next two days held in store for me upon reaching Dublin and how thankful I was to have found my ancestral home at this time in my life. Had I found it 20 years sooner, would the weight of the years been enough to ground me in the appreciation of all that I had accomplished due to the sacrifices and prayers of those who came before me? If I had known of my enslaved great grandmothers or that my own second great grandfathers owned them, would I have avoided any deeper discovery of their existence? The strains of Ray Charles' "Georgia on My Mind" serenaded me those last few miles - a song I had heard many times but never had greater meaning than it did on that day.

I woke early the next morning determined to see Laurens Hill with my own eyes. Frances had given me the address during one of our many exchanges, and I could not honestly predict how I would feel upon seeing it, so I was determined to go alone first. After a leisurely breakfast with orange juice, I took my coffee to-go and entered the on-ramp to I-16 W driving 14 miles back in the direction I had come the day before. I exited at Hwy 26, turned left and proceeded about a mile down the highway once known as Blackshear Ferry Road. Pine groves on the right and a tree farm on the left created a channel that poured me forth to an intersection with a barely visible old cemetery on the left.

I slowed as a white wooden fence roamed far south and west framing the perimeter of a large field on my right, the southwest corner of Laurens Hill Church Road. Beyond the fenced field I beheld the towering cypress trees planted by Mary Fish Harvard 182 years prior. The 6 square white columns set in place by David Harvard still watched over all who approached and departed. A for-sale sign was planted outside the main gate, which was open, and I spun the wheel right, into the dirt and gravel driveway.

As I walked past the boxwoods flanking the brick path and climbed the 5 steps to the porch, I had not considered what I would say to anyone who confronted me or who might answer a knock. The sound of my own knuckles rapping on the large doors echoed the thudding of my heart. Boom, Boom. Boom, Boom. Boom, Boom. The noise and feel of something touched by so many of my ancestors reengaged my purposeful brain, which until that moment had muted every other stimulus. The sounds of the wind in the pines and faraway cars and trucks returned me to my senses, and I quickly rehearsed something. "I am so sorry to arrive unannounced, but I'm visiting for a family reunion and I happened to be driving by when I noticed the sign. My second great grandfather built this entire plantation and home on the backs of slaves who are also my relatives. Would you mind showing me around, please?" No, scratch those last parts. I knocked again. Was I being watched from an upstairs window? This was a once-in-a-lifetime opportunity, I rationalized. If I don't see this house while I'm here, who knows if I'll ever have another chance? One more knock—staccato this time—and I accepted that the property was empty, retreated to my vehicle, turned around in the drive and headed toward the highway.

My armpits were soaked, my legs and arms ached, and my head throbbed. I closed the windows, turned the air conditioning fan to max, and took a deep breath, and again, and again. The physical exertion of the visit was minimal, but the emotional workout delivered real physical effects. I was angry that David Harvard imprisoned and took advantage of Louisa for 20 years. I wanted to purge every segment of every chromosome inherited from him. I was angry that he profited from the forced removal of the indigenous people from their land. I was angry that great grandmother Amelia and her siblings were born into slavery, yet I was beyond thankful they survived to see freedom and to thrive in spite of their early circumstances.

I was angry with myself for admiring the restoration of the house David built and the grounds his hateful wife landscaped so artfully. I was thankful to have the chance to see with my own eyes and touch with my own hands the place my ancestors called home, that they built from a true wilderness. All of this was a part of me—the bad as well as the good—but I reckoned it did not define me. I was much more than the actions and ideas of these people, but I existed because of them, and for that I would always be grateful.

I told Frances that evening of all I had seen and she smiled knowingly, having seen it many times herself. "Have you ever been inside?" I asked. "Well, no." she answered quizzically. Of course, she had never been inside. No one in our family had since Louisa left with her youngest ones in 1865. We dined with our second cousin Cecil, grandson of William and Amelia's youngest son Thomas. We talked about the big picnic the following afternoon and about how special it would be if we could arrange a showing of Laurens Hill. As it happened, Cecil's niece Tiffany was a licensed realtor. Within 24 hours the appointment had been set and word spread among everyone attending the reunion.

About 30 of my closest, newest cousins showed up at 5:00 p. m. to set foot in the place only Amelia had been allowed before and until emancipation. The side door opened into a dining room. A butler's pantry and kitchen, which was a subsequent addition to the original structure, were to the left. A parlor and living room were to the right. The ceilings were 12 feet high, baseboards at least 12 inches tall with wide-plank dark wood floors throughout the first level. We all wandered quietly through the magnificent home reverently communing with the lives that created and once sustained it, and grateful for those who lovingly restored it in the following century.

I looked out of the upstairs bedroom window and felt Amelia's presence. Her eyes became mine as the wavy antique glass revealed her father, half-brothers Quinn and William and several hands working in the green fields below. Missy sat in a chair in front of the window playing with a doll as Amelia stood behind brushing and braiding her half-sister's chestnut hair. I heard Louisa's voice in the front yard calling for little Reuben and Tobe to fetch eggs from the coop. I walked from the bedroom into the main hallway and opened the double doors and screens leading to the balcony overlooking the front porch. The wide hallway sucked a warm breeze through the cypress trees grown high above the roofline. Cousin Terrance and I stood where David must have stood many times overseeing his estate. We looked down at box hedges and up through the cedars, across the road to the cemetery where David was buried, and we inhaled the decades and filled our lungs with humility and gratitude to have made it as far as we had—and to have been able to return in freedom, strength and love.

We strode the grounds and peered into the 5-person outhouse. It was obviously a reproduction, but it was a very curious effect. It offered 5 seats side by side with a smaller one farthest right for the youngest (white) family member. I wondered if there were times when all 5 of them sat astride, discussing the day's events as they relieved themselves. I chuckled as I imagined Louisa bolting the door shut from the outside and shouting, "Run, chirrens! Run!" The only other outhouse I had ever seen was at my great grandmother's home in Mississippi. It had only one seat and her family took turns when duty called. There was nothing left of the slave quarters; however, an irregular area including a large ditch about 50 yards behind the big house seemed to be a logical location for them.

As I walked around the ditch, I imagined it may have been used as the emptying place for the planter's outhouse and a latrine for his slaves. We chatted about pooling our money to make an offer on the $400,000, 10-acre property, but how would we structure it, how would it be managed and sustained? This was too much to decide in the remaining days of the reunion, but it would not be forgotten.

Saturday morning was glorious. The day's agenda included a meeting with Pastor Gregory Jones of Laurens Hill Baptist Church as well as a survey of the Harvard Family Cemetery across the road from Laurens Hill. I waded through the tall grass of the field

210

having been warned of the venomous snakes. If any observers had been present, they would surely have found my stomping and whooping noises to warn and dispel critters as frightening and perhaps worthy of professional therapeutic assistance. I made as much noise as possible as I trudged through the hip-high weeds to arrive at the obelisk inscribed with the name David Harvard.

*David Harvard Born in Washington County, Ga. May 7, 1809; And fell asleep in Jesus at this residence at Laurens Hill, GA., Oct. 29, 1865. He united with the Baptist Church at Rockey Creek 2nd Lord's day, Sept 1837 of which he was ordained Deacon. He aided in the Constitution of Laurens Hill Church Oct 8, 1848 at which he was a Pillar till the day of his DEATH.*

"My, oh my," I sighed. What a "pillar" of Christianity he was to have warranted the carving of these words in stone for generations to admire. I photographed each side of the obelisk erected to his memory.

*He is joined with the happy throng of cherub and seraphim ... And he sees as he looks o'er the regions of peace The souls that escaped from this world of distress And his is the joy no tongue can express For he knows no sorrow there ... He was an honored member of the Cool Spring Lodge for years.*

Years later I discovered meeting minutes of the first Laurens Hill Baptist Church co-founded and constructed by David. In his own hand and later in that of his son Quinn, the words reflect a civility and respect for personhood in stark contrast to the institution of slavery. Slaves are referred to as "Colored Servants." Louisa is called "Sister Louiza." The ability of a man as acquainted with the Holy Bible as he to condone and profit from the dehumanization of those called his sisters and brothers, is a quandary I cannot claim to have satisfactorily resolved.

The only answer that seems probable is one that I cringe to accept. Benevolence may have been the cruelest weapon. David Harvard viewed himself as something of a savior to Louisa. By purchasing her for his own, he prevented her and her children from a far harsher existence in the possession of men of "lesser character." Bristling at the thought of this paternalistic subordination, I reluctantly understood how even the idea of a better life could be stolen from enslaved people. Instilling and reinforcing the notion that their lives are "good" and their needs are met, many lost not only the desire to be free, but the very concept and meaning of freedom. The insidious usurpation of individuality and self-agency through benevolence did more to keep people in servitude long past emancipation than any threat of violence ever could. One who is born free, as Louisa was, can never forget.

The original site of the first Laurens Hill Baptist church was a half mile southwest of the home on Blackshear Ferry Trail (now GA Hwy 26) where it crosses Rocky Creek. In the mid-19th century, Baptist churches were often built on the banks of streams and creeks to facilitate baptisms by immersion in water.

# CHAPTER TWENTY-NINE

---

## BEASLEY AND MOODY BRANTLEYS

The ability to connect living African-Americans to their enslaved ancestors is rare. Connecting them to the white men who were their captors as well as progenitors is virtually impossible without DNA. Before 1870, the given names splinter into shards of spelling variations. Surnames that lend clues in the present fade into the morass of the middle passage by 1850. Jenia Brantley, my biological paternal grandfather known as J. B., was the son of Simeon Brantley and Mollie Wright. The paper trail ends at the 1870 census with 18-year-old Simeon and 11 siblings in the home of their parents John (Jack) and Charlotte.

According to family lore, Simeon's wife Mollie Wright was born to a slave woman who was "hired out" to a man named Beasley. After Mollie was born, her mother was shunned by the other blacks in the community because she was open and not ashamed of being

Ronald G. Levi Jr.

with a white man. That was surprising for me to hear. Rather than the perspective of a white man ashamed to have known intimacy with an enslaved woman, cultural norms within the black community predicted that she should have been ashamed of being known to associate with a white man. When people saw Mollie's mother walking down the road, they would cross over to the other side to avoid passing next to her. Beasley owned the local grocery in Dublin, which allowed him to provide for his families. The number of my Beasley descendant DNA matches (63) confirms that Mollie was indeed the daughter of a Beasley male. Each one of us can be traced back to James and Mary Beasley (nee Cropley), immigrants from England circa 1715. The dates and proximity as well as other DNA matches to Brinsons, Mikells and Deals of Bulloch County make David Beasley, son of Thomas Beasley and Pharaby Brinson, the strongest candidate for Mollie's father.

David was born in 1801. He was a tax collector, Ordinary (now known as Probate Judge), and a state legislator. He signed many marriage records of the time CCOBC – Clerk Court Ordinary Bulloch County. The minutes of the Inferior Court on December 5, 1864 reveal that "This being the day appointed by law for holding the Court of Ordinary of said county. But the Yankees were here in Statesboro and burned the courthouse and there was no court held." David, the Ordinary, and my second great grandfather "was aware of the approach of Sherman's Army, and had heard that the soldiers were burning both private homes and public buildings...(he) had the Bulloch County records removed from the courthouse and concealed near his home where they remained until the danger had passed."[8]

Mollie's maiden name, Wright, can't be verified in public documents of the time, however, DNA matches support an argument that her mother may have been a daughter of John

[8] The True Story of the Bulloch County Courthouse, 2004, Parrish Blitch, Bulloch County Historical Publications, Bulloch County Historical Society Collection, page 4.
214

Benjamin Wright of Washington County. Instead of taking the surname of her Beasley father, she took the surname of her enslaved mulatto mother. Wright's home is one of the oldest houses in South Georgia. The wealthy landowner who "had the fifth largest number of slaves in the state" was also a legislator. He's best remembered as the namesake of Wrightsville, as he gave $1000 toward the founding of a new town that would become the seat of Johnson County, established in 1866.

> The house is vernacular in style, and the somewhat unusual second floor with its shuttered windows was used for storage. The house has apparently never been painted, either. In his seminal Architecture of Middle Georgia: The Oconee Area, John Linley noted in 1972: "Evidently, Mr. Wright never forsook his modest way of living: the house is still simple and sturdy, and far from pretentious." Linley also noted that slave cabins were still scattered on the property in 1972."[9]

The most challenging mystery to solve is the pedigree of great grandfather Simeon. Knowing from the first Y-DNA test I took that my patrilineal line is African, I can infer that the name Brantley did not come from Jack's father. Interestingly, however, we present-day Brantleys have DNA matches who are descendants of John and Hannah Brantley (nee Harper). The names Larkin and Moody match these Brantleys while they do not match the Lowthers, Harvards, and Hagans of J. B.'s wife Gertrude. Nor do they match the Beasleys of Mollie Wright. That leaves only the branch of Simeon's mother, Charlotte Hart, wife of Jack Brantley.

Ken Brantley, founder and president of the Brantley Association of America, is the foremost expert on the surname and patrilineal

---

[9] https://vanishingsouthgeorgia.com/2012/08/01/john-b-wright-house-circa-1799-johnson-county/

origins. Ken was able to locate in the minutes of the Williams Creek Church of Warren County Georgia a tantalizing connection. On March 19, 1814

> *"The Church met in conference agreeable to appointment. Brother Brantley's Charlotia a woman of colour, came forward and made an acknowledgment, that she had acted very wrong at a certain time when accused wrongfully & struck one of her fellow servants for which she appeared to be very sorry & was continued in fellowship."*

I find it fascinating and confounding that in church minutes of the early and mid-19th century, slaves are referred to as servants, brothers and sisters. People who were not only denied inalienable rights but their very personhood, deemed chattel—not fully human—were called *brother* and *sister* on Sundays at least in this part of middle Georgia. This was not unique to Wrightsville. The same practice is found in the minutes of the early Laurens Hill Baptist Church in Laurens County.

The years, ages, and locations of these people considering the context of DNA matches, makes a compelling case that Simeon's mother Charlotte was the daughter of "Brother Brantley's Charlotia." Charlotte's father was Phillip Brantley died in Wilkes County May 12, 1824. With Charlotte's maternity decided with as much certainty as might ever be possible, I looked to the identity of her father. I can be certain that our family's 102 Moody matches on Simeon Brantley's branch are not his father's father's limb. They are either his father's mother's people or they are his mother Charlotte's father's relatives. Narrowing down the candidates to years and location, all matches point to Jesse Isaac Moody II as the father of Charlotte Hart. Not quite a smoking gun, I concede, however, as circumstantial evidence goes, this is a satisfactory hypothesis until proven otherwise.

# Chapter Thirty

--------~⌒~--------

## The Big Ditch

After visiting the Harvard Family Cemetery across the street from Laurens Hill, I ventured a quarter mile southeast on Laurens Hill Church Rd., to an unpaved access road on the left. From that point I drove a quarter mile northeast to a 1-acre grove of trees in the middle of a large clearing. Densely overgrown with thorny vines, tall weeds and branches, the innermost regions were impenetrable. Blue paint on the largest perimeter trees signaled the presence of a burial ground. The Laurens Hill Church Cemetery is the presumed resting place of some of the Harvard slaves and their descendants. Cousin Frances explained that the Harvards offered a spot in their family plot to Amelia; however, when the time came, she was clear that she wanted to be buried with her husband William in the Laurens Hill Cemetery.

Ronald G. Levi Jr.

When Frances and I visited in 2018, Great Grandmother Amelia had been resting peacefully for 65 years. Although the older graves may have been unmarked or marked with materials reclaimed by nature and time, Amelia's remains were transported from Detroit back to Georgia in 1952, and there should be a durable, permanent marker of some type. If there is such a marker, it is impossible to discern in all that overgrowth. I determined that day that I would return and find a way to clear that vegetation, identify the graves and in doing so pay my respects to those ancestors.

On the same trip, I caught up with Cousin Jackie, who took me to see the *Big Ditch*. Jackie's maternal second great grandparents William and Amelia are my great grandparents. In addition to Lowthers, her mother's family also includes Kimbers, and Roziers to whom I am not genetically related. Compared to the Laurens Hill Cemetery, the Ditch is well-maintained. In fact, if the names were at all representative of the conditions, they would be swapped. Laurens Hill Cemetery looks like a ditch and the Big Ditch looks like a cemetery. The grass is trimmed and the stones are all visible and legible.

I read the inscriptions for Jackie's great grandfather Thomas Loyal Lowther, my grandmother Gertrude's youngest brother. His wife Amanda Kimbers is nearby as are several Roziers, ancestors of Thomas Jr's wife, Ruby. The stones are in remarkable condition considering the dates of death. I consider the possibility that the stones were erected years after the interments. If Mandy Hall's stone was truly placed in 1932, then surely my great grandmother Amelia had one in 1952. With all the talk these days of preserving monuments of the past, headstones and other grave markers are among the most valuable and worthy of care for genealogists.

Jackie and I swept dirt away from the stones and tidied the graves of our relatives as we walked and got acquainted with one another on that glorious summer's day. I looked uphill over my left
218

shoulder where I saw many more graves that were more prominently placed in front of and higher than the those we tended. "What's that?" I asked Jackie, pointing to the rows of erect head stones. "That's the Stanley Cemetery—for the white folks," she answered. "Hmm, a cemetery within a cemetery," I pondered. The graves of the slaves and their descendants were not so much hidden from the Stanley plots as they were subordinately oriented. As we walked up the hill toward the Stanleys, Jackie explained how our family now owned all of the surrounding land. The birds sang and the sun warmed our faces as we recognized the unspoken irony. In a manner of speaking we now owned the people who once owned us. I came upon a large stone expertly engraved with a name I recognized—Major Rollin A. Stanley Sr., Co A, 3 GA Regt, CSA, June 30, 1830 – March 14, 1893. "Where have I seen that name?" I pulled out my iPhone, opened the Ancestry app, and typed in the name. "Whoa, Rollin was the husband of Martha Rebecca Lowther, my second great aunt!" Martha is the white half-sister of my black great grandfather William Lowther and daughter of my white second great grandfather John Lowther. There she was, lying next to her husband in a place called the *Ditch*. As I walked along the rows of stones, I recognized so many of the names. When I entered the cemetery, I thought only of my relation to the descendants of the enslaved ancestors. As we left, I read the sign that I had overlooked on the way in.

*Stanley Cemetery, also known as "The Ditch", was begun by James Stanley II, born Jan. 23, 1771 and his wife Leah Fordham, born Sept. 6, 1771, who came to Laurens County, Georgia from Jones County, North Carolina about 1811. This is one of the oldest private cemeteries in the state still in use. Here sleep six or more generations of kith and kin; the slaves and their descendants in an adjoining plot.*

That's the kind of marker we need on the Harvard and Laurens Hill Church Cemeteries, I noted, cast aluminum, bold white letters on a black background. As a black man, as an American who believes our founding principles are sound if faithfully applied to all citizens, I believe it is in our collective best interests to remove any impediment to our assured success. Monuments to crimes of the past, to those who fought against our union are such impediments. I do, however, appreciate all efforts to preserve our history—that of which we are proud as well as that which blemishes or shames us into action. Monuments to such people and events belong in cemeteries and museums, not as sentinels in halls of government or entrances to places of community and progress such as schools, libraries and parks. It makes sense to have a monument of Robert E. Lee at his tomb. It makes sense that such a monument would have symbols and imagery of his life. It does not make sense to have a monument to him in front of a city hall or state capitol building. I would like to see all monuments to racist, Confederate, or fascist ideals removed from public places, but I do not think they should be destroyed. They have artistic and historical value if curated objectively and accurately.

I came to this conclusion viewing the obelisk of David Harvard at Laurens Hill and of John Lowther at the Old Dublin Cemetery. Although none of my second great grandfathers served in the armies of the South, and their counties were among those in Georgia who voted not to secede, they enslaved my second great grandmothers and their own children. They were also complicit in the obliteration of records, names, languages and customs of the families of those women. As much as I abhor celebrating their lives, I am grateful to be able to see evidence of their existence. Studying their headstones and reading the inscriptions deepens my connection to this land and to the story of this nation. The enduring physical records of their existence also prove the existence of those they discounted, those non-persons they fathered, and of myself.

Genetic Genealogy is so much more than building trees from publicly available documents, it is a stamp of authenticity affirming those documents *and* it is an unquenchable cyborg seeking new nodes to assimilate. Resistance is futile. If an Ancestry tree is accurate and connected to the owner's DNA results, the Borg connects matches mathematically and prompts the owner to accept or reject the assimilation into the tree. Of the 142 Lowther DNA matches I have since verified, one close connection to the Ditch stands out. About one year after I stood at the graves of Rollin Stanley and his wife Martha Lowther with Cousin Jackie, a familiar name appeared in my DNA matches— Stanley. As people continue to test their DNA, the match lists of their relatives continue to grow. Because my tree was accurate, Ancestry (the *Borg*) was able to suggest that Martha Stanley is my third cousin (we share a set of second great grandparents).

Careful genealogy dictates confirmation from multiple sources, and sure enough, public records such as census, birth, marriage and death records confirm that Martha is the great granddaughter of Rollin Stanley and Martha Lowther. She is the second great granddaughter of John Lowther and his wife Eliza Coyl. I am the second great grandson of the same John Lowther and his servant Sarah from Africa. Martha Stanley and I, therefore, are half third cousins. In this way, DNA validates both the documented and undocumented history of our family and our world. It fills in many gaps. From my research and the DNA matches piling up on Ancestry, I concluded the Ditch was a lot more kin than kith.

# PART III

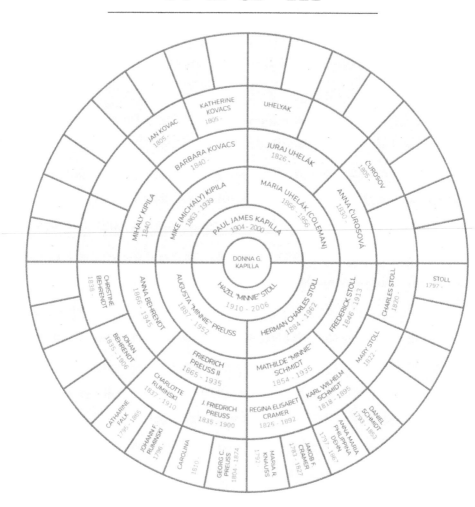

*Figure 3 Biological Maternal Family – 6 Generations (1795 - 2007)*

# CHAPTER THIRTY-ONE

## CONFIRMATION

A picture of my maternal relations was beginning to emerge in Linny's mirror tree. AnnaMay13x matched a couple of others who did not match A.S. and FRANCESSTEPHENS140. These were clearly two different lines and one was white and the other was multi-racial or black. One was Eastern European and the other was a mixture of African-American and British/Irish ancestry. AnnaMay13x and M.U. both showed as my second cousins once removed on the Eastern European side; however, they were not related to one another. This could only mean that one of them was my birth mother's paternal second cousin and the other was her maternal second cousin. Both of them made their family trees public—visible to their respective DNA matches. Linny quickly triangulated a connection between the two. The great grandfather of AnnaMay13x was Joseph Kapilla, the brother of Paul Kapilla who married Hazel Stoll. M.U. (Myrna) was the granddaughter of Mattie Stoll, aunt of Hazel. She was easy to find on Facebook.

The proud wife and grandmother was my first contact on my maternal side, and she was surprisingly open and happy to correspond. A member of the Latter Day Saints, Myrna already had a complete tree of her family and she printed a report and put it in the mail to me. Once I plugged the names into my tree, I had a complete view of my grandmother Hazel's family. By using public records, Linny made quick work of finding the marriage of Hazel Stoll and Paul Kapilla. Based on genetic distances and shared DNA matches, it was clear that Hazel and Paul were my genetic maternal grandparents. To find my mother, we only had to identify the children of Hazel and Paul and establish their locations and relationships at the time of my birth. Census records and obituaries are easily available online. Google and Facebook are invaluable tools as well. Using every method available, it was clear that Hazel and Paul had 3 daughters and 1 son. My haplogroup was proof that my father and his forefathers were of African origin, so that eliminated the Kapilla's son David immediately. That meant that 1 of their 3 daughters—Donna, Doris, or Janet had to be my biological mother.

The hints that Ancestry provided led to census records, obituaries and newspaper articles indicating that Doris had a son in April of 1964. I was born in October, so she could not have been my mother. Paul and Hazel's daughter Janet gave birth to a daughter in June of 1964. That eliminated her as well, leaving only Donna. I worried that I might find yet another child born to her in that year which excluded my existence. As plain and clear as the evidence was, I continued to dig for contradictions. In a time and place when it has become common to accept views and opinions that support our own biases, I refused to leave any stone unturned, especially if there were any chance of error. In the face of all evidence that Donna was the only possible remaining candidate, I still needed proof positive. Such proof was only possible if she or a descendant of hers were living and willing to test.

Donna died in 2007. I missed the opportunity to meet my birth mother by 8 years, but her sisters were still living and her obituary confirmed that she had one child—a daughter! I had a big sister? Five years older than I, I hoped that Susan would be willing to test. I dropped another c-note to order a test for whichever of them would say yes first. If she or our Aunts Doris or Janet were willing, it would confirm definitively that Donna was my biological mother.

From the tree of Donna's family that was emerging, we were able to identify many if not all of the children and grandchildren of Doris and Janet. Doris had a Facebook account and her friends were visible. It was easy to match the names of many of them with the obituaries of Hazel and Donna. Janet's daughter Rachelle was also on Facebook. My first contact was Doris's granddaughter Samantha who was very cordial and appropriately curious. She confirmed via Instant Messenger that Doris was her grandmother and she agreed to ask Doris if she would mind speaking with me.

In retrospect this was not the best approach to take. I believe that surprising people—showing up on their doorsteps unannounced—is impolite and inappropriate. In the case of Aunt Doris, however, it might have yielded better results for me. Perhaps she would have been so shocked by the truth staring her in the face, she would have immediately seen her sister and parents in my likeness and been relieved to unburden herself of long-kept secrets. Approaching through her granddaughter, however, gave her time to think of myriad outcomes.

Doris forbade her children and grandchildren from corresponding with me. Samantha apologized that she would not be allowed to speak with me further. She was so sweet and gentle about it that I certainly couldn't hold anything against an obedient granddaughter. The curt response from Doris only made me more certain and determined. Why would she not want to speak with me and offer the simple courtesy of telling me what she knew? Clearly she knew something. I imagined that the revelation only refreshed painful memories she thought had been put to rest long ago. Whether 50 years ago when Donna left me at the hospital or 8 years ago when Donna died, perhaps Doris thought she had moved on from the trauma Donna put her through by confiding in her. Maybe speaking with me would open old wounds, or maybe she thought I was looking for some sort of inheritance—to contest the disposition of Donna's estate. I was getting tired, tired of conjuring up hypothesis after futile hypothesis. In every message, email and phone call, I made sure that each person understood at the very outset that I was only interested in the truth of my origin. I was not interested in money, property or in disrupting anyone's relationships. I just wanted to know.

Google and fee-services to which Emmilie and Linny subscribed had mailing addresses, phone numbers and email addresses for everyone. Yes, *everyone*. If you have ever had an address or phone number, your privacy is an apparition. Anyone willing to pay a few dollars can find out every address, phone number, email and court case related to you in a matter of minutes. Emmilie shared every phone number and address ever associated with Donna, Doris, and Janet, and I began my measured campaign of infiltration. The myriad accounts of heartache and failure published in Foundling Finders informed a more cautious, circuitous approach. I considered that these women had families with whom they had never shared the truth of my existence. One of them had borne the child of a black man. My assumptions of their feelings and motives were based only on my Levi and Jamerson experiences—biases of lives in the Jim Crow South. Black children born to white women were a shame, to be hidden and denied.

I connected with Susan's daughter Amber via Facebook also. A series of instant messages and phone calls ensued. My adult nieces questioned the reliability of the tests, but Amber was most open to learning and communicating.

Susan (12/19/2015, Facebook IM)

*Hi, Susan. I'm doing some family tree research. I'm related to the Stolls and Kapillas. Is Janet your aunt?*

Within days I was on the phone talking with my half-sister about her life and our mother. Amazingly she verbally expressed the thoughts I'd kept only to myself for 50 years, "I always felt I had a sibling somewhere in the world." I explained that I had purchased a test and that if she was willing, we could meet in a public place of her choosing. She would spit in the tube, I would send it in and share the results with her. She agreed and we set the date for lunch at the National Coney Island in Roseville. Roseville is in the heart of Macomb County, and Macomb County, Michigan is solidly red Trump country. Seeing her sitting across the table from me was incredible, puzzling, funny, amazing, and gratifying all at once. I already knew that she was my half-sister.

The DNA test I bought for her was only to give her and her children the proof of what pure deductive reasoning had already sufficiently proven to me. I studied her face and hands looking for a resemblance. Her forehead and hairline were similar. But her hair was blond. Her eyes were blue. When I imagined a sibling as a child, I never considered the reality of sharing only one parent. She was not as tall as I am, but I never expected her to be a six-footer. We talked about our children and she told me a little about our mother. Susan's father was a Greek immigrant. She confided that it was difficult for her to learn English as fast as other children because her dad spoke Greek at home. She didn't look very Greek to me, but I didn't look very white to me, so confidence in my own deductive powers was waning fast. She told me that Donna was tall and that she was smart. "She graduated from high school when she was 16," Susan announced. I graduated from high school when I was 16! Yeah, this was really happening. Susan had 4 daughters and several grandchildren. I had 3 sons and no grandchildren yet. Our grandparents had 3 girls and a boy. Our great grandparents had 8 boys. My paternal grandparents had 3 boys. This generational gender oscillation was tantalizing. It was a pleasant first meeting, she spat in the tube, we hugged and I took it straight to the post office.

A few weeks after my meeting with my paternal cousins, the Brantleys and Frances, I received an email that Susan's AncestryDNA results were in. Linny, Emmilie and I communicated via Facebook Instant Messenger daily. "'Predicted relationship: Close Family-1st Cousin.' What does 'close family' mean?" I asked. Mine was one of many foundling cases Linny had worked and solved. She had long ago committed to memory the ranges of centimorgans corresponding to each type of relationship. The newly initiated referred to a chart—a cheat sheet to make the determination, but I didn't yet trust my interpretation of that tool. "Half-siblings!" Linny cheered "Congratulations!" She giggled as excitedly as I did. This was the only proof I needed. There was no need to test Donna's sisters: the answer was irrefutable. It didn't tell me how she met my father or anything more about her life, but I hoped that the news would encourage Susan to open up and share details that I certainly would not be getting from Aunt Doris.

I shared the results electronically with my sister and her daughters. The initial skepticism dissipated as I gave them time to make calls to Ancestry, verify that I was indeed interpreting the results correctly, and that they were truly correct and reliable. I encouraged them to ask health professionals they trusted, their physicians and pediatricians. Susan began sharing more very quickly. The 2016 election threatened to throw the entire collaboration into chaos, however. I found it hard to ignore my niece's Facebook posts supporting baseless conspiracies, dog-whistle racism, and grotesque misogyny of the Trump campaign. It struck and remained on a very particular nerve of mine.

As Susan described my mother's life and the abuse she and her mother experienced from her father, it echoed the memories of my own mother's abuse. The sympathy I had for them all was matched only by the anger I had toward those men and toward myself for being powerless to prevent it. What is it with men who intentionally hurt women and use them as tools for personal gratification or enrichment? The faceless, nameless women who were slaves of my white second great grandfathers in Georgia cried out to me. My mom, my birth mother, and my half-sister were victims who, although they appeared free, were similarly captive to men who abused them physically and or emotionally. This painful and unsettling commonality could only be addressed through prayer, forgiveness and rededication to ensure that it would not be allowed to continue in my life or those of my sons.

Susan didn't know how her parents met other than her dad was a bus driver and her mom worked at Great Scott grocery. From many short conversations over the course of several weeks with my sister and 2 of her daughters, a composite, if obscure, picture of her father emerged. He was reviled in the community, Susan believed it was because of his Greek heritage. He built a house with his own hands and neighbors burned it to the ground. Susan was taunted and bullied because she was different—not for the color of her skin, but because of how she spoke. Today Macomb County is not known for its inclusivity or diversity, hence its affinity for Trump; however, I was not aware of any particular bias towards Greeks in the 1960s.

Greeks began arriving in Detroit in the 1890s. Henry Ford's $5 per day pay ratcheted up the number of Greeks to tens of thousands by 1930. A quick check of the Social Security Applications and Claims Index on Ancestry showed that Alex was born in 1929. He was a full 10 years older than Donna. His father was born in Greece, but Alex Jr. was born in Ann Arbor. It didn't feel right that a kid born in Ann Arbor to a Greek immigrant would grow into manhood and revert to speaking only Greek in the home of his American wife and daughter. Susan attributed her difficulty in learning English to this fact, however.

A passenger list of the Olympia arriving in New York on April 22, 1955 included the name of an Alexious Gikas born about 1929 from Piraeus, Greece. Census enumerations of 1930 and 1940 show an Alex Giokas born 1929 in Michigan living in Macomb County. Assuming a person cannot be born in 2 different countries in the same year, I thought it reasonable to disregard the immigration record which also contained a spelling variation of the surname and accept the census records as fact. What kind of game was this man running on my mother? Did the American Giokas assume the identity of the Greek immigrant Gikas? My imagination spiraled. What happened to the one who arrived in New York in 1955?

Sonny Bono, Jack Van Impe, Wayne Dyer, Bill Bonds, Jerry Hodak... all of these national and local celebrities attended Denby High School in Detroit about the same time as Donna. Perhaps they even rode the same bus in 1956 when the 16 year old looked forward to graduation as one of the youngest in her class. Maybe they made small talk with the dark-haired driver whose ready smile greeted them every morning when they boarded the Gratiot bus for school or when he waited a few extra minutes before pulling off when they were running late. How could they have known the same bus driver who picked them up every day and extended so many kindnesses was laying an inescapable trap for one of their own? He wasn't an old "square" like their parents; he was only a few years older than they were. He was already working a real job making real money while they were in high school. He was "connected." He had cool stuff and would sometimes give them brand new music records—45s as they were called then. Kids were used to 10-inch vinyl discs that spun at 78 revolutions per minute, but smaller 7-inch discs spinning at 45 rpms could hold a single hit on each side.

As usual Donna boarded the bus Alex was driving January 26, 1956. They had only returned from Christmas break a few weeks earlier, and she had noticed his eyes on her in the rearview mirror above. She didn't think he ever saw her looking back, but this morning he shyly smiled as she boarded and handed her a flat, brown paper package tied with red shiny ribbon. Feeling confused, embarrassed, and flattered, she took it quickly and dropped it in her bag. As she took her seat alone toward the middle of the bus in front of the rear exit on the right side, she knew he would be able to see her clearly.

Assured that no one noticed the exchange, she reached into her bag and removed the ribbon carefully in case the gift was something horrid and inappropriate. She unfolded the single sheet of paper and saw immediately the black vinyl center with Nipper the terrier and the Edison Bell cylinder phonograph. "RCA Victor" "The Finest Record Ever Made" emblazoned in maroon on the tan paper sleeve. She almost missed her bus stop for school as she read the title of the song, "Heartbreak Hotel" by Elvis Presley. The sixteen-year-old floated off the bus and through the rest of her day. Sonny, Jack, Wayne, Bill and Jerry never had a chance with her. From that moment, she never had a chance either.

How else can a son reconcile the abuse of a woman described by her daughter and children as chained to a bed and beaten, and followed by a "black body guard" as she collected rent from income properties or a pizza parlor she owned? She was never allowed to be alone. I discovered there's never any reconciliation. There is only forgiveness. Our destructive, selfish actions can never be reconciled. But repentance and forgiveness are the only ways to clarity and freedom. I could nourish the anger and

231

resentment, or I could starve it. I chose the latter and channeled my effort into building relationships with my biological relatives and putting the ugly past behind us as much as possible.

Susan and 3 of her daughters opened up and began to share more about their experiences. I attended the birthday parties of my grand-nieces and enjoyed spending time with them all. One niece, however, remained reluctant. She seemed to have had an especially close relationship with her grandmother. Perhaps it was idealized. I believe she could not accept the love I offered because I represented not only an imperfection but an ugly truth about her grandmother that could not coexist with her memories of her. Her grandmother was not perfect, she was a victim, or even more difficult to accept, she may have been voluntarily complicit.

# CHAPTER THIRTY-TWO

꒰ ꒦ ꒷

## NOT THE DADDY

In addition to public records and obituaries, cemetery records are another excellent way to learn about the lives of our forebears, especially those who were born after 1940. There were no online records of Donna's burial. Susan attended our mother's funeral. She agonized that Donna's sisters took all of her possessions and left Susan with nothing. Not being able to speak with Doris, I could only hope to meet with Janet someday to get some sense of her understanding. The relationships in this family, I was discovering, were extremely fractious and isolated. Susan knew the names of some of her first cousins, but not all of them.

This was very different from my own experience. I knew the names of all of my adoptive first cousins growing up, and I even knew some of their birthdays. We played together often, and I was comfortable around all of my aunts and uncles. I sensed a resentment in Susan but could not ascertain the source of the estrangement. Susan admitted that her father kept her and her mother apart from her aunts and cousins. My nieces confided that family members (presumably our aunts) tried unsuccessfully to intervene and "get Donna out." She could not or would not say why they failed. Did Donna want to stay in the relationship, was she threatened physically, or was she afraid for the safety of her daughter?

There was another reason Susan believed me when I first contacted her. When she was 5 years old, she said, Donna left home for "a long time." It took months before her dad was able to "bring her back." Susan was born in 1959. She was 5 in the year I was born, 1964. So there it was. When she began to show, Donna escaped. I believe that she escaped to protect both of us from violence, and that she certainly could not keep the child of a colored man in the home of her *Greek* abusive husband.

I could see it clearly now. Before I discovered that David was my father, I imagined that his brother, Rev. Joseph Brantley may have been. The abused, frightened woman sought advice and refuge. Completely without intent she fell into the strong arms of a kind, generous sympathetic, man of the cloth. She visited him as often as she could steal away from her husband and daughter. She discussed ways of leaving him and helplessly threw herself on the mercy of a man who was weakened and unable to resist giving her and himself a moment of true compassion and love. The aftermath was difficult for them both. He knew in his heart that he should have resisted the temptation and that this must be ended immediately. He would repent and seek God's forgiveness, but he would never tell a soul, especially not his wife. Donna begged him to help her. He apologized profusely and gave her the names and phone numbers of Lutheran social workers who might be able to help, but he could not see her again. The temptation and danger were far too great. He would not risk his salvation or his livelihood again.

Donna didn't contact the social workers as advised, but she did tell her sister Doris when she discovered that she was pregnant. She would not reveal the pastor's name or contact him ever again as he requested, but she did tell her Aunt Grace who invited her to stay with her and her husband Dr. Cook when the time came. Aunt Grace took Donna to Saratoga hospital on October 5th and I made my arrival. All the pieces fit neatly together. Douglas, Michael and Pam were my paternal half-siblings, I concluded— incorrectly.

Michael's DNA test proved the fallacy of this idea and many others I concocted.. Beyond any doubt Michael's results revealed definitively that he (and Doug and Pam) were my first cousins – not my half siblings. Their father Rev. Dr. Joseph Brantley was not my father, he was my uncle. His brother David and Donna were my biological parents with certainty. I had my answer. That's all I asked for, and maybe that would have to be more than enough.

I continued to receive notifications of DNA matches daily and Linny and I kept fitting my third and fourth cousin matches into my tree. Those who matched Susan were obviously on my maternal side. All the others were paternal. It started getting easier for me to see the connections. Trees with Slovakian and German branches were almost, though not always, maternal cousins. Similarly trees with many generations in Southern states such as Georgia, South Carolina and Virginia were paternal. Many of them had detailed trees and we looked for common names and used the public records to identify prior or later generations wherever possible until a common name appeared—my nexus.

Susan invited me to visit the cemetery where her dad and our mother were buried. She may have told me previously that our mom was cremated, but I didn't know that her ashes were buried in the same cemetery as her first husband. That seemed very strange to me because she remarried after Alex died in 1978. Why would anyone bury her anywhere near the man who treated her so wretchedly? As the weekend of the visit approached, I also began to examine Susan's DNA matches. I recalled a story she shared with me not many weeks after our relationship was first confirmed that one of her daughters took some sort of DNA or genetic test in Tennessee that identified her ethnic heritage as Eastern European and British. Susan said she was surprised that there was no mention of Greek ancestry in her daughter's results.

Those who matched Susan, but did not match me were necessarily her paternal matches. At such close genetic distance (half-siblings) everyone who matched us both was very easy to segregate. Interestingly her paternal matches were largely of British and Irish descent. I was seeing names such as Franklin, Evans, Rowell, and West. These people were from Michigan, Missouri, Illinois, Ohio and Connecticut, but none were Greek. She had about three or four second and third cousin matches that enabled me to build a complete tree leading to one of the sons of George and Aris Rowell Franklin as Susan's biological father. Patrick and Peter had 4 sisters. In order to determine which of the 2 males was her father, we'd have to test one or the other. Their sisters would all resolve as aunts to Susan. One brother would be revealed as an uncle and the other as father.

As with my own tree, I scoured Google and Facebook and a few other sites for information on these close matches and my mouth formed the word *wow* as I viewed photos of Tessa Rowell and Carla Friend. Just as the photo of my paternal uncle Joseph stunned me, these women could have passed for sisters of Susan. She looked more like their sister than she did mine, yet she was genetically more closely related to me. I messaged a couple of the most active users of the social media platform and shared my findings and questions and waited for a response.

As I drove to the cemetery Saturday knowing that her biological father was not the man buried there, I felt quite ambivalent. I was relieved that she shared no biology with the man who had controlled our mother's actions. I remained saddened that our mother was buried with him. If it were possible to exhume her urn and move it elsewhere, I was determined to make that happen. It was a warm sunny summer afternoon as I pulled up the path and parked behind Susan's vehicle. She and one of my grand-nieces were already out walking and tidying around the headstones. We hugged and she showed me the inscription in the bottom left corner of the granite stone originally intended for only Alex.

Susan explained that Donna's ashes were given to her second husband when she died, and that Susan had nothing of hers except a few pictures. She paid to have our mother's name and dates of birth and death inscribed on her father's stone so that she could remember them both. My heart was in pieces. This poor child, my big sister, in spite of all that she had witnessed, much of which I am certain she had repressed or become unable to verbalize, still chose to honor and remember both of her parents in this way. I couldn't possibly tell her that this man wasn't her father. Here I stood at the grave of a man unrelated to either of us with my mother's inscription and her whereabouts completely unknown.

# CHAPTER THIRTY-THREE

---

## ANSWERED

How could I tell Susan that man whose grave she had been visiting for 30 years was not her biological father? I certainly couldn't just drop that on her, but maybe I could suggest the possibility. I recalled the confusion she expressed about her daughter's test results that showed no trace of Greek ancestry. I asked if she would want to know if anyone ever contacted her regarding matches or if she wanted me to investigate her connection to all those matches who did not also match me—her paternal matches. She was hesitant, but she agreed that she would like to know even if it meant that her dad was not her biological father. I told her I'd look into it and get back to her. I didn't tell her that I'd already narrowed it down to two men, but once I had her permission, I would try to contact the family to see if either of the males remembered my mother or if they would be willing to test. One of their sisters was quite active on Facebook. The brothers were not, so I messaged her and considered the implications of all that I found.

The facts were clear if not comfortable. Donna married a man who was known by all of her family to be very physically and psychologically abusive and controlling. While she was married, she conceived and gave birth to a daughter with a different white man whom no one in her family knew and five years later she conceived and gave birth to a son by yet another man not her husband—a black, recently-released felon 22 years her senior. The snippets of conversations were reshaping every scenario I ever imagined. My parents were not the careless high school heavy-petters. My mother wasn't the free-spirited hippie on holiday. She wasn't dragged through the passenger door of her car, pistol whipped and raped in an abandoned building in the Cass corridor either, as far as I could tell. Once I knew for certain that Rev. Brantley was my uncle and that his brother David was my biological father, it became clear that none of the things I imagined were true, but the most likely scenario forming was perhaps even more tragic. I had been wrong so many times, but now in my bones I believed that she was prostituted by her own husband.

She was never left alone, always followed or accompanied by her husband or "body guard" and none of the children she bore were her husband's. If she had 2 children with 2 different men, how many more johns might there have been? She could pass Susan off as the daughter of her husband, but there was no chance of that with me. I bet that bastard knew he was not Susan's father. When David was released early from prison, one of the first things he did was find the comfort of a woman—even if he had to pay for it. Somehow, Alex had Donna in a place at a time that intersected with David. It saddened me to think that Alex benefitted so much from the extraordinary grief he inflicted upon Donna. The other possibility I preferred not to entertain, but could not entirely dismiss, was that every act was voluntary. That her husband was not the pimp, but the voyeur. Maybe this was how she made the money they used to buy rental properties and a pizzeria.

"You're lucky," Susan once told me. "You got the better end of the deal." "I'm so sorry," I answered. I told her about Ronald, the spaghetti-covered walls, and the walking on eggshells. I saw that she identified and needed no elaboration to understand the isolation, fear and hypersensitivity we shared. We both grew up as only children in tumult, but with mothers who tried beyond measure to shield us from the very worst of their trauma. It may have seemed that things turned out better for me, but we each carry scars that only those closest to us can see. We each developed impenetrable shells that not even we ourselves can intentionally crack. I was certain that I would not have survived in her home with her father. Hell, I barely survived in my own and my father Ronald never even laid a hand on me.

I finally had the answers I sought when I began my quest. The identities of both of my birth parents were known, I discovered a half-sister and I knew the names of many cousins on both sides of my biological family. My genetic tree was complete to three generations. I know all four of my grandparents and all eight of my great-grandparents. My father was 47 when I was born. His parents were born in 1886 and 1887. All 4 of their parents had been born into slavery. Every one of my paternal great grandparents was the child of a white slave owner and a first generation African female or American-born "mulatto" female. The sources and documentation already gathered and devotedly organized by cousin Frances allowed me to delve even further into my paternal roots, and the bottomless bounty of DNA would continue revealing secrets no living person on either side of my family has ever known.

# CHAPTER THIRTY-FOUR

## PLANET JANET

Susan's paternal aunts became quite engaged with solving the question of her paternity. With several of their family members already tested, only two people in the world could have been her father. The younger of the boys was certain that he could not have been. The elder, however, was 90 years old when we first made contact and hearing loss made telephone conversations with him difficult in the best of circumstances. His sisters bought a DNA kit and paid him a face-to-face visit. Peter had no memory of Donna, or he did not admit to one. After reading innumerable accounts of blood relatives who stonewalled adoptees and foundlings who only sought honest answers and closure, I counted Susan's aunts as exceptionally persuasive for beating the odds and convincing their reluctant brother to provide a sample.

Since I submitted Susan's sample and was the administrator of her results, I saw the match before Peter's sister contacted me. "Shared DNA: 3,446 cM across 61 segments. Predicted relationship: Parent/Child." As anticipated Peter was Susan's father, not the "Greek" whose house was burned to the ground, who chained my mother to a bed, who made it difficult for my sister to speak and who isolated them from the love and support of their family. Peter was married to another woman when Susan was born and no one wanted to upset his wife with the news of a dalliance 56 years ago. He preferred not to have contact with Susan, but his sisters welcomed her and they all seemed grateful to have found a shared truth.

By the time of Susan's introduction to her paternal genetic family, we still had not located our mother's ashes, which were given to her second husband. I already had received more information about my biological parents than I ever thought possible. I didn't expect to possess her cremains, but I thought the ultimate closure would be to know where she was, so that I might lay a hand on the urn once and say a prayer of thanksgiving. If that were possible, it felt worth a try.

Finding no trace of her second husband, I circled back to Donna's youngest sister Janet. Aunt Doris had not lifted the cone of silence from her family, but if Janet were willing, I might be able to learn more. Her daughter answered instant messages and after confirmation that Susan was indeed my sister, they agreed to meet for lunch. We share roughly the same amount of DNA with aunts and uncles as we do with half siblings. Visiting Susan's home on occasions, she shared a few photos with me. I saw a few of Donna when she was older and one or two from what appeared to be the 1980s. My favorite was a color photo of Grandpa Paul's 70th birthday celebration. He, bespectacled in a tan suit, solid brown neck tie and white shirt, was seated next to Grandma Hazel with a big yellow corsage pinned to her purple dress. Standing behind them are all four of their children, Donna 45, Janet 30, Doris 31, and David 40. I look more like Janet and Doris with their brown curls than Donna, but the foreheads, hairlines and chins are all mine.

The luncheon was set for the Black Rock Café in July of 2016. As my wife Fran and I arrived, Aunt Janet was already seated with her daughter, son-in-law and grandsons. My nose came from this side of my family, I am certain, and Janet has my younger self written all over her. Pictures spanning decades of my mother, her sisters and parents flowed freely after this luncheon. The blondes were all originally brunettes. Susan's high school photo revealed the same sandy brown coloring as my own. I looked more or less like one or the other depending on the year the photo was taken. I looked most like Donna when she was 10 and I was 8.

Through writing Denby High School, I was able to find her yearbook graduation pictures, which turned out to be a great stroke of fortune as my own high school graduation photo at the same age of 16 bears a striking resemblance to hers. The DNA results are proof, but the family photos are the essence of my longing. I have found the people who contributed most to my appearance, the impression of me first perceived by the world. I must say, Aunt Janet takes the cake. The distance from my brow to the tip of my nose is slightly longer, but the nose, cheeks, eyes, forehead, chin and even her ears were mine. It is also fairly easy to see a resemblance between Susan's daughters and me. Now, the Brantley ears were substantial all by themselves, but the confluence of Kapilla ears emphasized any fantasy of autonomous flight. The only difference to the untrained eye was that the Kapilla ears sat a smidge lower on the skull than the Brantley ears.

After pleasantries were exchanged, the conversation turned to Donna and Janet's relationship with her big sister. Janet had no knowledge of Donna's pregnancy. Growing up in a close-knit family with cousins, aunts and uncles bustling about

Grandmother A's home as if it were Grand Central Station, there was grown-up talk from which young ears were spared, but we all knew a great deal about one another's lives. If 3 sisters were pregnant in the same year, everyone surely knew it. Janet gave birth to a daughter in October of 1963, Doris delivered a son 6 months later, and Donna checked in under an alias 6 months after that. I found it unusual that Susan and Janet and many in the Kapilla family were so isolated and distant from one another as if they lived on separate planets.

Janet recalled a time when it seemed Donna was on the verge of telling her something of importance, but the words failed and the subject changed. Maybe she wanted to tell Janet about the child she left at the hospital long ago. Janet didn't know or wasn't willing to speculate why Doris was unwilling to speak with me. She explained how "everyone" tried to get Donna away from Alex unsuccessfully. Susan's estrangement notwithstanding, Janet was as sweet and pleasant an aunt as I could have hoped to find, but she had none of the answers I sought. I could not tell if her filters were up or if she honestly didn't know.

# CHAPTER THIRTY-FIVE

<hr>

## HUNKY TOWN

By following the trail of census and birth records, I learned that Donna's paternal lineage was Slovakian and her maternal side are German with a touch of Polish. Bežovce is a small village in the Sobrance District of Slovakia, which in the 1840s was the Kingdom of Hungary under the Habsburg Monarchy in the Austrian Empire. In 1843 a law was enacted making Hungarian the country's official language to the great displeasure of the Slovaks, Serbs and other ethnic minorities. German and Bohemian administrators managed the region and German became the language of government and education.

In the 1850s Austria suffered two defeats, first by France in 1859 and then by Prussia (Germany) in 1866, resulting in the Compromise of 1867 which created the Austro-Hungarian Empire. The Empire consisted of 51 million people with the two largest ethnic groups being Germans (10 million) and Hungarians (9 million). There were many ethnic minorities including Poles, Slovaks, Czechs, and Romanians who spoke more than 15 different languages. Michael Kapilla and his bride Barbara Kovacs were among these minorities who resented the imposition of the Hungarian language and customs called Magyarization and the suppression of non-Roman Catholics by the Empire.

This was a period of great expansion and industrialization. By 1873 Vienna had doubled in size to over 1 million residents, but global inflation following the American Civil War, unchecked speculative investments in railroads, property losses from the great fires in Chicago and Boston all conspired to strain bank reserves beyond capacity. New York bank reserves fell from $50 million to $17 million in less than a month giving way to the Panic of 1873. The financial collapse, political persecution and military conscription pushed the Kapilla children Michael Jr., Elizabeth and Stephen to seek a better life for themselves in the U.S. Hundreds of thousands of Czechs colonized U.S. cities from New York to Nebraska and Texas. About 30 percent of Slovaks who arrived in the U.S. were illiterate and forced to take unskilled work in coal and steel towns of Pennsylvania, Illinois, and others.

It was Mt. Carmel, Pennsylvania that received Michael, his wife Mary, and their sons Mike and John. The Philadelphia and Sunbury Railroad was completed from Shamokin to Mt. Carmel in 1854 prompting the birth of many coal mines and attendant infrastructure. The Locust Mountain Coal and Iron Company held tremendous coal lands and eagerly assimilated the Slovak labor as quickly as it arrived. Thomas Edison had recently installed one of his first generators here, and Michael and Mary were amazed at the sights and sounds of this miraculous new world. There was no shortage of work. If not in the coal mines, there was employment in the businesses that made miner's clothing and tools, silk mills, foundries, machine shops and dry goods. George,

Stephen and Andrew were the first American-born sons of Michael and Mary.

As white cotton was king in the 1850s Dixie, black coal was king in the North and would remain so for a full century. As Eastern collieries like Mt. Carmel absorbed the huddled masses, western sprawl promised relief from the depressed wages brought on by the glut of immigrant labor. Their wide-eyed idealism dimmed as wages stagnated and the Kipillas sought better opportunities for education and employment for their growing family. In addition to the labor difficulties, anti-foreign sentiment was heightening precipitously.

The response by Americans to Slovaks reflected the common anti-foreign attitude. Furthermore, the desire by Slovaks to live cheaply, the large number of males, and their concentration in unskilled industrial jobs reinforced beliefs that immigrants were creating social and economic problems for the United States. Slovaks were not usually singled out as presenting special problems. Since Slovaks did not have a separate identifiable homeland and most Americans did not know that there was a Slovak people, they often referred to Slovak immigrants simply as Slavs, Slavic, Slavish, or by the pejorative terms Bohunk or Hunky (contractions of Bohemian and Hungarian). Based on their geographic origin, Slovaks fell into the general category of undesirable immigrants. Judging persons from both eastern and southern Europe as biologically and intellectually inferior and a threat to American society, some native-born Americans demanded that these "undesirables" be barred from the country. The immigration laws of the 1920s that curtailed southern and east European immigration severely reduced the number of Slovaks who could enter the United States. [10]

---

[10] June Granatir Alexander, "Slovak Americans," Countries and Their Cultures, http://www.everyculture.com/multi/Pa-Sp/Slovak-Americans.html

Ronald G. Levi Jr.

Michael confided in his wife, "Mary, I tell you there is no improvement on the horizon in this place. The conditions are miserable. I see men dying and injured and I fear that if we do not leave now, I or our sons will fall victim to violence if not some failure in the gut of the mine. We are forced to work in conditions that are unsafe and there has been no increase or improvement in our situation since the first year of our arrival. I have heard there is demand, greater safety and higher wages in mines to the west. When eating lunch last week I saw a newspaper from a place called Staunton in Illinois. The article said that everyone should buy land quickly because the city is expected to triple in size within 5 years. John Coleman from the Reading Engine House crew in Shamokin says that things are much better there for families."

Anthracite has the highest carbon content of all varieties of coal—between 92% and 98%. It burns with a blue, smokeless flame without any tarry or hydrocarbon vapors and is mined in only a few countries. Also known as Black Coal, it has greater hardness, higher density and luster than the more common bituminous coal. During the Civil War, Confederate blockade-runners burned anthracite in their ships to avoid detection by Union naval forces. Railroads advertised the soot-free advantages of their black diamond fuel under the guise of Phoebe Snow, "My gown stays white / From morn till night / Upon the road of Anthracite." Purity and superiority in the trodding of whiteness upon and at the expense of blackness was diabolically ingrained in every facet of 19th century American life.

Several small strikes were organized by the United Mine Workers of America throughout the region from 1899 to 1901, but the workers wanted recognition and a stake in the direction and policies of the industry. The miners, supported by the maintenance employees who did not work in the twisted bowels of the mines, voted to strike in 1902. Eighty percent of the

248

workers supported the strike, but about 10,000 returned to Europe and another 30,000, unable or unwilling to sacrifice their weekly pay envelopes, headed for mines in the Midwest. Michael Kapilla packed up his wife and 5 sons and boarded the Pennsylvania Railroad bound for Staunton, IL.

Michael and the thousands who left correctly predicted the violence that would ensue. The Pennsylvania National Guard, local police and private detective agencies clashed with those who remained that summer. Michael missed no more than a single week's pay as he resettled his family. Upon reading the news of the strikes in October, Michael was inspired by the words of Clarence Darrow who represented the workers:

> *"We are working for democracy, for humanity, for the future, for the day will come too late for us to see it or know it or receive its benefits, but which will come, and will remember our struggles, our triumphs, our defeats, and the words which we spake."*

The ideals were noble, Michael thought, and that's what makes this such a great country. "We have many problems but we also have many good people working to improve things for us all. Our children and grandchildren may yet have the lives we always imagined for them," he said to his wife with a sigh. In spite of continued hardships, the Kapillas felt they had made the right decision and counted their relocation as perfectly timed.

Paul James Kapilla was the 6th son of Michael and Mary and in 1904 was the first to be born in Illinois. The family worked hard and coal mining provided economic stability if not grandeur and luxury for them. Everyone did not follow Michael into the mines, however. At the onset of World War I the eldest boys Mike Jr., John and George enlisted and served with distinction. Mike Jr. was a saloon keeper and John was a tire builder for the Morgan-Wright Company. All three had moved from the family home in Staunton to the industrial hot bed of Detroit. Younger siblings Paul, Joseph, and Frank still lived with their parents and attended schools in Staunton. The addition of Joseph and Frank brought to 8 the number of sons that Michael and Mary produced, and Andrew was the only one of them to follow his father into the coal mines.

Andrew Kapilla was the fourth son of Mike and Mary and the third born in America. He married Anna Bednar in 1923, 5 years after joining his father in the Mowequa Coal Mine. Andrew and Anna were blessed with two children, Clifford and Shirleyann. Andrew was one of 115 miners earning $6.10 to produce 30 tons of coal each day and counting themselves fortunate to do so at the height of the Great Depression. On Christmas Eve, about half of the miners enjoyed the holiday with their families, and 54 reported to work as usual. At 8:15 a. m. Mary and Mike were having breakfast, discussing preparations for the holiday meal that evening when they heard the steam whistle blow. They were momentarily paralyzed. Although 7 of their sons had recently moved to Detroit where manufacturing and other jobs were plentiful, they still had one in Staunton and he went to work at the mine that morning. The steam whistle was an alert that something was wrong. Mike and Mary were already dressed and needed only to don their rain coats and grab umbrellas. They hoped and prayed that Andrew was safe, but there was no discussion about waiting to hear news or turning on the radio. That whistle meant trouble for someone, if not their son, and they would be there to help in any way possible. Hundreds of family members like Mike and Mary filled the streets and headed for the mine in the cold December rain. Before they were within site of the entrance to the mine word spread that an explosion occurred deep within and trapped many of the miners. State rescue workers, the fire department, the Red Cross, and the Mowequa hospital mobilized quickly. Townspeople pitched in to provide meals for the rescue workers. The Illinois Central Railroad provided sleeping cars and food for the rescue teams as well. Rescuers warned that the explosion was caused by poisonous gas, and all feared the collapse of shale and rock some 2,000 feet from the entrance may have crushed the mine's ventilating system. The rescuers swung picks and shovels as relentlessly as the cold rain drenched the families and remaining miners who were kept back from the mouth of the mine.

There was no Christmas in Staunton in 1932. The crews labored for 2 days to recover the fallen men. Back pay and insurance payments did little to assuage the grief of their loss. The death toll, 54 souls, was the second largest for any mining disaster in the state since 1909. While Christmas would never be the same for Mike, Mary, and Anna, the legacy of Andrew in their children and grandchildren remained a source of strength and comfort throughout their remaining years.

# CHAPTER THIRTY-SIX

## SPRINGWELLS

Donna's maternal grandparents were Herman Stoll and Augusta Wilhelmina (Minnie) Preuss. Germans were among the largest groups of immigrants to America in the 19th century. Between 1820 and 1870 the number of Germans coming ashore more than doubled the population of the entire country. Shortages of land, religious intolerance and political oppression in Germany drove many to seek greater opportunities and freedom in America. There were so many Germans in the U.S. by the end of the 1800s that German-speaking towns were common. Newspapers, banks, haberdasheries and diverse businesses of all kinds catered to Germans in their native language making the transition to America much easier for them than their Eastern European and Italian cohorts.

At the age of 16 Friedrich Preuss boarded the S.S. Oder in Bremen for the 14-day journey to New York. From Manhattan he transferred to rail for his final destination, Detroit, where employment with the Griffin Car Wheel Company had been pre-arranged. The network of parishes and extended family allowed Fred to work and save money to bring his parents and siblings to America. Fred became a molder apprentice in a foundry that manufactured 570-pound, 33" diameter, cast-iron car wheels for railroad cars.

The German enclave of Springwells was growing rapidly and by his 18th birthday, he was well known and liked by co-workers and neighbors. Although Fred had arrived at Ellis Island two years prior, his parents and siblings arrived in Baltimore because the B&O railroad signed an agreement with the North German Steamship Line that allowed passengers to purchase a single ticket that carried them across the ocean and to points west via train. When his family stepped onto the platform at Fort Street Union Station on the first day of spring in 1884 their relief and exuberance was euphoric. Seeing Fred again and reuniting their family safely after the long journey overwhelmed his mother Charlotte. Tears of joy left streaks through the dust that had begun to coat her cheeks as the family made its way to a tidy new house in Springwells. His older siblings Minnie, August, and Augusta and their parents pooled their savings from years in Germany in order to buy a home, which Fred had negotiated on their behalf prior to their arrival. The same day they arrived in Detroit, the Preuss family paid cash for a home in Springwells and went to bed exhausted, thankful, and debt-free. The family integrated quickly into the community. German was spoken almost exclusively in the churches and businesses of Springwells. For the Preusses, the sights and sounds were new but the customs and culture were familiar and they made friends with neighbors and co-workers easily and quickly. St. Paul's Lutheran Church welcomed them and the community was nothing short of idyllic for these recently arrived immigrants. The ease of their transition and the speed of their assimilation could not have prepared them or anyone in this rapidly growing community for the "most pitiable and horrible tragedy that has been recorded against Wayne County in years," according to the Detroit Free Press.

On the morning of December 16, 1885 Fred's mother Charlotte awoke early as usual. She rose before the sun just as she always had in Germany to prepare meals for the school and work day. Little Otto was only 5 years old, but Herman, Gustave, and Ida attended the Springwells School founded by Father Gabriel Richards. They were looking forward to the last three days of school before Christmas break. Their home was already decorated with the tannenbaum and *CMB 1885* was inscribed in chalk above the doorway signifying the initials of the Three Kings, Caspar, Melchior and Balthasar. They giggled constantly about the gifts Christkindl ("Christ Child") would bring them on Christmas Eve and teased about the Americanized version, "Chris Kringle." As Charlotte made breakfast for the children, she noticed a dim reddish glow in a reflection on the glass of the kitchen wall clock. She turned to find the cause, but nothing in the room proved revelatory. The outdoor darkness and the electric light in the kitchen created a mirror effect on the glass, but Charlotte thought she could see people, men, running southward. She cupped her hands around her face to shield the reflection and saw faces masked in shadows with glowing, ruddy highlights. Fred's father Johann appeared in the kitchen doorway just as the doorbell rang—"Das Haus von Herrn Knoch brennt!" called a voice from the porch. "The Knoch house is on fire! Bring buckets!" Without opening the door, Johann bounded up the stairs and ordered August to join him. The men stepped into their boots, threw on overcoats and crossed the street to Fred's home. Fred greeted his father and brother at the door with a bucket in each hand and the three men joined the procession headed only a couple of city blocks away to the farm of Frank and Susan Knoch.

Johann's heart sank as the Preuss men came within direct sight of the flames illuminating the entire pre-dawn horizon. They took their respective places in the bucket brigade line that stretched nearly a quarter mile from the nearest creek, but it was already becoming clear that their efforts to save the house were futile. Word spread that the family could not be reached and someone had seen movement through the windows earlier, but no one had emerged and no one was able to enter to save the young family. Frank, Susan, their 2-year-old George and baby Frank Jr. all perished that morning.

The close-knit community took the loss squarely on the chin, but the uppercut that sent them to the mat was the revelation by authorities that the deaths had not been accidental. Wayne County Physician Dr. F.W. Owen determined through autopsy that Frank and Susan had been fatally shot by a .22 caliber pistol found next to a sewing machine in the charred wreckage. A hatchet blade found in the ashes had been used, it was determined, to chop George's head into pieces. There were too little remains of the infant Frank Jr. to determine the circumstances of his demise.

Weeks later Fred and Herman sat in the dining room of their parents' home discussing the horror that had gripped their neighborhood. Charlotte poured coffee as August opined. "Sheriff Stellwagen swears he will find the murderer, but everyone remains in fear. Frank and Susan had no enemies, and we all know one another. This must have been done by someone from outside." Fred disagreed, "Everyone is more fearful that the person who did this is from within our own community, August. Frank had two brothers, Gustave and Herman, and you know Herman was committed to an asylum for a while. Sheriff Stellwagen is talking with them and their mother, I have heard." Charlotte shivered at the thought of Frank's own family being complicit in his gruesome death. In German she spoke, "Was für eine hasserfüllte Sache das war!" (Such a hateful thing this was.)

Ronald G. Levi Jr.

Only a monster could summon such hate and anger to kill his own brother's family." August was not convinced. "You know Aleck, the man that boarded with them last summer? Have you seen him lately?" "I saw him driving a manure wagon to Detroit the week after the murders, but not since," added Johann entering from the kitchen. "They had to move the inquest from the courthouse to the hall above the Fort Street Saloon because so many people wanted to listen. Newspaper reporters and people from all over the country are following this with great interest. Even the New York Times is writing about this horrible thing that happened in our home," he lamented.

Word reached the sheriff on New Year's Eve that Frank's mother, who had become ill, wanted to make a statement. Those involved assumed that it would be a confession or incrimination of her sons. The prosecuting attorney accompanied the sheriff to her home the following day, but Elizabeth had fallen into a coma and died early that morning. Authorities suspected poisoning, but an autopsy performed by candlelight in the living room of her home revealed a skull fracture. Herman and Gustave were arrested and public sentiment against the brothers raged over the headlines, Mother Murdered! The boarder, Alec, was found the following summer and proved to be ignorant of the events. According to the Detroit Daily, the community believed "that the present generation will not see the mystery solved and that further investigation will be fruitless."

By the time Fred fell in love with and married Anna Behrendt in 1887 the case was at a standstill and the widespread fear was beginning to dissipate. Their first daughter, Augusta Wilhelmina "Minnie" and the 11 children that followed would only know of the dreadful massacre through bits and pieces of the story their father and uncles would tell when they were older. They refused to allow their own memories of one terrifying Christmas to steal the joy and magic of the holiday from their children in the years that followed. Minnie would later notice a sadness in her mother at Christmas—not constant, but fleeting and reflective—that she witnessed on a few occasions. As she became more aware of the history, she never asked her mother or father about it because she understood the pain these memories inflicted upon them.

# PART IV

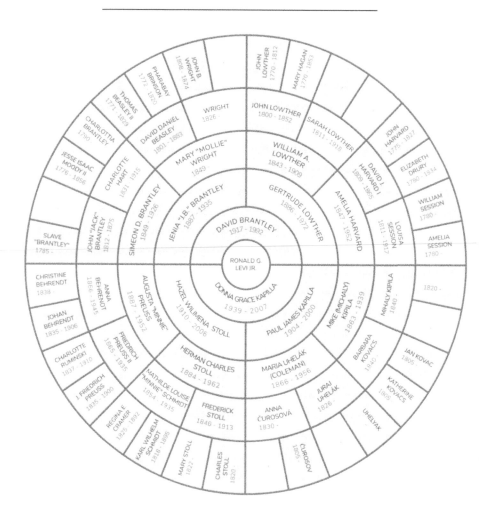

*Figure 4 Combined Biological Maternal and Paternal Chart*

# CHAPTER THIRTY-SEVEN

*

## THAT'S ALL

When I began my search in 2009, I dared not hope to find more than the names of my birth parents. History and life prepared me to live with resignation that the identities of my enslaved ancestors would never be revealed. Although I have long considered myself a hopeful person, I consciously chose to believe that a welcome reunion with flesh and blood relatives was not in the cards for me. The word *coincidence* is commonly understood to mean random chance. Literally, however, it also applies to events that coincide—occurring at the same time. Such was the coming together of my maturity, spirituality, the science of genetic genealogy and explosive growth of social networking. To say that the coincidence of these elements in 2015 exceeded my wildest expectations is a gross understatement. My cousin Emmilie and my Search Angel Linny guided me on the adventure of a lifetime and introduced me to a history that few Americans

Ronald G. Levi Jr.

and even fewer African-Americans are able to experience. They connected me to Frances, who knew more about our shared ancestry than I ever thought possible. They connected me to paternal cousins who welcomed me with open arms and have become such a blessed addition to my own extended family. They connected me to my maternal half-sister with whom I have developed bonds spoken and unspoken as well as a cherished fondness. None of this would have been possible in 1990, 2000, or 2010. It happened when it was supposed to happen, and the greatest part of it was being able to share it with Mom openly and honestly before she departed this life.

Once I knew who my biological parents were, I asked Mom if she wanted to know. When I told her that I was looking, she said that she figured I would eventually take up the challenge. I told her that I had a half-sister, and I told her a little about Donna and David. I told her how wonderful and warm Aunt Claudia and cousins Frances, Douglas, Michael and Pamela were. I invited them to our home on a couple of occasions for cookouts to meet Mom, my wife and sons. It was great to see her relax with them and them with her. The fears allayed, I suppose she realized after 50 years, there was no risk of "losing me" to my genetic family. Mom never said so, but it may have helped that Donna died before I could find her. It was much easier for Mom to "compete" for my time and attention with someone who could never be seen or heard.

At 83 years of age, Mom made an admission that I never saw coming. "When we went to Lutheran Social Services, the child we thought we were taking home was sick. We brought you home instead." All I could say was, "Praise God." Those who have faith receive it from God. To the extent we exercise it, like a muscle it becomes stronger, more developed and useful to us. Mom knew that I could not have received that admission when I was a young person, and she knew that I was now strong enough to accept it and process it constructively. She didn't tell me to hurt me, she told me because she was herself amazed at all that God had brought us through. If it had been solely up to her and Ronald, they would have gone home with a different child that day. Who knows what would have become of me? But knowing as I do now, God has a plan for all of us and no matter what we want or what we do, He has a way of blessing us beyond our own understanding. In some cases, it takes a lifetime to recognize and appreciate His guiding hand. Charlie Mae prayed for a child and she got one, but as for which child—that choice was God's.

Mom succumbed to kidney disease 6 days after Mother's Day, 2018. I am thankful to have been able to arrange hospice care for her in our home. Each of her final days found her breathing a little more labored, a little more raspy, but never alone and never with strangers. The medications we administered on a strict schedule seemed to keep her free of pain. As I held her hand and knelt next to her bed, I thanked God for the gift of her life, for all of the love and sacrifice she poured into me, and her strength and endurance. I thanked Him for answering my prayers and allowing her to know all of her grandchildren and to see them grow into adulthood. I thanked Him for allowing me to find my nearest biological relatives and to introduce them to her while she was still able to interact with them. Finally, I told God that I wanted my mom to stay with me longer and that I knew He could make that happen, that He had the power to completely restore her right then and there, but if He would not, if that were not His will, then I asked, "Please don't let her linger and suffer here any longer. It's ok if you take her home. Amen."

I walked upstairs where my wife Fran was getting ready to begin her Saturday and told her that mom's breathing seemed to be getting more shallow. We brushed our teeth, combed our hair and went back downstairs. Fran went in to listen. "Ron, I don't hear *anything*. I think..." I checked, and she was gone. Not more than 10 minutes had passed since I left her side. Nothing left unsaid, no regrets, she departed on her own terms. The following week was a blur of making arrangements, hosting friends and family who called to console and support us. It was not a terribly sad time for me, however. It was a time of profound gratitude. My cousin Jenny (Ronald's niece) who opened the door every morning when Mom dropped me off at Grandmother A's house went with Fran and me to make the arrangements at the funeral home. My church family pulled out all the stops and Pastor David L. Roberson, First Lady Catherine Roberson, and Minister Calvin Southern officiated an absolutely beautiful celebration of Mom's life. Cousins from my "new" biological family as well as those who I've known my entire life, and co-workers of Mom and myself were there. Cousin Marcia, Jenny's elder sister and ordained minister joined with me in closing the casket and seeing Mom for the final time. We felt so loved and blessed.

For days afterward I reflected on the arc of my life and how fortunate I have been. I thought of all the foundlings who experienced rejection not once, but twice as the doors were closed and a parent denied them. I thought of all the babies discarded in dumpsters and alleys who didn't survive. I thought of the victims of physical and sexual abuse, forever scarred by the experience. I remembered the thousands still searching for their genetic truth and worried about those who are not ready to receive it. Doubts about one's worth, the fragility of one's self-image, and uncertainty of one's identity independent of one's parents are hairpin turns that can send a seeker headlong over a cliff of despair. I was able to rebound relatively easily from the very disturbing reality of my birth parents' circumstances because I never felt I was or would be defined by them. I believed myself to be the child of a King, a Heavenly Father through whom all things are possible. I am truly grateful to live in a time that compassionate, brilliant people like my search Angel Linny, CeCe and the DNA Detectives can use science to answer decades-old questions of the most personal and secretive nature. Linny's kindness and expertise connected me not only to living relatives, but to a specific relative who already had my paternal history documented thoroughly and tied off neatly with a big, shiny blue ribbon. Thanks to Emmilie, I met Linny. Thanks to Linny, I met Frances. And thanks to Frances, I met my late father David, his mother Amelia, her husband William, his mother Sarah of Africa, and my great, great grandmother, Louisa. It was as if they had all been watching me my whole life from a distance, unable to speak to me until now. I considered the perspective that it was all a jumble of happy coincidences, but I can't shake the feeling that *coincidence* is too convenient a label for an unwillingness to grapple with the alternative. It is intellectually lazy and altogether unsatisfactory to ignore the persistent drum of circumstance after circumstance crying for recognition as intelligent design.

Louisa survived 20 years of slavery with all of her children in tow, not by chance, but by her own will, her own faith, and the grace of God. What does a free woman sold into slavery, referred to as *Sister Louiza* in the church meeting minutes, do every Sunday? She prays. She prays for the safety and freedom of her children and she acts upon that belief every moment as if the affirmative answer is imminent. She keeps up her strength and theirs so that they will be able to stand, walk and run on their own when the time comes.

I was delivered from chaos and destruction throughout my gestation by Donna's courage and faith. Whatever control of her own life and body she lacked as a victim of sex trafficking, one thing she refused to relinquish was the sanctity of life—my life. She could have given birth to me in a public restroom and left me to be found, but she took a brave risk by checking into a hospital to ensure we both had the best chance of survival. I survived many a potentially deadly encounter in my youth, not because I was stronger, smarter, or better looking than anyone else, but because prayers on my behalf through the centuries were being answered in the present. The way I've seen black people treat white people and vice versa and the teasing and bullying I endured as a child, I had to consider the probability that my interracial coloring was akin to camouflage in the wild. It fooled the most pernicious predators (including myself) into perceiving me as more like themselves than unlike them. This was my unearned privilege. When I clung to the face of Detroit's Ford Auditorium high above the Independence Day fireworks crowd and my left foot slipped from the black offset smooth stones eliciting a collective gasp from thousands of onlookers, I knew nothing of Psalm 121:3, "He will not let your foot be moved; he who keeps you will not slumber," or Psalm 94:18, "When I said, 'My foot is slipping,' your unfailing love, Lord, supported me." The child my parents had chosen to adopt became ill the very day they were to take him home, and I alone became the son of a mother who gave everything she had to ensure my survival, safety, happiness and success. The hand of God was upon me long before I entered this life. I was steered through the prayers of Louisa, Amelia, Gertrude, Donna, and Charlie Mae by the work of the Spirit in them with one purpose—to share it with you. Providence and coincidence are indomitable allies.

Today, I held my first grandchild for the first time. The legacy I leave her is a family that is truly as diverse as America itself and far older. For her, this legacy is not a composition of topographical polygons. She has names, dates, public records of births, deaths, marriages, as well as thousands of triangulated DNA segments that are irrefutable proof of her genetic origins and relationships. She is the descendant of European monarchy and hardworking peasant immigrants. She is a descendent of Egyptian Pharoahs Seti I and Ramesses the Great. She is a sub-Sharan African, German, Polish, Northern Irish and English lady. She is Mexican American, indigenous and original to this continent. If she ever hears anyone tell her to "go back where you came from" she'll smile politely and say, "I'm already there." She has scores of ancestors, white, black and brown who were on this continent hundreds of years before later generations declared independence from the crown. Her parents named her Alba (dawn/sunrise) Lucía (light). Her initials A.L.L. will ever remind me that she is our *all* and she is the embodiment of *all* of America—its history, highest ideals, truest values, and professed faith. It's ironic that the Eastern European immigrants of my ancestors were actually the last to arrive on the shores of our nation over 100 years after she won independence. The most ancient Western Europeans (British and Irish) were here much earlier, but certainly not before the native peoples. Why is this important to mention? Because the differences used to separate and divide us are superficial and far beyond our control. Every immigrant to this land has faced discrimination and marginalization. Although is it folly to compare one person's pain to another, I think we must collectively acknowledge and do something to reverse the wrongs done to native indigenous and African people on this continent. It is not only an American sin— it is a collective sin of British, Dutch, Portuguese, Spanish... and other nations. The solution can and should be a global cooperative effort. Open and digitize all birth and adoption records, digitize all immigration records and connect all digitized databases electronically. Most importantly I have learned, and I hope you will understand, that we are all related to one another. When we accept that we are all related, we understand that perceived differences imposed upon us are false and contrary to our best interests. We understand that as family, we are far stronger united than divided. Admittedly, some people treat known family members as complete strangers, but I believe it is in our best interest—even in the interest of mutual survival—to help one another in every way we can. This wretched game of racism and colorism we play robs us all of the empathy and compassion required to make our world not only bearable, but beautiful.

Generalizations about white folks being privileged blot out our ability to see those in dire need, battling common societal woes that have no regard for skin color. Selectively recognizing people of color who achieve academic and professional success as proof that the same opportunity is possible for everyone is a recipe for conflict and violence by and toward everyone. This pernicious and false construct, whether called race or color, is never used to unite—only to divide. *My pain is worse than yours, my suffering is greater*—this is a zero-sum game that is truly laid bare when we understand that we are all factually biologically related.

I was given a story to tell, and it is a story of hope, faith, and love. It is the fire Sonia Sanchez implores us to catch – my fire that I pass on to you. Be not afraid, know who you are and whose you are regardless of or in addition to your genetic path to existence, and trust that God will reveal what you need when you need it. Accept that His time is not your time, that you may not get what you want when you want it, but you will get what you need when you need it. You are precious and valued no matter what the world hands you, and your future depends on you and God—no one else.

# AFTERWORD

ꝺꞬꝺꞬ

In June of 1999 then-governor of Texas, George W. Bush signed House Bill 3423 into law. It was the first of many safe-haven laws throughout the states, initially known as Baby Moses Laws.

*Every day countless women around the world face the reality of an unplanned pregnancy. Sadly, a small number of these women hide or deny the fact that they are pregnant. They often lack family or friends to confide in and have not reached out to any of the crisis pregnancy or adoption services that are available to them. These women carry their babies to term, give birth in secret, and then out of fear, shame, confusion, or desperation, they abandon their newborn baby in an unsafe location—leaving their child to die–hoping that the pregnancy will never be discovered. Unfortunately, it may never be known exactly how many newborns are abandoned every year. A statistic that is often quoted is a*

*1998 study in which 108 newborns were reported abandoned, and of those, 33 died. This study was conducted by surveying a relatively small number of newspapers, and it is important to recognize that to be counted, the newspaper had to be large enough to be included in the study, and the newborn had to be found. In other words, this number significantly underrepresents the severity and scope of the problem.[11]*

The Safe Haven Laws, enacted between 1999 and 2008 in every U.S. state, address this heart-breaking tragedy by providing a safe alternative to abandonment and infanticide by offering mothers the opportunity to surrender their healthy newborn infants to a designated Safe Haven location, such as a hospital. In some states, additional Safe Haven locations are included in the law, such as fire stations, free-standing emergency centers and emergency medical services (EMS) stations. Under the Safe Haven Laws, a mother may anonymously and without penalty, relinquish her unharmed infant within a designated timeframe to a Safe Haven location without question. Once relinquished, the baby will receive proper medical care and is placed with an adoptive family within 24 hours.

When I was abandoned in 1964, these laws were not on the books. According to a federal study reported by the Los Angeles Times in 1993, at least 22,000 babies are left in hospitals each year by parents unwilling or unable to care for them. I was one of these lucky ones. Thankfully, my birth mother had the courage to check into a hospital, even under an alias so that I could be attended to by professional caregivers. It is my fervent hope that my story, in addition to giving hope to adoptees and foundlings who are searching for their genetic identities, might also bring awareness to the resources that are available in every state to prevent

---

[11] http://www.babymosesproject.org/background.html

unwanted or abandoned babies from being harmed or left unprotected to die.

To that end, a portion of the proceeds of this book will be donated to the National Safe Haven Alliance, the leading Safe Haven experts in the nation. If you would like more information or would like to support directly, please visit their web site.

Please talk about this important subject with your friends and family members and do anything you can to let potential mothers know that there is a 24/7 Crisis Hotline available. If they feel they can't keep a child, encourage them to call 1-888-510-BABY or text *SAFEHAVEN* to 313131. You can also visit their web site to find the nearest designated Safe Haven location and the details on your state's Safe Haven law. Thank you for buying this book, and contributing to this life-saving cause. You can also support this effort by writing a glowing review of Spitting Image at Amazon or your online point of purchase.

# ACKNOWLEDGEMENTS

O f the many generous friends and family to thank for their support and contribution to this labor of love, I must begin with Frances Lillian Stephens. Hers and our cousin Annie's were the first close DNA results leading to the discovery of my genetic paternal family. Although Frances confided that she only tested to learn more about her own ethnic diversity, if she and Annie had not tested, I might never have found them. Of equal importance to the emergence of this book are the years of unrelenting research that Frances devoted to memorializing her family's history—our family's history. Connecting to her was like plugging a lamp into an electrical outlet, illuminating a room full of artifacts previously hidden in complete darkness. Most of all, even if I had never written this book, I am grateful for her acceptance, sincerity, generosity, and love. She is a careful and reserved person, but once you're in her circle, you are in it all the way. I will be forever grateful to have her in mine as well.

Another debt of gratitude is owed to our late cousin, Simon Michael Brantley whose agreement to test was the single determining factor of my father's identity. His siblings Douglas and Pamela, and the entire Brantley, Harvard, and Lowther families have been nothing but welcoming, and I have been richly blessed by them all.

I am especially grateful to my search Angel, Linny Yint, and to all of the amazing, talented, selfless genetic genealogists who give so much of their time and their hearts to helping foundlings and adoptees discover their biological identities. Linny's laser focus and brilliant deductive powers notwithstanding, her cheerful encouragement along this journey really kept me going and gave me hope every time doubt reared its head.

I offer a heartfelt thank you to my fellow foundlings and adoptees for their courage in sharing their stories, trusting the process, and daring to hope. Here's to the Foundling Finders, DNA Detectives and the pioneer who really started the ball rolling, CeCe Moore.

Thanks to my sister Susan for opening up and sharing so personally with me. We always thought we had a sibling "out there somewhere" and we were right. I wish we could have been there for each other sooner, but we have each other now, and for that I am humbled and truly appreciative.

To my family, the ones I grew up with, my Levis, Williamses, Martins, Calverts, Thomases, Clemonses: You are my first love and always will be. Thank you for loving me, encouraging me, teaching me, raising me. Thank you for being my home, my tribe, my people.

Finally, nothing I have experienced or achieved can compare to the fierce love, unmitigated patience, and tireless care and kindness of my wife Frances and my late mother, Charlie Mae Levi. I owe everything I hold dear to these two women, and I will continue trying to be worthy of their sacrifices and their trust.